THE CHALLENGE

Addressing challenges arising from Christian–Muslim encounter, this book engages with the primary challenge—enabling outsiders to understand the religion of Islam.

Douglas Pratt offers distinctive perspectives that complement much other literature in the study of Islam and in particular of Christian–Muslim relations and the relation of Islam and the West. Whilst in recent years there have been many introductions to Islam, a book that combines introductory material with issues of the relationship of Islam to Christianity and Judaism, and issues of dialogical engagement, is rare and offers an important complementary perspective to other texts.

For
Abdul Rahim Rasheed, LLB (NZ), BTheol (Auck), QSO
of Auckland, New Zealnad

An exemplary Muslim leader and champion of interfaith dialogue

The Challenge of Islam

Encounters in Interfaith Dialogue

DOUGLAS PRATT
University of Waikato, New Zealand

ASHGATE

Published by
Ashgate Publishing Limited
Gower House
Croft Road
Aldershot
Hampshire GU11 3HR
England

Ashgate Publishing Company
Suite 420
101 Cherry Street
Burlington, VT 05401-4405
USA

Ashgate website: http://www.ashgate.com

British Library Cataloguing in Publication Data
Pratt, Douglas
 The challenge of Islam : encounters in interfaith dialogue
 1. Islam – Relations 2. Islam 3. Islam – Relations – Christianity
 I. Title
 297.2'8

Library of Congress Cataloging-in-Publication Data
Pratt, Douglas.
 The challenge of Islam : encounters in interfaith dialogue / Douglas Pratt. – 1st ed.
   p. cm.
 Includes bibliographical references and index.
  ISBN 0-7546-5122-3 (hardcover : alk. paper) – ISBN 0-7546-5123-1 (pbk. : alk. paper)
 1. Islam – Relations. 2. Islam – Relations – Christianity. 3. Christianity and other religions – Islam. 4. Islam – Relations – Judaism. 5. Judaism – Relations – Islam. 6. Islam – Essence, genius, nature. I. Title.

 BP171.P74 2005
 261.2'7—dc22

2004013984

ISBN 0 7546 5122 3 (Hbk)
ISBN 0 7546 5123 1 (Pbk)

Printed and bound in Great Britain by MPG Books Ltd, Bodmin, Cornwall

Contents

Preface

The study of Islam, a particular concern with Christian–Muslim relations, and research into interreligious dialogue more broadly are fields of interest I have grown into over recent years. However, the earliest—somewhat indirect—contact I recall having with Islam was travelling on a ship, the MV Kuala Lumpur, in the days when it spent half the year plying pilgrims from Malaysia to Mecca, and the other half ferrying tourists and schoolchildren from New Zealand around the Pacific. In 1966 I was one of an all-boy school party enjoying the adventure of a 17 day educational cruise. Such school groups were quartered in the bow section, which was permanently set up as dormitories for the Muslim pilgrim trade. The mid-section of the ship had been converted to accommodate first-class tourist passengers. Little did I know that, years later, I would make a number of visits to the city after which the ship was named.

The first, in 1990, was to attend an International Conference on Islamic Civilisation. This was held under the auspices of the Malaysian Ministry of Tourism and Culture and the Islamic Affairs Division of the Prime Minister's Department. It was a most informative and worthwhile event for a non-Muslim New Zealander (or 'Kiwi') to attend. At the time I was teaching Islam as part of an introductory course in Religious Studies at the University of Waikato; indeed this was something relatively new to me as only two years previously, from a background in philosophy and theology, I had been appointed the foundation lecturer in Religious Studies at what was then New Zealand's newest university. This conference was my first opportunity to have contact with Islam outside of New Zealand. I found myself in a triple minority—one of only a handful of Westerners, the only representative from New Zealand, and thus the only non-Muslim New Zealander. For me, that conference was very revealing and stimulating. Speakers, both Muslim and non-Muslim, came from many parts of the globe.

Many issues were addressed, but the underlying theme was the question: whither Islam in the contemporary world? Questions of Islamic civilisation and western modernity were tackled by a number of speakers who gave both an insightful critique of modern secularised mentality and cultural norms, and also some penetrating self-reflective analysis of Islam in relation to that. A number of possibilities for further research and investigation suggested themselves to me, among them the issue of the ways in which each religious community perceives the other as religiously and ideologically 'other'; the way in which Islam is perceived by the West in general; and the prospect for engaging in theological dialogue that goes beyond polite, mutually monological, presentations of the status quo.

I returned to Kuala Lumpur in 1995 for a brief period as a visiting scholar at the International Islamic University of Malaysia, where I gave a series of seminars on dialogical matters, and to speak also at the University of Malaya and the National University of Malaysia. This was followed the next year by attendance at an International Seminar on Islamic Theology and Philosophy at the National University of Malaysia. These visits afforded opportunity to pursue some lines of research and thought, and to sound them out in the context of actual dialogical engagement. This had also been the case with my encounters with Islam and Muslims in Birmingham, England, when I undertook a period of sabbatical leave in 1993, spending much of my time working at the Centre for the Study of Islam and Christian–Muslim Relations. While there I had the opportunity to participate in a Summer School on Islam and Christianity at which I co-led, with a Muslim colleague from Malaysia, a theology dialogue group that met daily for the duration of this eight-day event.

Further, and also in 1995, I had the privilege of travelling to Egypt to attend, as a guest of the Egyptian Ministry of Waqfs (Religious Affairs) and Al-Azhar University, the convention of the Supreme Council for Islamic Affairs. This event was held in Alexandria and my attendance there was the result of being nominated by Muslim leadership in New Zealand. This was a rare opportunity for a distant New Zealander, and one that was both stimulating and instructive. It gave me, quite literally, a front seat perspective onto the then contemporary world of Islam and the dynamics that operate within the context of a major international Islamic gathering. The paper I had been asked to prepare was included in the published pre-conference material. I was graciously hosted by the Egyptians, just as I had also been by the Malaysians when in Kuala Lumpur. A number of other international travel experiences and research opportunities in recent years have allowed me to gain further knowledge of, and insight into, the wider dimensions of the relationship between Islam and Christianity and the broader context of Christian–Muslim dialogical activities.

This book is a limited and tentative attempt to explore some of the concerns and issues that have exercised me in the field of Christian–Muslim encounter over the past decade and more. It is a small contribution to a vast ongoing conversation. While seeking to maintain my integrity as a critically reflective Christian theologian and scholar of religion, I seek nevertheless to engage empathetically with, and to deepen my understanding of, Islam. Indeed, I am of the opinion that there is much in Islam that can be affirmed in good faith by a Christian. I would like to think that the reverse is also true. Much the same could be said with respect to Jewish–Muslim relations also. The ongoing challenge is to tease out what these affirmations might be, and how they might be appropriately expressed, both to the honour of each and to the honour of the One God in whom all three religions believe. In all I seek to affirm the integrity of the process of dialogical engagement, and to respect the uniqueness and integrity of my dialogical partner as the religious 'other', with whom I am challenged to relate and engage in interfaith encounter.

The main corpus of this book is divided into three parts. Part I constitutes an introduction to Islam, Part II delves into aspects of the wider encounter with Islam, and Part III explores issues in regard to the prospect of engaging in dialogue with Islam.

Part I comprises my attempt to meet the primary—and preliminary—challenge of interfaith encounter, namely, of understanding the religious 'other' with whom I am to engage in dialogue. This intellectual task is a necessary concomitant to real-life encounter. There are, of course, many introductory works on Islam, and many that are more substantial and far ranging than I have attempted here. My intention is to serve the reader who is interested in dialogical issues with Islam and who needs to have immediately to hand a succinct introduction to the religion, or at least something sufficiently substantial, but not overwhelming, to refer to. For the reader already familiar with the Muslim religion, this section can be skipped over. However I am of the view that, apart from academic professionals and others highly versed in Islam, all 'introductions' serve the purpose of reinforcing knowledge and expanding understanding. For, as with other non-Muslim writers on the subject, each author has his or her own interpretive slant and presentational perspective. So the non-specialist reader ought to gain something instructive and illuminating yet, of course, ought also to consult other works on Islam in the quest to gain a fuller and deeper understanding.

Part II explores some elements of the relationship of Islam in regards to the wider religious context in which it is set, on the one hand, and of the nature of Islam as a religious phenomenon encountered within the contemporary world, on the other. In particular, patterns and paradigms of interfaith engagement may be discerned from a review of the history of Christian–Muslim encounter and the trajectory of Jewish–Muslim relations. Issues of contemporary Muslim identity and ideology are imperative to grasp if dialogical encounter is to be rooted in the real world. In Part III, I make a tentative start on the business of dialogical engagement by way of discussing a number of pertinent issues, ranging from matters of media-driven perceptions of Islam to some thorny theological topics.

As with many scholars in the Western world, I have had numerous speaking engagements and allied opportunities for reflection and writing in the wake of the rise of interest—if not outright concern and anxiety—in things Islamic following the events of 11 September, 2001. Like it or not, we live today in a post-9/11 world. Global affairs and our nightly newscasts remain dominated by troubling events in and with the world of Islam. The imperative to understand and dialogically engage with Muslims and the religion of Islam is urgent and paramount. I trust my work will assist the reader to do just that.

Douglas Pratt
October 2004

Acknowledgements

I am grateful to the many people who have contributed—for the most part quite unknowingly—to this book, or at least the processes that made it possible. Not everyone who has supported me personally will necessarily agree with me in all that I have written, at least at points. I crave their indulgence in the spirit of raising issues for reflection, discussion and debate, and as a further stimulus to meeting the real challenges of interfaith dialogue.

I have been greatly encouraged over the years by colleagues and senior figures in the Religious Studies and Theology establishments of New Zealand. This has been most heartening. In particular, in respect to this book, Associate-Professors Peter Donovan and William Shepard have been particularly supportive and offered valuable comment and advice at various stages. Ken Walker, an honorary Research Associate and long-time friend to Religious Studies at the University of Waikato, also helpfully read early drafts and has been diligent in drawing my attention to relevant books as they have arrived at the library.

I thankfully acknowledge the encouragement and support that I have received from Muslim leaders in New Zealand over a number of years, including in particular Dr Anwar Ghani, former President of the Federation of Islamic Associations of New Zealand; Mr Mohammad Afiz, for many years President of the Waikato–Bay of Plenty Muslim Association; and Mr Abdul Rasheed who, as a significant leader over a long period within the Auckland Muslim community, and also serving regionally and internationally in various Islamic leadership roles, has embodied an Islamic spirit of tolerance and dialogue to the extent of undertaking, in retirement, a degree in Christian Theology. I was privileged to have had him as a student at the University of Auckland during my tenure there as an honorary lecturer in theology. I regard him as an esteemed colleague in the cause of interfaith encounter.

I am most grateful to authorities in Malaysia, in particular the International Islamic University of Malaysia; and Egypt, particularly Al-Azhar University, for making possible significant visits to parts of the Islamic world. These have been most informative and stimulating for my own understanding of Islam. Likewise, to the University of Waikato, specifically the Faculty of Arts and Social Sciences, and prior to that the School of Humanities, which has supported my research and related travels, I express my thanks. Without such support, the work that has led to this book could not have been undertaken.

I am particularly grateful for the hospitality and encouragement which I have received on a number of occasions from colleagues and advisers in England, Italy, Switzerland and Germany, including Professor Jørgen Nielsen and Dr David

Thomas of the Centre for the Study of Islam and Christian–Muslim Relations and the Graduate Institute for Theology and Religion in the Department of Theology, the University of Birmingham; Archbishop Michael Fitzgerald and the Pontifical Council for Interreligious Dialogue, the Vatican; Professor Justo Lacunza Balda and colleagues at the Pontifical Institute for the Study of Arabic and Islam, Rome; Dr Hans Ucko and Dr Tarek Mitri of the Office for Interreligious Relations at the World Council of Churches; Professor Dietrich Ritschl and colleagues at the University of Heidelberg and Professor Christoph Elsas of the University of Marburg, Germany. I am also most appreciative of the Visiting Scholarship to the Oxford Centre for Hebrew and Jewish Studies during 2002, which enabled me to undertake research leading to Chapter 7.

Despite corrections and helpful critical comment, without which this book would be the poorer, I alone am responsible for the final form and content. I have only myself to blame for any error or misunderstanding. I plead simply the limitation of my humanity, of which it is said that erring is a defining mark.

Books do not appear overnight, not even once the initial manuscript is finished. To Sarah Lloyd, Emma McBriarty, and the team at Ashgate I offer my profound thanks for taking this project on and for assisting me through the production tasks of publication.

I am most grateful for permissions of publishers kindly given to reprint material from cited works as follows:

John Esposito, *What Everyone Needs To Know About Islam* (New York: Oxford University Press, 2002)
Mahmud Faksh, *The Future of Islam in the Middle East: Fundamentalism in Egypt, Algeria, and Saudi Arabia* (Westport, Connecticut: Praeger, 1997)
Jean-Marie Gaudeul, *Encounters and Clashes: Islam and Christianity in History* (Rome: Pontifico Instituto di Studi Arabi e Islamici, 1990)
Husein Haykal, *The Life of Muhammad,* trans. Ismail Raji al-Faruqi (Kuala Lumpur: Islamic Book Trust, 1993)
Ibrahim Karawan, *The Islamist Impasse* (International Institute for Strategic Studies. Adelphi Paper 314. London: Oxford University Press, 1997)
Charles Kimball, *Striving Together: A Way Forward in Christian–Muslim Relations* (Maryknoll, New York: Orbis Books, 1991)
David Waines, *An Introduction to Islam* (Cambridge: Cambridge University Press, 1995)
Sami Zubaida, *Islam: The People and the State. Political Ideas & Movements in the Middle East* (London: I.B. Tauris, 1993)

Finally, I express my heartfelt thanks to my wife, Jenny Dixon, for her collegial encouragement as a fellow academic, and her loving support as my partner in life.

Chapter 1

Introduction

Of all the world's religions, Islam seems to be the one that is forever in the news. And the news, more often than not, is bad. Islamic issues and Muslim politics seem to feature constantly in a negative light in the media. Why should this be so? Are Muslims getting a fair deal? At the same time, Islam has been the focus, in recent years, of much dialogical activity and the fostering of good relations within both academic and ecclesiastical circles. Islam has the attention of Western scholars and the Christian Church as never before. Religious architecture other than Christian adds new shape to our skylines. The contours of dome and minaret are emerging as identifiable features. Today, perhaps as never before, questions about Islam and our relation to it are being raised. What is Islam? What may we make of it? What has been the nature of the relationship of Islam to its 'sister religions' of Judaism and Christianity? Why has the religion of Islam always been something of a puzzle—to put it mildly—to Western societies? How does Islam relate to the modern world? What issues are raised when we contemplate the prospect of a dialogical relationship with Islam and Muslims? In order to begin to answer, we need to understand where this religion comes from and how it sees itself.

> The Islamic world remains today a vast land stretching from the Atlantic to the Pacific, with an important presence in Europe and America, animated by the teachings of Islam and seeking to assert its own identity. ... Muslims wish to live in the modern world but without simply imitating blindly the ways followed by the West. The Islamic world wishes to live at peace with the West as well as the East but at the same time not to be dominated by them. ... It seeks ... to create better understanding with the West and to be better understood by the West.[1]

As a major religion of the world, Islam is, historically speaking, relatively recent. But Islam traces its origins, at least theologically and mythologically, to the very beginnings of creation. Historically, the religion of Islam began in the seventh century of the Common Era with the Arabian prophet Muhammad. But in Islamic thought and ideology, the religion really began some twenty-five centuries or more before that with the Semitic (Jewish) patriarch, Abraham. Some would even say it

---

[1] Golam W. Choudhury, *Islam and the Modern Muslim World*. 2nd edn (Kuala Lumpur: WHS Publications, 1994), 217.

began with Adam as the first created human being: here the idea is that Islam represents the 'natural religion' of being human.

The Arabic word (*Islam*), which connotes the idea of making active submission, and the Arabic for peace (*salaam*) are linguistically connected. Islam is to be understood as, in essence, a religion of peace. More specifically, it is a religion of peaceful submission to God and God's law (*Shari'a*). Furthermore, as with other enthusiastic believers in God, Muslims are passionate for their faith. Muslims care about their religion. And for conscientious Muslims everywhere, their religion is their life. It is given expression in daily prayer, in frequent mosque attendance, in an intentional recognition of God in all things at all times. The vast majority of Muslims throughout the world seek to live in peace and to honour the One God who is merciful and compassionate, just and fair. Muslims on the whole seek to submit themselves to God (*Allah*), to live godly and good lives. A Muslim is one who lives life in submission to the Will of God. In Islamic thought, all human beings are born innately '*muslim*'; that is, all are born according to, and so innately in submission to, the Will of God, the Creator.

Struggle—the essential meaning of *jihad*—with unbelief from within, or threats to belief and the believing community from without, has steeled this religion through the centuries. Thus throughout history, and in the contemporary Western world, Islam has been perceived by many as a threat. A standard reaction is one of fearful concern, of anxiety about an unknown quantity, of prejudice propagated through media bias and popular distortion.

I prefer a more positive outlook: Islam poses a challenge to Western society—religiously, ideologically, and culturally. A threat is something that evokes a defensive response, even hostility and reactive aggression. A challenge is something we rise to meet. It evokes a reaction of anticipation; it stimulates the desire to attain new accomplishment, and it excites expectation at the prospect of new encounter and the chance to attain new vistas of experience and understanding. The degree to which any 'other' is a challenge or a threat is a function of the perspective, or interpretive viewpoint, that one takes toward that other. The perspective I bring to the topic of Islam is that it constitutes a challenge, or perhaps, more aptly, a matrix of challenges.

The primary challenge is that of understanding Islam, of allaying anxiety and fear through proper knowledge, information, and appropriate investigation. This is the element of ongoing educational engagement. It is a necessary precursor to, and concomitant requirement of, dialogical encounter. For each to understand the other better is the first goal of interfaith encounter and interreligious dialogue. For there to be any hope of countering misperception, correcting false image, and combating mischievous prejudice, then learning for the sake of genuine, critical, and yet at the same time empathetic, understanding constitutes the first challenge. In the case of Islam and the West, in respect of cultural and social dialogue—as well as dialogical relations between Islam and Christianity on the one hand, and Islam and Judaism on the other—it is certainly the first challenge to be confronted. Furthermore, the challenge of dialogical engagement is not something that can be taken for granted: it is an endeavour requiring an exploration of issues that functions as a prolegomenon, so setting the scene for realistic dialogical encounter. This book has been written in the spirit of attempting to meet these challenges, if only in a limited and initial fashion.

An educational and informative encounter with Islam is itself challenging, of course. The notion that Islam forms a single monolithic entity may be quickly debunked as a Western myth, based on misconception and fear. Underneath a veneer of apparent normative 'sameness' there can be found a rich diversity of religious expression, piety and Muslim cultures, which is not unlike the internal diversities that mark the variegated identities within both Christianity and Judaism. On the one hand there is obviously much stridency and exclusive rhetoric emanating from vocal quarters within the Islamic world; on the other hand there is evidence aplenty of urbane forms and modalities of Muslim life: most Muslims live by an ethic of tolerance; many are open to the enriching possibilities of genuine religious pluralism. In reality, there is great diversity and dynamism within the present-day Islamic world; indeed, there always has been.

Islam represents approximately one-sixth of the population of the globe. Islamic cultures are seemingly omnipresent; the religion of Islam is virtually next-door everywhere, and is overwhelmingly predominant elsewhere. Or so it seems. Certainly, as we will have cause to explore, the contemporary revivalist phenomenon within Islam—most often referred to as Islamism—has made Islam, in one context or another, a daily news item. But does Islamism represent 'true' Islam? One Muslim scholar says of Islamism that it

> refers to the movements and ideologies that claim Islam, as they interpret it, as the basis for restructuring contemporary states and societies according to an idealised image of Islam's founding period ... Hence, Islamists talk of the need to return to Islamic roots and a 'golden age'.[2]

Very often, when political leadership and the media are confronted with Islamist excess the cry goes up, 'But they are not representing true Islam'. But on whose say-so? How can we judge? How much do we know and understand of this religion and its people to be able to intelligently assess the claims and counter-claims for 'true representation'? As with many situations in the field of religion, there is often no easy or simple black-and-white answer. It always hinges on interpretation. But interpretation, if it is to be authentic and not just a wishful projection, must be grounded in informed understanding. Consider the following:

> Islamists commonly believe that Islam has to be implemented in society *as a whole*. Individual adherence to the faith cannot in itself lead to an Islamic society. For

---

[2] Ibrahim A. Karawan, *The Islamist Impasse*. International Institute for Strategic Studies, Adelphi Paper 314 (London: Oxford University Press, 1997), 7.

Islamists, Islam encompasses the three 'Ds'—*din* (religion), *dunya* (life) and *wa dawla* (state)—and has to be implemented in its entirety. ... Islamists consider it their duty to overcome challenges to Islamic teachings and norms to bring about the rule of God in place of the rule of human laws.[3]

What clues does this give us about Islam as it is today? What does it tell us of the motifs, modalities and metaphysics of this religion? Clearly there is a primary value given to the community over the individual. Further, Islam is not just a political programme: there is a transcendental reference and transcendental values involved. This religion centres everything on God.

That said, what do make of this: 'Achieving an Islamic *society* is predicated on establishing an Islamic *state*'.[4] Does this not mean that the political agenda will inevitably predominate, despite assurances to the contrary? And does it not suggest that it is the local—that is, regional or national—interest that is the primary focus for Islamic activity? But then what about transnational expressions of Islam—and of Islamism in particular? 'Islamist ideology does not recognise state boundaries, which it sees as an artificial colonial legacy. Islamists have exploited this argument to expand their influence'.[5]

It would seem that there is something about Islam which is at least as imperialistic and universal in scope as the heyday of European Christian imperialism: one religious sociopolitical blueprint to fit all. At least, that appears to be the claim and case from some quarters. And it is the contemporary expression of the imperialist claim that garners international economic support: today there are many Muslims, as well as Christians, for whom their imperialist and fundamentalist crusade in the modern world is self-righteously expressed through the donation box.

Of course, from a Muslim point of view it has been very often the history and ongoing heritage of economic and cultural dominance arising out of Western colonialism and its progeny of globalisation (on Western secularised terms) that pose both a cultural and metaphysical problem evoking, in response, various forms of opposition. Thus,

> Political and militant Islamists both believe that the West is a major threat to Muslim societies. ... Islamists see their primary task as resisting growing Western influences on the institutions, policies and, more importantly, the *identity* of Muslim societies. They vow to eradicate Western secularism in the Muslim world, and to confront policies aimed at bringing about Arab and Muslim recognition of Israel.[6]

---

[3] Ibid. 14.
[4] Ibid.
[5] Ibid. 39.
[6] Ibid. 52.

Nowhere is the clash between Islam and the West more evident, it would seem, than with the situation of Israel/Palestine, even though the current context of both Afghanistan and Iraq, consequent upon Western invasion, also fuels the fires of Islamic oppositional rhetoric. Widespread Islamic opposition to Israel, which seems nowadays to be something of a modern Muslim mantra, is not merely a matter of religious rivalry—although one gets more than a hint of that at times—as it is a touchstone of Islamic opposition to Western hegemony as such. Within Islamic countries themselves, where Muslim leaders are seen as compliant with the West, this can fuel the Islamist's intensity of response and reaction. Yet more often than not it is Muslims, more than any others, who suffer at the hand of Islamic violence.

Often, of course, much of this is lost on the West, but the fact remains that the effect of the history of colonisation of Islamic countries has led to poor Muslim self-image on the one hand, and now, in the wake of contemporary forms of Islamic resurgence, Western anxiety over Islamic terrorism on the other. The noted scholar Edward Said once remarked that 'the economic and political threat to Europe posed by the birth and rapid expansion of Islam led to a kind of systemic paranoia which has been reinforced over the centuries'.[7] The Muslim world in general, and the Arab world in particular—with an additional emphasis on the Middle East—both fascinates and frightens the West. This is not without good reason. And even in Indonesia, for example, the turn of the century and millennium has seen an upsurge in tensions between Christian and Muslim communities. The largest Islamic population belongs not to the Middle East, nor even to the Indian sub-continent, but to the islands of Indonesia. Mutual assaults and bombings, together with horrifyingly savage inter-communal and ethnic violence, all give cause for concern.

A decade or more before the end of the twentieth century, Rafiq Zakaria noted the tension within the Islamic world between liberal and secular tendencies, on the one hand, and reactionary conservative fundamentalisms, on the other. In general terms, Islamic fundamentalists argue 'a truly Islamic State is the antithesis of a secular state. They believe that a secular State is a by-product of Christian "heresy" or of Hindu "hypocrisy". They argue that secularism, whatever its form, is basically materialistic and a negation of spiritualism'.[8] Sami Zubaida has further remarked that

> current Islamic movements and ideas are not the product of some essential continuity with the past, but are basically 'modern'. Even when they explicitly reject all modern political models as alien imports from a hostile West, their various political ideas,

---

[7] Edward Said, *Herald Tribune*, 11 March, 1996, 6.

[8] Rafiq Zakaria, *The Struggle Within Islam: The Conflict Between Religion and Politics* (London: Penguin, 1989), 11.

organisations and aspirations are implicitly premised upon the models and assumptions of modern nation-state politics.[9]

Islamic fundamentalists, or—and more accurately—political activists and extremists, tend to act on a mandate that holds, in effect and for the most part, that Muslim governments are apostate: they have acted contrary to, and so thereby implicitly denied, the profession of faith. The *Sunnah* (Islamic tradition) that is invoked and adhered to in this regard encapsulates the perspective that the apostate must be killed, even if they are in no position to fight. Thus, during the twentieth century, such notable leaders within the Islamic world as Presidents Sadat of Egypt, Khan and Bhutto of Pakistan, Indonesia's Sukarno, and the Shah of Iran were either assassinated or forcibly deposed.

The apparent resurgence of Islam in the wider world certainly reflects an element of religious fundamentalism and fanaticism from some quarters, but for the most part Muslims are moderates. To be sure there is a tenor of strictness and discipline that adheres more or less naturally to Islam by virtue of the very nature of the religion. But headline-grabbing excesses are just that—an excess of fervour and zeal rather than an expression of the essence of the religion. The majority of Muslims are passionate for the cause of right. They are not terrorists. They are not destroyers of civilisation. They are not harbingers of hate. They are as much the victims of those who usurp Islamic ideals in the name of an intransigent and exclusivist ideology as the rest of the world. They do not deserve to be viewed with suspicion. Rather they require to be listened to, understood, and accepted so that together we may combat an evil that, in the misused name of religion, stalks the world today.

In the opening decades of the twenty-first century of the Common Era we are all called to join in the struggle to overcome the evil of terrorism. At the same time we must not succumb to the easy reaction of hate. Justice must always be tempered with mercy and compassion, and that is as much an Islamic as a Christian or a Jewish perspective. Islam cannot be ignored in the modern world. Worse yet is the response that dismisses or otherwise tries to negate it. Islam, the religion of peaceful submission to the God who is merciful and compassionate toward all, is not so much a religion to be feared as a faith to be acknowledged and understood; a religion inviting respectful appreciation and dialogical response. In this regard it is worth noting Karen Armstrong's suggestion that Muhammad's fundamental view was that

> all rightly guided religion that submitted wholly to God, refused to worship man-made deities, and preached justice and equality came from the same divine source. Hence Muhammad never asked Jews or Christians to accept Islam unless they particularly wished to do so, because they had received perfectly valid revelations of their own.[10]

---

[9] Sami Zubaida, *Islam: The People and the State. Political Ideas and Movements in the Middle East* (London: I.B.Tauris, 1993), ix.

[10] Karen Armstrong, *Islam: A Short History* (London: Phoenix Press, 2001), 9.

Early Quranic revelations include the oft-repeated general statement 'there shall be no coercion in matters of faith' (Sura 2:256) and, when it comes to the specific matter of relations of Muslims with both Jews and Christians—whom the Qur'an refers to as 'People of the Book' or, more accurately, as Armstrong points out, 'people of an earlier revelation'—then the injunction of Sura 29:46 applies:

> Do not argue with the followers of earlier revelation otherwise than in a most kindly manner—unless it be such of them as are bent on evil-doing—and say: 'We believe in that which has been bestowed from on high upon us, as well as that which has been bestowed upon you, for our God and your God is one and the same, and it is unto Him that we [all] surrender ourselves.[11]

Islam contains within its scriptural source and ideological heritage the possibility for dialogical engagement and peaceful co-existence with peoples of other faiths. This has been both confirmed and countered within Islamic history. The task today is to take up the challenge of dialogical engagement and the quest for sustainable peaceful co-existence with renewed vigour.

This book attempts both to understand Islam and to engage in a dialogical response to this important world religion. Accordingly, the first part comprises my own introduction to Islam, written not so much as a textbook piece (although it could be used as such) but more particularly as an attempt, by a non-Muslim scholar, to express respectful appreciation by as accurately as possible describing, and with critical empathy discussing, Islam. Therefore I begin with exploring themes of origins, scripture, and tradition: the component elements of the 'foundations' of a religion. I then move on to probe the unique particularities of Islamic community, beliefs, practices, and the nature and place of law. Thus the twin components of historical background and contemporary expression, requisite for a critical understanding of any religion, are covered to a greater or lesser degree. And the context for all this is, of course, as a precursor to dialogical engagement. For my interest is not that of making my mark as an expert scholar of Islam—I am not an academic Islamist in that sense—but rather, as a Christian theologian and student of religion *per se*, concerned very much with the phenomenon of, and prospects for, interfaith dialogue—most particularly that of Christian–Muslim engagement—to contribute to the pressing contemporary global discussion of and about Islam in the world today.

My wider interests become clear in Parts II and III. My approach will presume a background knowledge such as is found in Part I, at least to a certain degree. Where it seems appropriate some cross-referencing will be flagged, but otherwise the chapters of both Parts II and III are designed pretty much to stand on their own. In Part II, I explore the wider context of the encounter with Islam by way of, first, the encounter through the centuries of Islam with Christianity and, second, the encounter of Islam

---

[11] Sura 29:46 of the Qur'an from Muhammad Asad, trans., *The Message of the Qur'an* (Gibraltar, 1980) cited in Armstrong, ibid.

with Judaism. It is not possible, in two short chapters, to do justice to the sweeping and complex histories of these two arenas of interfaith encounter. So my approach has been to temper historical overview with interpretive analysis and comment for, once again, the purpose is to stimulate thinking about interfaith relationship with Islam and, hopefully, make a positive contribution to the prospects for dialogue in our time. And this does not mean painting rosy pictures and fostering shallow hope: the approach I seek to take is that of critical realism.

There have been, and are, very serious issues at stake in the context of both Christian–Muslim and Jewish–Muslim engagement and dialogue. They may appear insurmountable. They are profoundly important. They require serious attention in order to reach any sort of satisfactory resolution, for resolution—or perhaps reconciliation—of deeply held antipathies is no easy task. I certainly make no claims to have done that in this book, but I hope I have made at least some small contribution to the process required to get there. Further, it would be an injustice to the integrity of each religion, and the process of dialogue, to minimise the difficulties that each has with the other. What I have attempted to do is identify operative paradigms and leitmotifs that apply to these areas of interfaith encounter which, even as they beg further questions, may yet assist the process of realistically grappling with salient aspects and issues of the interfaith relations involved. And a key component in those relations, as well as the more general question of cross-cultural and inter-social relations—such as may be thought of under the rubric of 'Islam and the West'—is, of course, the question of the contemporary religio-political contours of Islam. Chapter 8 looks closely at matters of Islamic identity and ideology as constituting much of the 'drivers' for contemporary events.

In Part III I have attempted to discuss what I see as three important areas or elements of dialogue with Islam, notably the matter of perceptions of Islam that contribute to the barriers that prevent dialogue taking place; a range of elements that arise out of experience of, and reflection upon, interfaith encounter with Islam; and finally a foray into the potential minefield of theological dialogue. The work of this book is then drawn together in a closing chapter. I trust the reader who makes it through will be at least satisfied that a worthwhile venture has been enjoined.

In the Appendix I have provided something of a beginner's guide to reading the Qur'an, which might be of some help to guide the first-time student into unfamiliar scriptural territory. There is also a Glossary comprising a selection of Arabic words and other more technical terms that pepper the pages of a book such as this. While for the most part I have endeavoured to explain such terms as they appear in the text, and reinforce their meaning and usage by repeated translations and explanations given in parenthesis, the provision of an explanatory list may also prove to be a worthwhile aid for the newcomer to Islam and the field of Christian–Muslim interfaith dialogue. The bibliography is a representative list of relevant works that goes beyond those directly cited, and the Index, of course, is given as a guide to both the persons and the subject matter that can be found within the pages of this book.

PART I
UNDERSTANDING ISLAM
A PRECURSOR TO DIALOGUE

Chapter 2

The Origins of Islam
Prehistory and Prophet

The word *Islam* means, in essence, 'surrender' or 'submission' and carries the idea of 'being in peaceful submission' to God (*Allah*). The words *islam, muslim* and *salaam* are derived from the common Arabic root, s-l-m, and yield the meanings, respectively, of *willing active submission* (to God); *one who makes or practises such submission*; and *peace*. This last term is especially used as a greeting. A Muslim is one who lives life in submission to the Will of Allah. In Islamic thought, all human beings are born innately 'muslim'. This means that everyone is born according to, and inherently in submission to, the Will of God, the Creator; it is a fundamental feature of a created being. In the Bible—and of particular importance to Muslims—the wandering Near Eastern patriarch, Abraham (*Ibrahim*), who lived some two thousand years before Jesus (*Isa*), provides an originating model of what it means to be in perfect submission to God, that is, to be *muslim* or in the state of *islam*. For, in complete submission to God's command, Abraham prepared his first-born son for sacrifice. However, at the point where the sacrificial act was to be concluded, God intervened and declared Abraham's submission to be well demonstrated. Abraham was then directed to a ram caught in a bush close to hand, which he offered as the sacrifice in the place of his son. The biblical story is recorded in Genesis, Chapter 22, and names the son Isaac (*Ishaq*), from whom is descended the Hebrew tribes and thus the religion of Judaism.

However, Abraham had another son, Ishmael (*Isma'il*), older than Isaac, although not of the same mother. Isaac's mother was Sarah, the wife of Abraham. Sarah had conceived very late in life, prior to which she had allowed her husband, as was custom, to produce a son and heir by her Egyptian-born maidservant, Hagar. Hence paradoxically, it would seem, Abraham had two first-born sons: the elder being the first-born in time; the younger being the first-born of his wife. According to the biblical record, Ishmael and his mother Hagar were exiled from the land of Abraham soon after Isaac was born because Sarah did not want them around. So they emigrated to the deserts of Arabia, and thus, so the story goes, from Ishmael are descended the Arab tribes and, in due course, historically speaking, the religion of Islam. Ideologically speaking, Muslims view their religion as, in fact, coming directly from Abraham, if not from Adam, the first created man. In this sense Islam is the religion bequeathed by God. (But more of this below).

Although the Qur'an is silent about the identity of the son offered for sacrifice, the issue has been much debated by Islamic scholars who have concluded that it was the first-born Ishmael whom Abraham offered in obedient response to the divine command. Thus, from the Muslim point of view, the seal is set on the special place, indeed the priority of place, of the Arabic heritage within the unfolding story of divine revelation. Debate on detail aside, what is exceedingly clear is that from Abraham's exemplary act comes a common thread binding Jews, Muslims, and also Christians, together. Abraham is the patriarch not just of ancient Near Eastern peoples, but of three great world religions. For Jews he demonstrates fidelity to Torah, the 'Law' or, better, the 'Way' of God. To Christians, Abraham demonstrates sublime faith: wholehearted obedience to God. To Muslims he demonstrates perfect submission to the Will of Allah, the One and Only God. But if Abraham is the common link, the subtle variations of understanding him reflect nuanced difference in religious perspective. To understand the Islamic viewpoint, we need to turn to Muhammad, born towards the end of the sixth century of the Common Era, more than twenty-five hundred years after Abraham. However, before doing this, we need to understand a little of the contours of the social and religious context of Muhammad's time.

Pre-Islamic Arabia

Arabia, by the seventh century of the Common Era, was divided into three geographic regions, each with its own distinctive and predominant racial, cultural and linguistic heritage. At times there was much strife and animosity between these regions. A nomadic lifestyle coupled with cultural diversity meant there was neither any unanimity among Arabic peoples nor any sense of a fundamental unity in religion. Nonetheless it would appear that, given the existence of trade and commerce, with the central role played in this by the city of Mecca (*Makkah*), then some forms of economic interaction and social relations certainly existed among the tribes and regions as the order of the day, albeit a somewhat tenuous order. Certainly it would not take much to precipitate an ongoing feud. Furthermore, there were many harsh customary practices indulged in by Arabs at this time, such as the 'exposing' or burying alive of infant daughters. Life was harsh. Women were predominantly, but not always, the chattels of men. Children were of low status, and the female child was the most vulnerable of all.

By the time of Muhammad the geopolitical context of Arabia, for some time, had been set off to one side, rather in the manner of a spectator so far as the arena of encounter between the two great Near Eastern empires of the day, the Roman Byzantine and the Persian Sassanian empires, was concerned.[1] There were, of course, other lesser powers in the region, but the main tension was between the competing claims for political dominion and cultural superiority of the Byzantine

---

[1] See Fred M. Donner, 'Muhammad and the Caliphate: Political History of the Islamic Empire up to the Mongol Conquest', in John L. Esposito, ed., *The Oxford History of Islam* (Oxford: Oxford University Press, 1999).

and the ancient Iranian (that is, Persian or Sassanian) empires. This tension was echoed in the main religious rivalry, namely, Byzantine Christianity on the one hand and Persian Zoroastrianism on the other. Both were religions that espoused belief in a single supreme deity who had sent prophets and a revelation to humankind. Byzantium and Byzantine Christianity faced off against Persia and the religion of Zoroastrianism. Furthermore, populations in the region were by no means homogeneous. Considerable emigration, often fomented by religious dissent, meant that Diaspora Judaism and heterodox Christianity infiltrated the region of Arabia as elsewhere. So, even before Muhammad, Arabia certainly knew of the phenomenon of prophets and of scriptural revelation, both in terms of contemporary events and in respect to its own ancient heritage.

However, in Islamic thought it is held that, by the time of Muhammad, Arabia had forgotten its ancient beginnings. Abraham and the One God were but a faded memory. As a people, these descendants of the great patriarch had fallen into a state and age of ignorance—*al-jahiliyya*—a term referring to the forgetting of the truth and knowledge of the One God, and also to a cultural climate of somewhat wild, savage and uncivilised behaviour, whether thought of in terms of an historical epoch or a more broadly applied idea of the human condition or state. Tribal diversity and rivalry was reflected in polytheistic variety as well as cultural diversity. Although there were some individuals, known as *hanif*, who clung to a residual notion of monotheism—and Muhammad appears to have been of this persuasion—the Arab tribes worshipped many gods. As well as the notion of a distant supreme deity, many lesser deities and spiritual entities abounded. As Fred Donner remarks, 'In addition to the scriptural religions, Arabia also was home to a host of local animist cults, which attributed divine powers to natural objects—the sun, the moon, Venus, certain sacred rocks and trees, and so on'.[2] Different forms of animism, as well as variant polytheisms, were features of this 'time of ignorance'.

A great variety of cults and religious influences were to hand at the time Muhammad appeared. From South Arabia, for example, an astral cult based on the idea of a moon-god and reflecting Babylonian and Zoroastrian influences predominated. The majority of Arabs worshipped local gods and goddesses, and gave veneration to a variety of astral deities—Jupiter, Venus, Mercury and so on—reflecting also Roman and Greek influences. In some areas the incursions of the Jewish Diaspora, and the settlement of heterodox Christians, had led to a reawakening of interest in, and focus on, the idea of there being one God only. Variant forms of monotheism were being espoused, but Christian debates and differences of opinion concerning the doctrine of the Trinity further confused the picture. To be sure, in Arabic lore there was reference to a one High God *(al-ilah)*. However, the ancient shrine in Mecca, of which it is believed Abraham had it built to the honour of God when he paid a visit to his son Ishmael—indeed many

[2] Ibid., 4.

Muslims believe it was first built by Adam in honour of the one Creator and that Abraham in fact rebuilt it—by the time of Muhammad housed the images and idols of the many Arabian deities. This shrine, a cubic building made of hewn stone, had ever been known as the *Ka'ba*, and for many centuries veneration had been given to a stone—thought to be a meteorite, a divine portent from the heavens—built into a corner.

Furthermore, according to Islamic history, the Meccans rebuilt the Ka'ba during Muhammad's lifetime—before he began his prophetic life—and that, at the crucial point when the stone was to be replaced, Muhammad's practical intercession prevented the eruption of deep disharmony among the four Meccan tribes involved in the reconstruction. His answer to the question 'Who has the honour of replacing the stone?' was to instruct representatives from the tribes to take the four corners of a piece of cloth upon which the stone had been placed and together carry it to the corner of the shrine where he, Muhammad, on behalf of them all, then placed it into position.

The involvement of Muhammad at this point notwithstanding, the shrine had become, and had continued to be, a kind of polytheistic centre: all gods were welcome and many were represented there. Within the Ka'ba there were many idols ranged around Hubal, the chief male deity. At the time, the idea of 'the one God' (*al-ilah*) was a vaguely conceived notion of a faraway High-God creator. This deity was venerated by some, especially the tribe into which Muhammad was born. But also there were believed to be three closely related goddesses worshipped as the three 'daughters' of Allah. Thus the Arabs boasted a veritable pantheon: Hubal, Allah, the daughters of Allah, and so on, all of whom could be worshipped at the Ka'ba in Mecca.

Mecca, at the time of Muhammad, was very much a mercantile centre within the Arabian Peninsula. The peninsula itself stood astride a most important trade route, namely that which went from the Roman Empire and other territories of the West over to India and the lands of the East. Whether by way of Egypt or the Persian Gulf, Arabia formed a trade-bridge between East and West. In this situation, nomadic Bedouins played a significant role and were deemed the 'princes of the desert routes'.[3] Mecca had become, in respect of both international as well as local trade, a most important economic and cultural centre.

Meccans themselves belonged to different tribes and clans. At the time there were essentially two forms of tribal life: those of the tribes who had become settled and established around towns and cities, and the more nomadic Bedouin lifestyle of the desert. This difference made for a complex situation for both social relations and any notion of corporate identity. Life was a constant state of flux and there was really no sense of cohesion beyond that of the immediate tribal context. As Husein Haykal comments, in the desert

---

[3] Husein Haykal, *The Life of Muhammad*, trans. Ismail Raji al-Faruqi (Kuala Lumpur: Islamic Book Trust, 1993), 4.

the basic unit of life is not the state but the tribe. Moreover, a tribe which is always on the move does not know of any universal law nor does it ever subject itself to any general political order. To the nomad, nothing is acceptable that falls short of total freedom for the individual, for the family, and for the tribe as a whole.[4]

Although Muhammad's clan was one that had been settled in Mecca over a long period, and one that shared in the administration of the Ka'ba, it was nonetheless one of the poorer tribal groups.

Annual pilgrimage (*al-hajj*) to the Ka'ba, with its accompanying trade, had constituted the lifeblood of Meccan existence for centuries. The pilgrimage, with its festivities and engagement in allied commerce, involved a pact to desist from any inter-tribal strife and warfare for the duration. Close by the Ka'ba is a well, with the name *Zamzam*, an onomatopoeic word representing, in Arabic, the gushing sound of water when first released, as in the initial discovery of a well site. It is believed that while his mother Hagar was frantically searching for water for herself and her son, the young Ishmael uncovered the well and so released the aqueous flow. Visiting this well and retracing Hagar's frenetic search by running between the two low hills nearby has since been incorporated into the activities of the Hajj.

The point to note is that many elements of pilgrimage were in existence long before the institution of the practices of Muhammad and the religion he founded, historically speaking. Such elements became *islamised*, that is, subject to the process of Islamisation wherein they are taken on or over, redefined, and so incorporated into the new—Islamic—worldview. This phenomenon is not itself so unusual in the development of a religion. Such incorporations do not vitiate the religion and sully its motives; rather they demonstrate the pervasive and interpretative, or viewpoint-forming, power of religion, and this is no less the case with Islam.

Muhammad: a biographical sketch

Islamic interest in the historical person Muhammad is high indeed. There have been innumerable biographical studies undertaken by Muslim scholars. The tenor is largely one of subjective record and veneration. For the most part the sources that have been drawn upon in the construction of such works have been the Qur'an; the material known as the Sunnah of the Prophet—that is, sayings, deeds, and exemplary incidents of Muhammad other than the Quranic utterances themselves; and the earliest biographies written by those who directly knew Muhammad and lived in his time. Given that all biography, and especially that of religious subjects, is narrative history written from a particular slant or perspective, then biographical hermeneutics—or interpretation—needs to be acknowledged as an issue of

---

[4] Ibid., 15.

scholarly importance. Muhammad may have been a mere man, but the role he played, and the example he became for Muslims, has meant that legendary material and recorded historical data are intimately intertwined. Assessments and conclusions about Muhammad must be made with caution and in recognition that, as with any significant religious figure, we must discern historical essence and religious dynamic from, often, overlays of heroic legend and pious embellishment.

Biography, in this case, is not simply the telling of Muhammad's life-story. It is also an apologia, an active propaganda, for endorsing and promoting the authenticity of the messenger and his message. There is nothing necessarily improper about this: the academic issue is to discern the distinction between the pious narrative and the historical phenomena upon which it rests. Over against scholarly attempts to construct genuinely historical and critical biographic record—which itself, of course, implies a particular interpretive stance—there is the plethora of devotional and hagiographical biography. Each of these types of biography serves a different purpose. One seeks to uncover the concrete historical record in order to understand better the dynamics of Muhammad's life and situate both who he was, and what he achieved, in an objectively assessable context. The other tells the story of Muhammad so as to promote and reinforce a particular piety and perspective upon the validity of Muhammad's role. There is, integral to the biographies, an avowed assertion of the veracity of the faith tradition he founded. To this extent religious biography is, most often, religiously motivated. Muhammad's life and person has been long promoted therefore as uniquely exemplary and as proof of, and inspiration for, the Muslim faith.

There was also a particular reason for, and outcome of, the earliest biographies. If the predominant motive was largely pietistic, the early impetus for writing biographies of Muhammad was also very much political. Muhammad not only preached a principle of unity applying to both the concept of God and the formation of the Islamic community; he lived out and demonstrated the practical application of this principle in his life and in his overall leadership of the community. Prior to Muhammad's rule, attempts to bring about any form of pan-tribal unity within the Arabian Peninsula had failed. A key point of reference was missing. Muhammad supplied it, both with his own life-example and in his winning hearts and minds to belief in the One God. Thus Muhammad provided the concrete point of reference for the principle of unity. This principle is otherwise abstractly derived from the primary theological leitmotif of Islam: that God is 'One'—meaning the very idea of deity is that of an ontological unity—and there is no deity but the One God.

The unifying principle holding together human social diversity within one overarching social entity—the *Ummah*—is seen to be historically rooted in the life of this Apostle of God, the messenger of Allah. As John Esposito notes:

> Muslims believe that they are members of a worldwide Muslim community, known as the *ummah*, united by a religious bond that transcends tribal, ethnic, and national

identities. This belief is based on Quran 2:143, which declares that God created the Muslim ummah to serve as witnesses of God's guidance to the nations.[5]

The political development of Islam following the death of Muhammad was reinforced, if not actively guided, by the biographical interest in the life of the Prophet. More recently, however, Muslim biographies tend to focus on themes of excellence and uniqueness. The political impetus has been supplanted by the needs of piety. All this said, I shall nevertheless attempt to sketch the biographical contours of the life of Muhammad.

Although his exact date of birth is unknown, it is largely agreed that Muhammad was born in Mecca in 570CE into the *Hashim* family of the *Quraysh* clan (sub-tribe) of the tribe *Banu-'Abd-Manaf*. His father died before he was born. Then, from being but a young baby, in keeping with the customs of the time, he spent his infant years with a wet-nurse of a nomadic tribe living in the healthier environment of the desert away from the town of Mecca. Muhammad was returned to his mother at about the age of five. However, with the untimely death of his mother he was, at six years of age, an orphan and became the ward of his paternal grandfather *'Abd-al-Muttalib*. Later, after the death of the grandfather, when Muhammad was eight, he was raised in the care of his uncle *Abu-Talib*. In later life this uncle assumed a particularly important role as the protector of Muhammad. Abu-Talib remained close to his nephew, even though he never embraced the beliefs that Muhammad proclaimed. He died when Muhammad was fifty years old.

Emerging from humble and somewhat impoverished origins, it appears the young Muhammad developed a rather sensitive personality. Donner notes that:

> Traditional sources portray Muhammad as having been a promising and respected young man who participated in both Mecca's cultic activities and its commerce. He also seemed to have had an inward, contemplative side, however, which expressed itself in his periodic withdrawal to secluded spots for prolonged periods of meditation and reflection.[6]

It is said that Muhammad displayed revulsion to the worship of idols from quite an early age. However, he lived a life that was relatively normal for a young Qurayshi man, including the undertaking of various duties and obligations in respect of maintaining the Ka'ba. As a youth he was occupied as a herdsman, learned the arts of warfare and so on, and he engaged in much reflective thought and contemplation. As he grew into manhood it is clear he gained a reputation for being honest and trustworthy and he was well regarded for his active promotion of justice and fair play. He came to dislike many of the harsher customs and practices of his society and it appears, as he grew up, he was attracted to some of the ethical

---

[5] John Esposito, *What Everyone Needs To Know About Islam* (New York: OUP, 2002), 15.

[6] Donner, 'Muhammad and the Caliphate', 6.

injunctions and theological views encountered amongst Jews and Christians who visited Mecca with their own trade caravans, and whom he encountered on his own travels.

As a young man, Muhammad was employed by *Khadijah*, a tradeswoman of great honour and wealth. She had engaged a group of young Qurayshi men, including Muhammad, to take trade caravans around the region. This experience led him into contact with clans of Jews and communities of Christians who, by this time, had moved into Arabia. So it was that Muhammad learned afresh of belief in the One God. He heard about the prophets to the Jews since the time of Abraham. He found out about Jesus who, for some of these Christians, was also seen as yet another great prophet, but who, for others, was believed to be the divine Son of God. But both Jews and Christians were talking about a Day of Judgement, a day when God would call all to account and determine a final outcome: dispensing the rewards of heaven or the punishments of hell in accordance with the deeds and outcomes of one's life.

At the age of 25 Muhammad married Khadijah, his widowed employer, then aged 40. Muhammad enjoyed a relatively privileged life for many years. However, it was not without personal sorrow and tragedy. For although he and Khadijah raised a family, their two sons died in infancy, and of the four daughters only one, Fatima, survived Muhammad. She married Ali, a paternal cousin to Muhammad, and so was the only one of his children to provide Muhammad with direct descendants. Khadijah's death at age 65, when Muhammad was 50, and after they had been married for 25 years, occurred in the same year that Muhammad's uncle Abu-Talib also died. This double loss of the closest relatives and support people in his life is of significance for, as we will see below, it contributed to the turn of events that propelled a local and contentious reforming figure onto the world stage as the founder of what was to become a major religion of the world.

Following Khadijah's death, Muhammad eventually took several other wives, but the reasons for doing so were primarily religio-political and pastoral: the cementing of tribal alliances in the early formation of the Islamic community, and the taking in of widows of close companions who had died in battle, for, like infant girls, widows at that time were among the most vulnerable. Against any suggestion that Muhammad was a lascivious Arab leader indulging his earthly passions, stands the reality of social changes he was instituting, and concern for the welfare of close female associates. The place of Khadijah in his affections and the honouring of the role she played for him were never diminished. Muhammad apparently once said of Khadijah: 'When I was poor she enriched me; when they called me a liar, she alone remained true.'

By the age of 40 Muhammad was in the custom of taking regular time out in prayer and meditation in a cave not far from Mecca. It would appear he had been impressed by the belief, common to both Jews and Christians at the time, that there would be a last judgement. Those who committed idolatry—who worshipped false gods—would receive punishment by everlasting fire. The one true God, said both Christians and Jews, could not be represented by any image but only by prophetic leaders. Muhammad knew that such prophets had in previous times appeared in Palestine. In Persia also there had been just such a prophet—Zoroaster. So who would come to Arabia to give warning? Surely God would send a prophet to the Arab peoples? While on one of his regular meditation or 'time-out' sessions in a cave at the base of Mount Hira, near Mecca, Muhammad experienced a vision of a heavenly messenger, the Archangel Gabriel (*Jibreel*). This event is known and recorded in the Qur'an as the 'Night of Power and Excellence'. The angel commanded Muhammad simply to 'recite' words that would be directly given him. Muhammad was informed that God would provide the words of the recitations: Muhammad simply had to submit to the Will of Allah thus allowing God to speak through him. The Arabic for the command to recite is *iqr'a*, from which is derived the word *Qur'an*, which names the collection of these recitations, believed, of course, to be divinely given.

For Islam it is important that Muhammad's submission, humility, and his relative illiteracy, are acknowledged. For, to Muslims, in no way could a human being invent or create the recitations, which have since been collected and reproduced in book form as the Holy Qur'an. Muhammad's call to be the mouthpiece of God, and the commencement of the recitations that eventually became the scripture of Islam, took place in the year 610. The Qur'an itself records, in Suras 13, 30, and 37, the divine command to Muhammad to proclaim the message in public. Muhammad's initial reactions were of disbelief and doubt. It is clear that he did not consider himself worthy for the task: he required considerable prompting and encouragement both to believe that what was happening to him was real, and to act upon it by preaching, once the initial doubt was overcome. In this latter regard the support and encouragement of his wife was critical. She, along with Muhammad's cousin Ali (who eventually became his son-in-law, then the fourth Caliph after the death of Muhammad), was the first to accept Muhammad's prophethood and call and so 'submit' to the new faith. The one who would eventually succeed Muhammad as leader of the Muslim community, *Abu Bakr*, was the first person outside Muhammad's own household to submit to the call 'to worship God alone and to the repudiation of idols'.[7]

The endorsement of his uncle, Abu-Talib, was also of supreme importance to Muhammad. Although Abu-Talib never himself became a believer, remaining instead a traditional polytheist, he was nonetheless crucially supportive of Muhammad's right to preach the new faith and not to succumb to pressures to desist. Further, the support of the first few individuals with whom he shared his revelations and who believed in them, and so also believed in Muhammad and his divinely appointed role, was likewise crucial. So, in terms of both the early support he received and the recorded Quranic injunctions, the prophetic mandate and role of Muhammad is well attested and unequivocally endorsed.

---

[7] Haykal, *Life of Muhammad*, 82.

Nevertheless, Muslims then, and ever since, have viewed Muhammad as simply the 'mouthpiece' for divine messages which he received in the form of spontaneous utterance. Certainly, when it was clear that these strange locutionary experiences— in which beautiful poetic or sublime prose Arabic flowed across his lips—would continue to occur spontaneously, Muhammad came to believe that Allah was indeed using him as a mouthpiece. The verses he uttered, half in trance it would seem, were believed to be real divine revelations. The eventual collecting of these revelations meant that Arabia was at last being provided with a scripture. More than that, the revelations themselves declare that this scripture, of later date and authority than the scriptures of the Jews and Christians, is in fact the only unadulterated revelation of the message of the One True God.

In the next decade (610–20CE) Muhammad would repeat the recitations in public after they occurred, and also preach on them. In essence their message was the proclamation of the One True God over against polytheistic idolatry; a concomitant warning against idol worship and remaining in ignorance of the truth of the One God; and the proclamation of a Day of Judgement and general resurrection. The core of the message received and delivered by Muhammad was of

> a warning that only through devotion to the one and only God and through righteous observance of the revealed law could people attain salvation in the afterlife. Some revelations thus emphasized the oneness and omnipotence of God ... Others warned that the Last Judgment was near; and then those who had lived righteously would be sent to heaven and those who had lived evil lives would be sent to eternal damnation in hell. Other revelations laid out the general guidelines for a righteous existence. ... Still other revelations retold stories of earlier prophets.[8]

Much of what Muhammad said, and the language he used to say it, would have been familiar to his audience, thus contributing to making Muhammad's message that much more readily comprehensible.[9] At first Muhammad was listened to because of his good standing in the community and his reputation for truthfulness and for being trustworthy. He stressed the call to fellow Arabs to give up their idolatrous ways, to repent of their harsh customary practices, and to worshipfully submit to the One God, the ruler and judge of all. Needless to say, this did not go down well with the worldly Meccans.

> If the idols were destroyed, what would become of them, the keepers of the idols, and their renown throughout the land? How would they retain the allegiance of the neighbouring tribes who came to worship their several divinities at the Ka'ba? That a few should follow the ravings of a madman or a magician who preferred one God above the beautiful deities of Mecca was of small concern; but that some leading men of the

---

[8] Donner, 'Muhammad and the Caliphate', 7.

[9] Cf. Donner, *passim.*

city should join the sect, and that the magician should terrify the people in broad daylight with his denunciation of the worship which they superintended, was intolerable.[10]

The Meccan oligarchy was seriously disturbed; Muhammad was in earnest—and so was the opposition to him.

Apart from winning a few converts, the first years were harsh for Muhammad. He experienced much rejection and vilification from his own people. He was openly rebuked because of his unpalatable message. In particular, his activities aroused the ire of tribal and mercantile leaders and posed an affront to pagan polytheists. Some attempts to negotiate directly with Muhammad, as a fellow clansman, in order to dissuade him from his seemingly destructive mission, failed. Compromise was impossible. As Azzam remarks:

> The purest form of monotheism, which is the essence of Muhammad's faith, was an impossible doctrine for the Qurayshis to accept. The polytheism of Mecca had been established from time immemorial. It was not only the religion of their ancestors but the source of their distinction in all Arabia. If it went, with it would go their honour, power, and wealth.[11]

Hence Muhammad's preaching in Mecca brought adverse reactions including personal insult and challenges. Argument and dispute with Muhammad increased and intensified, together with direct persecution of many of his followers. Threats, repudiation, and an economic and social boycott against him and his clan who were protecting him, were instituted. As Haykal notes:

> Fearful of arousing the enmity and antagonism of Quraysh for their departure from idol worship, the new Muslims used to hide the fact of their conversion. ... For three years while Islam continued to be spread among the Makkans, the Muslims continued to hide.[12]

As negative social conditions intensified towards the first converts and, by association, to Muhammad's own family and sub-tribe, Muhammad took seriously his responsibility to these followers. Many were sent to Christian Abyssinia (now Ethiopia) where they were afforded the protection of the emperor who apparently thought the new Arab faith to be a derivative of, and parallel to, Christianity. Members of the Hashimite clan of the Quraysh tribe loyal to Abu-Talib, and thus protectors of Muhammad, withdrew to a valley on the outskirts of Mecca.

---

[10] Abd al-Rahman Azzam, *The Eternal Message of Muhammad* (Leicester: The Islamic Texts Society, 1993), 12.

[11] Ibid., 13.

[12] Haykal, *Life of Muhammad*, 83.

Bloodshed was avoided but harsh privations were endured. A boycott and siege at the hands of the Meccans was suffered for three years.

Although the majority of Hashimites were not converts, nonetheless tribal bonds provided the protection and context out of which the nascent Muslim community received its early nurture. After the three years of exile moderate forces within Mecca relented and allowed a return of Abu-Talib and the Hashimites to their homes. The converts in exile in Abyssinia also decided to return to Mecca, but soon they too were faced with renewed persecutions. Eventually, however, some gains were made, especially with the conversion of the Meccan leader, *Umar ibn al Khattab*. Haykal comments that the conversion of Umar 'reduced the power of Quraysh significantly in that Umar brought with him to the faith the tribal loyalties with which he had fought Islam earlier'.[13]

All the while, throughout these tribulations, Muhammad continued to receive revelations and to proclaim them, thus building up the body of recitations that were to become the Qur'an. According to various accounts and stories Muhammad is also reported to have had a variety of extraordinary spiritual experiences including a night of miraculous transportation (*al Isra*) to the site of the Jewish Temple in Jerusalem where he prayed with Abraham, Moses (*Musa*) and Jesus and then, miraculously transported (*al Mi'raj*) to heaven, he entered into the presence of Allah, conversed with God about his mission, and was shown the realities of paradise and hell. The point of this story, whether viewed symbolically or read literally, is to underscore the religious connections and relativities: Muhammad is a full member of this 'club' of religious leaders. However, the story also reinforces Muhammad's basic message: submit to Allah in the fear of damnation if you do not and the promise of paradise and reward if you do.

Despite the growing community of converts and the protective support of his clan, Muhammad was increasingly vulnerable. The precarious state of affairs in Mecca lasted some ten years, by the end of which, in 620CE, both Muhammad's wife and protecting uncle had died. This left Muhammad in a precarious position: he was still preaching the judgement of God to the intense irritation of Meccan society and now, as his own tribe was increasingly turning against him, he lacked personal protection. However, help was at hand. At another town, *Yathrib*, some distance from Mecca, tribal leaders were preparing to make an overture to Muhammad. When it occurred, it paved the way for his exit from Mecca and, at that critical turning point, the foundation of the community of Islam as a religio-political entity. A few merchants from Yathrib had been converted by Muhammad's preaching and had sworn their allegiance to him. In 621CE they returned to Mecca with news that others in that city had subsequently turned to the new faith. A further pledge was then made to Muhammad by representatives of the main tribes in Yathrib.

Early in 622CE a further and larger delegation again visited Muhammad, and pledged to him their loyalty and protection. In response Muhammad directed the

---

[13] Ibid., 115.

returnees from Abyssinia and other new converts to emigrate to Yathrib for their own protection. He himself delayed in going there until the last possible moment. The Qurayshis in Mecca did not wish to see Muhammad make it to a rival city so set out to eliminate him. However, Muhammad eluded his would-be assassins and in June of 622 fled to Yathrib together with his close companion and assistant, Abu Bakr. This dramatic exodus, known as *al-hijra* (the flight), was a critical event for Islam. Its dating provides the beginning of the Islamic calendar, for it marks the commencement of the first Islamic state, thus giving concrete socio-political expression to the notion of the 'universal' Islamic community, or *Ummah*.

By way of an excursus, it should be noted at this juncture that Islamic dating, on a lunar calendar basis, commences with the year of the hijra. Thus Muslims speak simply of a year as, using Arabic, '*hijri*', that is to say, meaning 'of the hijra'. In the West this has sometimes been given a Latin reference, in parallel to Christianity's *Anno Domini* (Year of [since] our Lord or 'AD'), as *Anno Hegira* (Year of [since] hijra − 'AH'). Thus the year 622CE is rendered, for Islam, the year of the Hijra, or AH1. However, for the most part the Muslim world simply refers to a year *as* hijri, thus H1, for the first year. The calendric equation of years is naturally complicated by the fact that the Islamic year is a lunar-based marking of time. If the calendars had been in parallel on the same solar system, the year H (or AH) 1400 for Islam would have equated with 2022CE (that is, 622 + 1400). However, in point of fact the Muslim year AH1400 fell in the year 1979CE.

The terms of Muhammad's relocation to Yathrib were significant. The town's leaders and people desired strong political and religious leadership in order that internal dissension and disputes might be resolved. Yathrib comprised non-believers, Jews and Christians, as well as Muslims who were either immigrants from Mecca (the *Muhajirun*) or those of Yathrib (the *Ansar*, or 'helpers') who had previously converted and so assisted the Meccan Muslims. Specifically, Muhammad was asked to arbitrate in a bitter feud between the two main Arab tribes there, as well as in respect to tensions between the Muhajirun and Ansar, and also between some of the Jews of Yathrib and the newcomers.[14] In general terms, he was approached to lead the restoration of the city's political life. Muhammad agreed on the basis of certain preparations taking place, including an undertaking that he be accepted by the city as prophet with full leadership functions and authority.

Thus was forged the conditions for the founding of the Islamic theocracy, a society where all of life is under religious direction, where politics and religion are effectively merged. In consequence the town was renamed *Medina al Nabi*—the city of the Prophet—or 'Medina' for short. Muhammad was well received there by the main converted tribes. And so, as Azzam comments, 'After thirteen years of intensive struggle to survive, the Prophet had at last found a friendly city where he

---

[14] See Donner, 'Muhammad and the Caliphate', 9.

could defend himself and base his future operations'.[15] The significance of the hijra and Medina lies in the fact that they mark the time and place where, as Armstrong puts it, 'Muhammad was able to implement the Quranic ideal fully … Muhammad had become the head of a collection of tribal groups that were not bound together by blood but by a shared ideology, an astonishing innovation in Arabian society.'[16]

Muhammad set about building the first mosque (*masjid*), or place of prayer, and shaping the Islamic theocracy by instituting the regularised practices of religion, which have become known as the 'pillars of Islam'. Promulgating the 'Constitution of Medina' was the first major political act undertaken by Muhammad in respect of establishing the Muslim community as a socio-political entity. It welded together otherwise disparate tribes into a new identity as Muslims belonging to a new pan-tribal community. Alliances with neighbouring Jews and pagan Arabs for the purposes of defence and security within Medina were secured. Haykal notes that, for the most part, biographies of Muhammad all emphasise a key significant point of Muhammad's initial policy at Medina, namely 'realizing the security of his followers and their right to worship as they pleased on an equal footing with men of other faiths'.[17]

> It was absolutely necessary that the Muslim, the Jew, and the Christian have an equal opportunity in their exercise of religious freedom as well as in their freedom to hold different opinions and to preach their own faiths. Only such freedom can guarantee victory for the truth and progress of the world toward perfection in the higher unity of mankind. Every war against this freedom furthers the cause of falsehood. Every limitation of it gives power to the forces of darkness ....[18]

But, to achieve his socio-political ends, nothing less than a total socio-political upheaval was required: the relinquishing of the ways of old and becoming 'muslim'; instituting a political and social order which, as Azzam remarks, was 'carefully established and observed in the here and now as a road to the afterworld'.[19]

The nascent Islamic Ummah now established in Medina, during the next ten years, to 632CE, saw a sequence of battles, negotiations, triumphs and defeats, as the community grew, consolidated, and eventually won Mecca over. Muhammad's leadership in all spheres—judicial, political, military as well as religious—grew in stature and capacity. According to Haykal,

---

[15] Azzam, *The Eternal Message*, 22.

[16] Karen Armstrong, *Islam: A Short History* (London: Phoenix Press, 2001), 12.

[17] Haykal, *The Life of Muhammad*, 175.

[18] Ibid.

[19] Azzam, *The Eternal Message*, 22.

Muhammad's thought was ... guided by one final objective, namely, the guarantee of freedom of religion and thought. It was for the sake of this freedom alone that fighting was permitted. It was in its defense that repulsion of the aggressor was allowed, that no one might be persecuted on account of his faith and that no injustice might befall anyone because of his faith or opinion.[20]

By the second year of the hijra Muhammad had adopted a tactic of mobile defence. In the third year this led to victory at the Battle of Badr where Muhammad's 300 warriors triumphed over an opposing Meccan force of 1000. The significance of this victory was that it established the Muslim community as a separate political and social as well as religious entity within the wider Arabian context, and confirmed the power and military leadership of Muhammad as Prophet-leader. But it was not itself a decisive victory for the forces of Islam. Nonetheless, prisoners were well treated, thereby enhancing the reputation of Muhammad as a beneficent leader, and it confirmed the Muslims as standing under a new ethical code of conduct.

In the fourth year of the hijra the Muslims again fought the Meccans at Mount Uhud. But this time they were beaten. The fierce battle ended with the retreat of the Muslims and the wounding of Muhammad. However, Muhammad managed to save his small army, again demonstrating his qualities of leadership. Islamic history records that *Abu-Sufyan*, who was leading the Meccans, called from the top of the hill, saying, 'Uhud for Badr; we call it even. We will meet again next year.' Both forces retired to their original bases. But that was not the end; Uhud, like Badr, was not decisive. The following year the Meccans laid siege to Medina with an army of some 10 000. This lasted two weeks but failed as Muhammad had changed tactics from standard mobile defence to an innovative static one, namely trenches and barricades, a tactic new to the Arabian military, and one which Muhammad apparently obtained from a Persian convert, *Salman al-Farisi*, thus constituting, for the Muslim world, an early example of the 'borrowing' of advanced technology.[21] Religious zeal, faith in God, a stoutly defended position—and a convenient dust storm—countered the enemy's superiority in numbers and arms. The morale of the attackers waned and they retreated, never to return.

In the sixth year of the hijra Muhammad moved on Mecca with a large force, but his purpose was to make pilgrimage to the Ka'ba, which was of course a long-standing Arab custom, made now more urgent for the Muslims once it had become the focus of prayer. The Meccans sought to block this manoeuvre and a truce was arrived at wherein Muhammad agreed to postpone his pilgrimage to the following year. This truce took the form of a treaty forged at a place called Hudaybiyah. The negotiations for the *Treaty of Hudaybiyah* gave right of entry to Mecca for the

---

20 Haykal, *The Life of Muhammad*, 176.
21 I am grateful to Dr William Shepard, retired Associate-Professor of Religious Studies at the University of Canterbury, New Zealand, for this information and comment.

Muslims, but under certain conditions.[22] At least the right of Muslims to make this pilgrimage, irrespective of other factors, was endorsed. And so, a year later Muhammad with an army of 2000 made a peaceful pilgrimage to Mecca. This event led to some further conversions of Meccans. But, two years further on, in H9, the Quraysh violated the treaty agreement. Muhammad then marched on Mecca, this time with some 10 000 armed and mounted troops. It is said he asked the Meccans 'What do you think I will do to you?' They answered, 'You are a generous brother and the son of a generous brother.' 'Go,' the Prophet rejoined, 'you are freed'.[23] So Mecca became Muslim and the Ka'ba became the geographic spiritual heart of Islam.

The peaceful victory and generous amnesty then given enhanced Muhammad's standing even further, and his action of cleansing the Ka'ba, of 'islamising' it—that is, removing all traces of pagan culture and polytheistic belief and restoring it to its pristine state as a shrine to the one true God—was both momentous for the site and significant for Islamic ideology. This action, as taken by Muhammad, arguably provides the paradigm for all forms of political 'islamisation' since. But struggles and victories on the battlefield were by no means over. For example, a tough battle later ensued in respect of the town of *al-Ta'if*. The Muslim force won in the end and Muhammad was again generously magnanimous in victory. Voluntary conversion was always the ultimate goal. Following his return to Medina, Muhammad received many delegations from various tribes and peoples of Arabia. Whether as a result of military engagement or peaceful initiative, all of Arabia was soon won over to Islam, all professed the new faith, repudiated the old, and gave homage to Muhammad, the Prophet of Islam, the Seal of Prophets, the Messenger of Allah.

Following the conquest and conversion of Arabia, attention turned to neighbouring empires. The Persian (Sassanian) and Byzantine empires initially rebuffed the Arab overtures, only to succumb to Muslim military conquest within a matter of years; by comparison the Copts (Egyptian Christians) gave a courteous response and have been allowed to continue their faith practice and identity ever since. As some of his emissaries to Syria were murdered, and the Byzantines determined to deal militarily with the 'Arab menace', Muhammad turned his direction northward and so set the scene for the first outward movement and expansion of the militarised Ummah.

In March of the year 632 (AH10), Muhammad made a particular and final pilgrimage to Mecca and the Ka'ba and, in so doing, established the paradigm for all subsequent pilgrimages. He asserted that only Muslims could make this pilgrimage (*al-hajj*). And while it echoed the actions of former times, he purged it from all previous polytheistic associations. The process of islamisation was thus completed with respect to a practice whose origins lay in the former time of

---

[22] Cf. Haykal, *Life of Muhammad*, 355ff.

[23] Azzam, *The Eternal Message*, 26.

spiritual and moral ignorance (*al-jahiliyya*). In the course of this pilgrimage Muhammad preached his famous sermon declaring the unity of all Muslims. However, having himself fulfilled the ritual performance of the Hajj, he returned to Medina and shortly afterwards he died.

So, in its tenth year, the Islamic community faced a crisis of leadership: who was to succeed the Prophet? Some felt Muhammad would return from death and come again to lead them—echoes of Christian sentiments about their Christ. Others felt Muhammad was not really dead, rather God had taken him directly into heaven—echoes of some Jewish views about prophets such as Elijah. In the event, the view that Muhammad was merely a man, a prophet charged with a divine task but now gone the way of all mortal flesh, prevailed. Muhammad's chief companion, Abu Bakr, asserted 'Muhammad is nothing but an apostle. Apostles have passed away before him' and so established that the Prophet Muhammad was to be viewed as a mortal man only, and God alone is to be worshipped. Thus there was to be no suggestion that Muhammad was in any way a divine being. Nonetheless, because he was indeed the Prophet through whom God gave the Qur'an, Muhammad was soon looked to as the model for what a Muslim is to be. In consequence, his own story and the record of his sayings and doings beyond the Quranic utterances became central for Muslims. Thus, his remembered words and actions provide a paradigm for interpreting the stipulations of the Qur'an and applying them to daily life.

The significance of Muhammad

The biographical contours briefly sketched out, and aware that many mighty tomes packed with detail and fleshed with anecdote abound on this subject, what may we infer or conclude about Muhammad? What is his significance for Islam? Clearly his life story is a tale of transitions: the man who married his boss, a wealthy widow, becomes the man charged to be the mouthpiece of Allah. This gentle son of Mecca, preferring the reflective quiet of cave retreats to the demanding tumult of the Meccan masses, seems to bear little resemblance to the feisty preacher confronting his fellow Meccans, let alone the assertive autocratic leader of Medina. Who could have imagined this orphaned Arab would become the fulcrum of a complete cultural turnaround in Arabia? Or that from such humble origins there could spring forth such a powerful force for religious change?

The life story of Muhammad, we could say, spans three phases. I call the first the *embryonic phase* for it encompasses his growth to maturity, that is, up to the commencement of his prophethood, marked by the initial divine injunction to recite the God-given utterances. During this phase he was a 'yet-to-be prophet', but his disposition, sensibilities and personality traits and characteristics were emerging such as to render him the right person for the task. In hindsight, of course, the veneration that has been given him by Muslims has made much of these sensibilities and qualities which fitted Muhammad for his prophetic role, and which indeed underscore the veracity of his being marked by God for such a role. After all, so the argument goes, Muhammad as a mere man, and despite his eminent human qualities, had neither the innate skills nor political acumen to himself carry off the immense leadership roles that fell upon him. To achieve what he did required more than just human capacity.

The second, which I call the *intermediate* or *developmental phase*, covers the first Meccan period of Muhammad's prophetic activity and the emergence, in response to this activity, of the early Muslim community up to the point of the *hijra*. Here Muhammad goes through a time of testing and coping with adversity, both developing his own sense of appropriate prophetic leadership in the process and responding to the many challenges and threats that are placed before him. Throughout this phase he is able to rely upon the bonds of tribal loyalty and protective social structures, and to draw strength from key family members and mentors, most notably his wife and uncle, who were able to support and sustain him.

In the third or *consolidation phase* the Prophet of Islam emerges into his full powers and influence as a founder and leader of a significant religious community. During this period he consolidates the theocratic community in Medina; he draws in surrounding tribes and Arab peoples; he triumphs in Mecca; and he completes his task as the 'mouthpiece' of God. With his death the Qur'an is concluded; the religion of Islam is well founded. Also, in his lifetime, Muhammad underwent a number of personal transitions: from mild mannered clerk to combative preacher; from deliverer of divine warnings to leader of inspired warriors; from peripatetic preacher to supreme ruler. In all this he embraced four main leadership functions, namely prophetic, military, judicial and political.

First and foremost—and quite irreplaceably—Muhammad was *the* Prophet: the Apostle of God, the Messenger of Allah, *par excellence* and in finality. This task was unique, although it empowered him to undertake others. Thus, secondly, Muhammad fulfilled the role of Commander-in-Chief of his military forces; thirdly, he was Chief Judge overseeing the welfare of his people; and fourthly he was the political head of the Islamic community. As military chief he was himself active in leadership: he led by example and from the front. He was seen to be in the thick of the fighting, not afraid to risk life and limb for the cause of God. He knew what it was to be wounded in battle. Clearly he was an intuitive strategist and innovative in his military prowess. He was a successful commander: yet he had received no formal military training. Likewise, as Chief Justice of the then nascent Islamic legal system, he had had no legal training. But for Muhammad he was not so much attending to a 'system' (which would come later in the development of Islam) but directly dispensing justice—specifically, God's justice—in respect of his people who came seeking it. In the process he clearly drew upon the guidance given in the inspired utterances, and he demonstrated his own innate qualities and sensitivities as one especially equipped to dispense justice.

In his role as political head, Muhammad displayed astute leadership and diplomacy, moulding together what had been previously a disjointed society quick to take offence, and cementing alliances and allegiances with personal initiative and active example. It was this latter role, and often subsumed within it the military and judicial roles, which defined the dynamics of the caliphate for Islam in the years immediately following Muhammad's death. To that extent the example and activities of Muhammad determined and delineated the institution of the caliphate. Only Muhammad could be Prophet. A 'Caliph' (*Khalifah*) was the 'deputy', one who stood in for Muhammad in the secular roles. Thus the first four such successors became known as the 'Rightly Guided Caliphs', the *Rushidun*. (But more of this below). For the moment, in concluding this study of the origins of Islam, I note simply the multi-layered significance of Muhammad for Islam and Muslims.

Muhammad is not only the fount of Islamic scripture, in the sense that it came via his utterances, he is also the source of the interpretive and guiding tradition— the Sunnah—which stands alongside the Qur'an, so constituting the two textual authority sources of Islamic life. Esposito speaks of Muhammad's life as translating the guidance given in the Qur'an. Thus Muhammad

> lived the revelation, giving concrete form to the laws that God revealed for the various conditions of ordinary human life. For Islam, no aspect of life is outside the realm of religion. ... (The) traditions of the Prophet provide guidance regarding personal hygiene, dress, eating, treatment of spouses, diplomacy, and warfare.[24]

Muhammad quickly became the focus of pious devotion, especially in respect of providing an example for Muslim life, both secular and religious, to the extent that these two categories can be distinguished. Indeed, 'Muslims look to Muhammad's example for guidance in all aspects of life: how to treat friends as well as enemies, what to eat and drink, how to mourn and celebrate'.[25] His name is upheld in terms of a creedal link to Allah, for in the *Shahada*—the creedal affirmation of One God—is added 'and Muhammad is the Prophet of God'. Later, Shi'a Islam adds further that 'Ali is the friend of Allah'.

Muhammad may be mere mortal, but he is well connected. Thus there is an implicit shared allegiance; the place of Muhammad is, at least in named veneration, seemingly a close second to that of Allah. Certainly, ontologically speaking, there is no association between Allah and Muhammad; but Muslim piety clearly links them in terms of both veneration and significance. For many Muslims this has led over the centuries to incorporating a focus upon Muhammad in respect of experiential piety, and a spiritual veneration of him derived from the Quranic assertion that Muhammad is, indeed, the 'Seal' of prophecy. In effect the name of Muhammad gives a spiritual guarantee of Muslim faith. Indeed, in popular piety Muhammad is viewed, in effect, as a saviour figure, albeit functioning differently to other saviour figures.

---

[24] Esposito, *What Everyone Needs to Know About Islam*, 11.
[25] Ibid.

Veneration, however, easily veers into hagiographical elevation. While it is well accepted that there is nothing divine about Muhammad as such—he is merely human after all—yet he is portrayed as holding quite unique and special qualities. There is an apparent paradox in the way he is perceived, on the one hand, to be so devoid of human capacity that it is claimed he was illiterate, and therefore could not himself have produced the Quranic utterances; on the other hand the noblest of attributes are ascribed to him suggesting, indeed, a person of refined literary character. To be sure, he had to be sufficiently literate to conduct commerce and interact intelligently with peoples of other faiths and cultures, nevertheless he was no man of letters in that sense. But, in any case, clearly he has had ascribed to his personality a range of superlative attributes. These include, for example, nobility, kindliness, honesty and trustworthiness (Muhammad was known, even before his prophethood as *al-Amin*, 'the Trustworthy'). He was marked with traits of sensitivity, reliability, astuteness and patience. He has been idealised as a devoted and loving husband and father; and as displaying great generosity, earnestness, undoubted sincerity and faithfulness. All these laudable ascriptions describe more a paragon than a mere man. The truth of who he was, as with any founder figure of a religion, is shrouded in veneration such as this. Without doubt he was a unique and special individual, and the ascriptions are indicative of that. Whether Allah used him and his gifts to achieve a divine end, or whether the end was achieved in spite of Muhammad's humanity, is a point of theological debate.

Chapter 3

Scripture and Tradition
Qur'an and Sunnah

The Holy Qur'an

The Holy Qur'an, or *al-Qur'an al-Karim* (also referred to as *Kitab Allah*—the book of Allah), is a compilation of oral recitations as uttered by the Prophet Muhammad and which were collected into written form in the years immediately following his death. The Qur'an is first and foremost a work of oral literature. The goal of Islamic piety has always been to recite it from memory; the written Arabic text is primarily an aid to this. Although there are translations of the Qur'an into other languages, the process of any translation necessarily requires or involves a measure of interpretation. Thus, for Islam, it is only in the original Arabic that the true depth of meaning, and the power of mystery, emotion and fervour pertaining to the original recitation, can be expressed and experienced: reciting the Qur'an is both a religious and an aesthetic act. As an Arabic language event, the Qur'an is 'primarily an aural-oral phenomenon' which, as Neal Robinson remarks, 'exhibits rhyme, rhythm, assonance, alliteration and other poetic qualities which are often lost when it is rendered into English'.[1] As Kenneth Cragg comments, reading the Qur'an 'in the quiet of the study, perusing it with the eye, silences the force of the text which properly belongs to the ear and the soul'.[2] The uttered recitation is the thing: indeed the context of the Qur'an began, in effect, with the angelic command to Muhammad: 'Recite in the Name of your Lord'.

Although the Qur'an is a single book and believed to be the exact copy of the Book of God that exists in Heaven—the 'Mother of the Book'—in its written form there were, early in the development of Islam, a number of variant editions in Arabic. An official recension (edition) of an Arabic consonantal text was issued by the third Caliph after Muhammad. By the tenth century CE there were no fewer than seven canonical readings of this text. That is to say, as written Arabic evolved, variant forms of vowel pointing were applied to the consonantal text as an aid to reading it aloud. Originally the consonantal text had provided a visual prompt to

---

[1] Neal Robinson, *Islam: A Concise Introduction* (Surrey: Curzon Press, 1999), 59.
[2] Kenneth Cragg, *Readings in the Qur'an* (London: Collins Liturgical Publications, 1988), 15.

the memorised utterance (or 'recitation'). In the end a 'normative' scriptural text emerged that is believed to reproduce faithfully the original oral text.

In this section on the Qur'an we will examine issues of structure and content, and then look at matters of development and compilation and also the issue of textual uniqueness. This will be followed by a discussion of the nature of revelation and some issues of interpretation from both Muslim and scholarly viewpoints.

Structure

The Qur'an consists of 114 chapters, called *suras*, arranged according to length from the longest to the shortest, excepting that the first sura in the collection, called 'The Opening', or *al-Fatiha*, is itself a short prayer. Each sura is divided into verses, known as *aya*. The division into verses is not according to subject matter, nor does it reflect structures of literary composition, but rather relates to rhyme patterns contained within the construction of the sura. Furthermore, each chapter is given a name, perhaps simply a word taken from an *aya*, but normally this gives no clue as to substantive content. The title may, for some, function somewhat as a prompt to memory for the purpose of oral recitation. Clearly the title is not meant to be descriptive of the substance, even if it happens in some cases to be indicative of the content, at least in part, of the chapter. As it happens, many individual suras, recorded in the Qur'an, are themselves compilations. That is, they are, in their final form, composed of recitations that were originally given, or recited, by Muhammad as a number of discrete units given at different times and which evolved, through repeated recitation, into a single sura. Others bear the hallmarks of a singly and holistically given unit of recitation.

Following the title of the sura there is an indication of the point of origin—that is, whether the sura was first uttered in Mecca or Medina—and a statement of the number of verses it contains. These headings are, in fact, editorial additions to the written text. They were not, of course, part of the oracular original. In all but one instance there then follows the *bismillah*: 'in the name of Allah'. In full, this is a prayer which states 'In the name of Allah, the Merciful, the Compassionate': *Bismillah al rahman al rahim*. Then there comes the chapter itself, although in 29 cases there stands, between the bismillah and the sura, a letter or group of letters. Usually, when the sura is read aloud, these letters are simply read out also. Their origin and meaning is a complete mystery. No one knows why the letters are there. However, as they have always been there, they are believed to have been part of the original text given to Muhammad; so they will always remain.

Many of the suras, or sections within a sura, can be identified with specific issues, developments, and situations that relate to the events and contexts to which Muhammad was responding, or with which he was interacting. For example, in response to rumours spread in Mecca against Muhammad in respect to his relationship with a Christian shopkeeper, there was given a revelatory counter by the following Quranic recitation: 'We know they claim that the Qur'an is taught to him by another man. But the man whom they suspect is Persian of tongue, whereas the tongue of this Qur'an is pure and clear Arabic'.[3] Later, as a result of the great victory achieved at the Battle of Badr, a revelatory response conceding both the impetus to battle and the resulting victory to be at the hand of God—echoes of which can be discerned not only throughout the Qur'an but also within the Hebrew scriptures—is found in Sura 8 (The Spoils—*al-Anfal*), verses 12 and 17.

Content

The substantive content, but not the structural arrangement, of the Holy Qur'an is believed to be authentically that of Muhammad's recitations. As noted, structural arrangement is simply by length. The style is predominantly poetic and reflects its originating context as an oral work. The content is rich with allusion and imagery, which is often obscure. So far as themes are concerned, the content is quite jumbled: there is a logic of sorts, but it has to be carefully extracted. References to battles, pilgrimages and other happenings, stories of other prophets and apostles, even relationships with other religions, together with much guidance for life and behaviour, are haphazardly intermingled. Most usually it is in some of the lengthy suras, later in time, but placed early in the written Qur'an, that a kind of compendium, containing many of the otherwise recurrent themes occurring throughout the Qur'an as a whole, can be found. Reading Sura 2, *al-Baqara* (The Cow), is an efficient way, for example, of getting an overview of the substantive content of Quranic ideas, injunctions and teachings.[4] Even so, there is repetition and a sense of randomness in the flow of the content of this sura. Nevertheless, despite any critical observation in respect of structure and content, Muslims believe the Qur'an to be the infallible Word of God, the transcript of the heavenly original.

While there are universal principles and teachings within the Qur'an, much of the concrete detail is specific to the situations and contexts in which Muhammad was located as a man of his time and place. This is worth bearing in mind when one first approaches the text of the Qur'an. Being aware of the original context within which a revelation is set, and to which it is addressed, is one of the first tasks of good exegesis and assists in genuine understanding of both the genesis of the text and the lasting 'word' or value it may have. For example, when the Qur'an refers to 'unbelievers' and 'associationists' it is naming pagan and polytheistic Arabs of Muhammad's day who were actively hostile to him and the first Muslim community, and who posed a very real threat to the life of Muslims. Hence the revelatory recitation tended to be harsh, although that harshness is most usually tempered by an affirmation of the wisdom and mercy of God, who will in beneficence receive those who repent and believe. For example, Sura 16, verse

---

[3] 'The Bee' (*al-Nahl*), Qur'an 16:103, as cited in Husein Haykal, *The Life of Muhammad*, trans. Ismail Raji al-Faruqi (Kuala Lumpur: Islamic Book Trust, 1993, 119.

[4] See also the Appendix, p. 229 below, for a guided introduction to the Qur'an by way of a structured selection of passages.

119: 'To those who do wrong in ignorance, but thereafter repent and make amends, thy Lord, after all this, is oft-forgiving, most merciful'.[5]

Development

There are suras that clearly belong to the early Meccan phase of Muhammad's prophetic leadership. These are short, fervent, ecstatic, and intensely poetic. Their content is dominated by the call to worship and submit to the one God, Allah; they contain references to an impending day of judgement, and the prophesying of doom for idolatry. Here the focus of content is Muhammad's address to fellow Arabs and the commencement of a new religious movement. Then there are those that belong to the middle and late Meccan phases. These are more measured and polemical or argumentative: they are responding and reacting to rejection and difficulty as encountered by Muhammad and the first Muslim converts. There then follows the early Medinan period in which Judaic and Christian elements and issues loom large, generally in a favourable light. Indeed, early relations between Muslims and Jews were very positive and sealed by a covenant.[6] Thus the emerging Muslim faith is viewed as relating positively to these forebears: Jews and Christians are to be equally honoured as people of the Book, even though they may have gone somewhat astray. Finally there are the suras that belong to the late Medinan period, in which there is a noticeable hardening of attitude to Judaism and Christianity, and a series of proclamations of the final triumph of a distinct teaching, namely that which Muhammad is now conveying. These Medinan suras are also marked by a pronounced legislative element. They are generally longer than the early chapters of the Qur'an. They are less combative in tone. Instead, they most often convey a sense of dominating authoritative pronouncement.

The content of the Qur'an was given through the Prophet over a period of 23 years. As the genesis of a scripture for a major religion, this is a relatively brief period of time. But of course at the end of that period there was yet no Qur'an in the sense of a completed text, a full and final divine revelation, only an apparently random collection of utterances. These were mostly committed to memory, although in some instances there might be a script of sorts as an aid for the purposes of recall. Indeed, there is reference to the earliest fragments of the Qur'an being found on 'date leaves and tablets of white stone' as well as 'the breasts of men'.[7] At this stage there was nothing in the nature of a literary document. The units of 'sayings'—which were to become the suras, or chapters proper of the Qur'an—were still to be gathered and compiled into book form. The process for doing this started soon after Muhammad's death: the motivation being the desire

---

[5] Abdullah Yusuf Ali , *The Meaning of the Holy Qur'an* New Edition with Revised Translation and Commentary (Beltsville, MD: Amana Publications, 1989), 668.

[6] See Husein Haykal, *The Life of Muhammad*, 179ff., especially pp.180–83 for the text of this covenant.

[7] See, for example, N.J. Dawood, *The Koran*, (London: Everyman Classic edition, 1987), 1

not to lose or forget that which Muhammad had delivered as the message from God, and the concomitant realisation that, as he was the last Prophet, with his death there would be no more such delivery of the divine message. There was, therefore, an understandable element of urgency, abetted by the fact that with the early rapid expansion of the world of Islam there were peoples coming into the community who had never directly heard Muhammad. The messenger was no more; but the message must yet be spread abroad. Therefore others must now learn it afresh and 're-iterate' it through repeated recitation. This required not only a reliable source of reference, but a source standardised in terms of textual structure and content.

Alongside the story of the development of the Qur'an as a completed text stands also the more complex story of development and change within the content of the Qur'an as uttered by Muhammad. This reflects changes to his circumstances. To the extent that the sequential development in the tenor, form and content of the suras reflects changes occurring within the life of Muhammad, the Qur'an itself 'registers the fundamental development of Muhammad's activity to include the work of statesman and ruler, as well as that of prophet'.[8] The challenge to the received tradition concerning the Qur'an consists in asking how much the Qur'an, in terms of detailed content, is a collection of transcendental and ahistorical messages, messages that stand outside time and history, as against how much, or to what extent, the content of the Quranic sayings directly reflects, addresses and responds to the particular circumstances of Muhammad's life and work, and the wider context of that. Clearly there is a mixture, with some verses more obviously referring to particular events directly and others being in the manner of more general instruction and comment. However, for the most part, even those that very obviously allude to concrete events, to be understood in context, from the Muslim perspective they nonetheless contain a valid message that transcends the originating context. This is a matter of the way in which revelation as such is understood, and involves a theological question concerning the balance between the universal and contextual dimensions of revelation and religion.

Compilation

There are a number of traditions regarding the history of the compilation of the Qur'an.[9] During the reign of the first two of the Rightly Guided Caliphs (*Rushidun*), the immediate successors to Muhammad as community leaders, it seems that a number of collections and codices of Quranic material appeared. The first known documentary record of the utterances was a manuscript compiled by a scribe, previously in the service of the Prophet Muhammad himself, one *Zayid ibn Thabit*. This same scribe and his original manuscript, passed on to *Hafsa*, a later

---

[8] Kenneth Cragg and R. Marston Speight, *The House of Islam*, 3rd edn (California: Wadsworth, 1988), 34.

[9] See W. M. Watt and R. Bell, *Introduction to the Qur'an* (Edinburgh: Edinburgh University Press, 1990), 40ff.

wife of Muhammad and daughter of the second Caliph, *Umar ibn al-Khatttab*, were involved in a commission authorised by the third Caliph, *Uthman ibn Affan*, that was critical in determining the eventual canon of the Qur'an. This commission was charged with gathering together the fragmentary record of the revelations, sifting through dialectical variations and making Meccan forms the standard. It determined what was to be included and what excluded, ensuring the written text was indeed both a complete and unadulterated 'copy' of the recitations given through Muhammad. 'Whatever may have been the form of the Qur'an previously, it is certain that the book still in our hands is essentially the Uthmanic Qur'an'.[10] Thus the work of the commission under Uthman was at the heart of the process of determining the text of the Qur'an as being faithful to the utterances as given by Muhammad. And, through the subsequent processes of reaching a standardised text for the purposes of public reading, the principle of unity was upheld without being forced: there is but one Qur'an.

The variations that were under consideration were not substantial in terms of content, but had more to do with the order or arrangement of suras, and textual variations in respect of how the suras were to be read aloud—the concern was more with form and structure of the actual recitation. The content of the Qur'an was given completely and directly through Muhammad as an oracular event. However, the Qur'an as a written entity in the Arabic language evolved textually with the development of the script of the language. In particular this development was associated with the technicalities that had to do with the change from a relatively simple consonantal script, designed to serve the purposes of a mnemonic device, to a standardised rendition of a full text, inclusive of vowel pointing. It was through this complex process that the variant readings that had emerged were harmonised. In other words the Qur'an itself became a textual entity, but only in order to be learnt so as to be recited, rather than being a recalling from memory of Muhammad's recitations with the aid of a written prompt.

The authenticity of the Qur'an is thus widely accepted within the world of scholarship as well as, naturally, the world of Islamic faith.[11] It is worth noting that the first printed edition of the Qur'an in Arabic, produced by Muslims, was not published until 1925, in Egypt. In part this was because within the Islamic world calligraphy—which had evolved with the hand reproduction of the Quranic text—invested the reproduction of the Qur'an with a sense of sacred art, and that militated against an early usage of printing technology. European productions of the *printed* text of the Qur'an had been in existence for quite some time before the first Muslim authorised printed edition. Today there are many different published versions of the Qur'an and in many languages. However, a Qur'an that is other than Arabic is not simply a translation, but an interpretation: it interpretively expresses the meaning of the Arabic original. For Islam it is the Arabic original, compiled as

---

10 Ibid., 44.
11 Cf. Ibid., 54.

it was into an authorised Arabic text, which *is*—not just contains—the Word of Allah.

Textual Uniqueness

It is important to recognise that, for Islam, revelation is both a linguistic as well as a religious phenomenon: the two are inseparable. The Qur'an is quintessentially an Arabic text. Islamic doctrine holds that 'the form (Arabic language) and the substance (meaning) cannot be separated. ...[Thus] if God willed the Holy Book to be in Arabic, submission to that Will requires that it should not be turned into another language'.[12] The Qur'an is not considered a literary compilation that admits of critical scrutiny in order to 'recover' an original literary text: it is believed to be precisely how God intended it to be. There are no standard (that is to say, universally accepted within Islam) translations of the Arabic text into another language: each 'translation' from the Arabic original is considered a distortion by virtue of the inevitability of interpretation. Islam holds dearly to its primary text in the original language.

However, a challenging argument runs to the effect that 'if the Qur'an is in Arabic so that Arabs can understand it, then translation for non-Arabs becomes imperative' and so by implication there is for Islam 'a duty of translation, since otherwise the central intention, namely understanding, would be thwarted'.[13] Nonetheless there is recognition of very real literary problems when it comes to translation. For example, in the translation of poetry from Arabic into any other language, perplexities of grammar and elastic Arab terminology conspire to render the result problematic. A considerable measure of interpretation is required which, for the purists, vitiates the translator's attempt. Of course, translation might be acceptable in respect of the work of *tafsir* (exegesis, commentary—especially linguistic when applied to the Qur'an) when the medium of such scholarly activity is not Arabic. But, in the context of religious activity, the recitation of the Qur'an can only be done in its original Arabic language, and such recitation tends to carry with it a sense of engagement in a religiously meritorious action. Indeed, as a consequence of all this, it was a long time before the Qur'an was translated fully into any other language. Continued Muslim hesitancy in respect to rendering the Qur'an into another language stands in marked contrast to the Christian propensity, via the work of Bible Societies for instance, to have its scriptures translated into all languages.

In respect to Islam, translation difficulties have led to an interesting doctrinal position concerning the status of the Qur'an as uniquely significant. The literary problems of translation give evidence of the excellence of Quranic Arabic: 'its matchlessness and incomparability', as is often said. And this in turn is evidence for

---

[12] Cragg and Speight, *The House of Islam.*, 29.
[13] Ibid., 30.

its divine origin. The nature of the Qur'an as a unique phenomenon—that is, it is inherently incapable of imitation or being matched by any human construction— yielded a doctrine of inimitability (*ijaz*) wherein the linguistic uniqueness of the Qur'an has been deemed a mark, or proof, of its divine source. Thus, the style of the Qur'an has meant that the 'incapacity of the Arab hearers ... to match or better the Quranic eloquence has always been interpreted as attesting its indubitable worth and its heavenly origin'.[14]

The nature of revelation

Modern critical scholarship detects a number of phases in respect to when the original recitation of the suras occurred. This analysis constitutes a refinement of the traditional dating of the suras.[15] These phases have nothing to do with final arrangement within the Qur'an as a written document; that was determined simply by the arbitrary criterion of length, as I have said. Rather, the analysis of phases has to do with the process of revelation in respect to the prophetic career of Muhammad. Now, from a traditional Muslim perspective it has been commented that the Qur'an 'was given by God in instalments so that the Prophet might be duly upheld and the people progressively instructed'.[16] Nevertheless, a pattern of progressive development of subject matter may be correlated with both the sequence in which the initial recitations were given as well as correlated with specific historical events in which Muhammad was variously involved, and to which revelation was given by way of a response, or specifically addressed item of input—guidance, advice, judgment and so on.

However, this kind of critical scholarly analysis tends to raise an acute hermeneutical issue for Islam, although it is certainly one that applies to other religions as well, especially those whose scriptural text is premised on the notion of a divinely revealed message being given to humankind *per se*. The issue has to do with the understanding of the nature of revelation as such. On the one hand, there is a position I would call *revelational positivism*. This denotes the view that the substantive message, as given in revelation and by virtue of its source, is fixed: it is not amenable to any change or modification whatsoever. The Absolute has spoken; what is given is, by implication, itself absolute and unchangeable, and so 'transferable' as it stands to other times, places, and contexts without any substantial modification of understanding or application. The divinely given datum of revelation is immutable.

On the other hand, an alternate position, which I would denote as *revelational relativism*, holds that the detail, or datum, of what is given in the revelatory event is

---

[14] Ibid., 32.

[15] See Watt and Bell, *Introduction*, 108ff. See also Neal Robinson, *Discovering the Qur'an: a contemporary approach to a veiled text* (London: SCM Press, 1996).

[16] Cragg and Speight, *The House of Islam.*, 33; cf. Sura 17:106; 75:16.

itself deemed to be in some sense responsive to the human situation. To that extent it is 'relative', even though the source—namely, God, or Allah—is absolute. Thus the datum of the revealed text is amenable, even necessarily so, to modification of understanding and application. Furthermore, this view discerns the essential relationality (or relativity) inherent in the dynamic of revelation as itself a key component: the medium is the message, if you like. In this way the real message of revelation is not so much in the specific context-bound 'detail' as in the essential 'dynamic' contained within, and also conveyed through and by, the very form and structure of the revelatory 'item' or text. Ideas, insights, guidance and understandings may be transferable, but not the actual event-specific details.

Of course, what I am referring to here is the distinction between an openly 'interpretive' (sometimes called a 'liberal' perspective, at least in a Christian context) and a 'fundamentalist' or 'literalist' perspective. It would be fair to say that Muslims tend most naturally to the latter, for that has been the dominant tradition within Islam, whether Sunni or Shi'a. However, whatever ideological position, or perspective of understanding, is held in respect of revelation, it remains the case that scriptural texts, for the most part, are susceptible to interpretation on the basis that they have emerged, or been received, over a period of time and in varying contexts, even where the components nonetheless end up as part of the one 'canon' or sanctioned corpus.

Some issues of interpretation

Insofar as Muslims themselves early identified evidence of apparent responsive change, even contradiction, within the Qur'an, the theory of abrogation (*naskh*)—conveying the possibility that internal revision took place—has been applied. Indeed, the debate would seem to be lodged within the Qur'an itself for there are verses that state Muhammad himself cannot revise or alter what is given him to reveal (cf. Sura 10.15–16), even when he is pressed to respond to pressures brought to bear to do so (cf. Sura 17.73f.). But God may initiate change by causing Muhammad to 'forget' some verses and replace them with others revealed to him.[17] The doctrine of abrogation that emerged to cope with the implications of these verses holds that some of the Quranic utterances were of a temporary nature and were replaced as circumstance warranted. But in at least one case significant revision took place with the excision of a portion of Sura 53 known as the 'Satanic verses'. The original utterance was understood by Muhammad—after the initial recitation of them—to have not come from Allah but was instead an interpolation of verses which, upon reflection, Muhammad realised were inauthentic. Indeed, the

---

17 Cf. Sura 87:6f: 'We shall cause you to recite, and you shall not forget except what God wills'; Sura 2:106: 'For whatever verse we cancel or cause to forget we bring a better or the like'; Sura 13:39: 'God will delete or confirm what he will; and with him is the "mother" of the Book.'

Qur'an itself (Sura 22) indicates this was a typically satanic testing of a prophet of God. However, it needs to be noted that in recent times many Muslim scholars tend to reject this account of change to the text and its interpretation.

It has been stated that, 'Islamic scholarship, regarding the Qur'an as the eternal Word of God, is unwilling to admit any development of thought in it'.[18] However the same authors also point out that, if the Qur'an is believed to be the Word of God addressed to human beings, then 'there is nothing inconsistent in supposing a change of emphasis according to the needs of the original hearers at any given time and according to what they were able to accept and understand'.[19] In other words, an analysis of the ideas found within the Qur'an itself can lead to a fuller understanding of the sequence of the revelations and their meaning and intent. Certainly this is the kind of task that scholarly exegesis of the Qur'an attempts. While acknowledging that the content of the Qur'an is wide-ranging, there are nonetheless key doctrines and issues that are repeatedly addressed. These include the being and unity of God; existence of and belief in other spiritual beings; the nature of prophethood and the relationship of Islam to other religions; the last judgement, or the 'day of doom'; and guiding regulations for the life of the Muslim community.[20]

Although the dominant subject matter of the Qur'an has to do with Allah and the Will of Allah, the major subject themes are those of law, the previous prophets, and final judgement. There is a distinct impression that the hearer or reader is expected to have background knowledge of both the Bible—the Qur'an makes many references to biblical material—and also indigenous Arabic traditions, into which context the recitations were primarily directed. The Qur'an is believed by Islam to be the final revelation from God and, the history of textual development and compilation notwithstanding, it has not been subject to human intervention and tampering. Its directness and immediacy attest its veracity. In Islamic thought it is not the only authentic scriptural revelation—God has given others such as Torah (*Taurat*) and Gospel (*Injil*)—but it is itself the consummation of, and corrective to, all that has preceded it. It is the benchmark against which distortion to previous scriptural revelation is to be measured. Thus the Islamic doctrine of the Qur'an has led to a corollary doctrine of corruption of previous scriptural texts, or the abrogation of distorted previous revelation, with the direct purity of the new and authentic Word of God as given through Muhammad. This is an understandable position although it has led to considerable problems in terms of relationships of Muslims to people of other religions, in particular Islam's relationship to other monotheistic faiths.

---

[18] Watt and Bell, *Introduction*, 114.

[19] Ibid.

[20] See Ibid., 148ff.

Sunnah

The Qur'an is, without doubt, the primary scriptural and authoritative source for Islamic religion and life. But it is not the only source. Through Muhammad came the Qur'an, the 'speech' of Allah, but Muhammad himself also spoke and acted. The 'traditions' recording what he said and did in this regard form the second authoritative source for Islam. For, even as Muhammad was giving voice to the recitations, he was preaching on and about them, and giving anecdotal illustration and interpretive direction. Further, he also gave practical instruction on matters of religious belief and life: he issued edict and command, responded to questions and provided clarification. On the one hand Islam is founded on the Qur'an, the unique Word of God. On the other hand, great store is placed on the words and deeds of the Prophet as both interpretive and instructive in living according to God's word.

> The detailed records of Muhammad's actions in war and peace, his interactions with family, friends, and foes, his judgments in good and bad times, and his decisions when under siege and when victorious recall and reinforce for Muslims what it takes to follow the word of God.[21]

The phenomenon of Islam as an historic living religion rests upon these two sources. On the one hand there are the divine recitations, collected together as the Holy Qur'an; and, on the other, prophetic discourse, command, discussion and so on, together with practical exemplary illustration, as given by Muhammad himself. All of this extra-Quranic material is the *Sunnah* ('trodden path' or 'tradition') of the Prophet, and comprises units of narrative material—*hadith*—which, over time, were gathered into a number of collections. These collections carry varying weight in terms of authority. Siddiqi comments that hadith literature originates from 'letters, laws and treaties which were dictated to scribes by the Prophet himself' and traceable also to documents 'compiled by the companions and Followers'.[22]

The earliest Muslims who lived in the company of Muhammad are known as the Companions of the Prophet, for which the title of honour—*al-sahaba* or *al-ashab* (Companion/s)—applies. Clearly, these first followers of Islam, the Companions of the Prophet, were keen to recall, learn and retain all that Muhammad said and did. So there emerged very quickly many items of report, hearsay, anecdote and so forth—in other words various stories of what Muhammad said and/or did. These items circulated among the rapidly expanding early Muslim communities, both in written and oral form. Over time these were collected into a number of comprehensive compilations considered, on the whole, to be reliable. However, many more were rejected as unreliable. The hadith collections of the Sunnah

---

[21] John Esposito, *What everyone needs to know about Islam* (New York: Oxford University Press, 2002), 11f.

[22] Muhammad Zubayr Siddiqi, *Hadith Literature* (Cambridge: Islamic Texts Society, 1993), 43.

(tradition) of the Prophet provide an authoritative guide for all aspects of Muslim daily life. Within the world of Sunni Islam there are six multi-volumed canonical collections, all compiled by the ninth century of the Common Era. Shi'a Muslims make use of these, but also have their own alternative collections.[23]

The science of hadith criticism developed to assess support for, and gauge the veracity and authenticity of, the stories and sayings that comprise, or contend for the status of, Sunnah. A set of criteria emerged by which hadith collections might be judged as belonging to one of three classes: sound, good, and weak. This structure reflects a descending order of reliability as to veracity and authenticity. The application of these criteria led to the judgement, within the majority section of Islam, of there being only two collections in the category of most highly regarded or 'sound' hadith. That is to say, it is the textual unit—the *hadith* item—that contains the substantive tradition—the *Sunnah* content—that is judged 'sound', not the collection as such.

As was noted in Chapter 2, Muhammad is revered as an exemplary man and his very life, as it is recorded and understood, impacts upon the everyday life of Muslims even to the present. The particulars of this impact vary: from deriving principles to be variously applied, to the emulation of example and obedience, to purported injunction and recorded directive. A distinction is sometimes made between obedience to Muhammad as 'Prophet' and obedience to him in his role as community leader, or *amir*. The one evokes an absolute response; the other is relativised, both temporally and instructionally. The temporal relativity is because Muhammad's amirship applies, strictly speaking, to his lifetime only. Instructional relativity lies in the fact that it is the principles of instruction (the Sunnah), enunciated in hadith, which may legitimately, at least according to some Islamic scholars and leaders, be differently and freshly applied as instruction to and within each age, and relative to contemporary place and circumstance.

On the other hand, there are those who would insist that such a division between the two roles of Muhammad could not be countenanced: in effect his Sunnah is to be applied and obeyed on a par with the strictures of the Qur'an. Submission to the Will of Allah in this case implies also submission to the Sunnah of the Prophet as it has been received, and without relativising. But, as we will see, there is much that is an open question when it comes to the matter of what, precisely, constitutes this Sunnah or hadith and which sources of it are to be trusted.

As already noted, the decision as to reliability of hadith was very important and required the application of finely tuned scholarly criteria, including in particular the introduction of the critical convention of a 'chain of transmitters'—the *isnad*. It was the demonstrated validity of the chain of transmission that attested to the authenticity of the hadith item so transmitted. In effect this was a matter of affirming the historical status of a hadith. Thus some hadith were discovered to be erroneous, even forged. However, by the third century AH there had emerged the

---

[23] Cf. John Esposito, ed., *The Oxford Encyclopedia of the Modern Islamic World* (Oxford: Oxford University Press, 1995), 84.

publication of the main hadith collections, critically attested, and which, by their very nature, would consolidate and conserve the Sunnah of the Prophet for the ongoing guidance of the Ummah.

Isnad criticism was the early and significant Islamic scholarly activity of checking and verifying the line of transmission and the genuineness of the transmitters of the items of hadith. A chain of transmission detailing the line of narrators, from Muhammad to a Companion or a Follower, down to the Compiler of the hadith, is established for each tradition within every hadith collection into the third century of the Hijra. The chain is the isnad. Checking and verifying the chain is the critical scholarly task, which led to the production of a comprehensive biographical literature about the narrators, establishing their authenticity and reliability. As a result there emerged a scholarly apparatus for identifying six categories of transmission.[24] As Siddiqi has remarked, the 'practice of specifying the *isnad* was of immense value in preserving the integrity of books in an age in which printing was unknown'.[25] Before the advent of copyright, the isnad secured some sense of authenticity.

Each item of hadith consists of two parts, the text (*matn*), which is the substantive item handed on, and the chain of transmitters (*isnad*). Hadith criticism closely scrutinises and analyses each of these parts, but in particular is concerned with the latter in order to assure the authenticity of the former. Thus an actual saying of Muhammad, for example, is preceded by a narration of '*z* heard it from *y*, who heard it from *x*', and then comes the substantive text. For example:

> Abdan related to us (saying) Yazid B Zurai informed us saying: Hisham related: Ibn Sirin related to us from Abu Huraira from the Prophet, may benediction and salutation be upon him–that he said 'If anyone forgets and eats and drinks, let him complete his fast, for it was Allah who caused him to eat or drink.'[26]

The actual *matn*, or textual item, is the quotation from Muhammad beginning 'If anyone forgets ...' and what precedes that is the isnad. In this case the item pertains to the matter of inadvertently breaking the fast: what should one do? What is one's status? The breach in the fast can be made up; the individual is excused the lapse by the gracious intimation that the lapse is not a matter of 'fault', but that Allah 'caused' it to occur in the first place.

In general terms, hadith are important as a source of data on both pre-Islamic Arabia as well as on early Islam. They also constitute a source for the development of Arabic literature, Islamic religious thought, and Islamic law. Hadith provide a common cultural framework for the world of Islam and still wield enormous

---

[24] Siddiqi, *Hadith Literature*, 77f.

[25] Ibid., 82.

[26] 'Abdur Rahman I. Doi, *Shari'ah: The Islamic Law* (Kuala Lumpur and London: A.S. Noordeen, 1989), 53.

influence in informing and shaping the modern Islamic mind. By adhering to hadith as the textual source of Sunnah, cultural continuity within and across the various communities of the Muslim world, as well as individual Islamic identity and focus, is effectively maintained. But this is, arguably, at the price of flexibility, adaptability and the ability of Islam to contextualise.

Within the Muslim academic community questions as to the centrality of hadith adherence, and the proper place of Sunnah, do arise from time to time. Typically it is the conservative 'hold the status quo' response that prevails. The reason is that, since the earliest days of the Ummah, not only has the example of the Prophet been of unique impact and importance, but also the process of the recording of and compiling all the details that comprise the Sunnah and the hadith collections has been subject to searching critique. Thus the first and foremost Islamic scholarly activity has been the attention paid to the origins and development of hadith, and to the task of hadith criticism. What has been the outcome of such scholarship?

The Islamic scholar Muhammad Siddiqi talks of hadith in terms of 'event'.[27] Hadith 'happened'. The term itself—*hadith*—carries with it the connotation of something new, in contrast to the 'old' particularly in the sense of a news item, a tale, story or report, whether legendary, historical or whatever. Culturally, Arabic storytellers were the purveyors of hadith. In other words, the term initially had a broad and general meaning, but that has since changed as a consequence of the influence of Islam and the particular application of the term to recording news of what the Prophet Muhammad said and did. As we have seen, the term hadith is closely linked with the term Sunnah such that they are often used synonymously. However, Sunnah carries the notion of 'custom' and 'precedent' and was early used to denote the accepted practice of the Muslim community; only later was it reserved for references to the reported traditions of the practice and words of the Prophet. We may say that Sunnah thus refers to the content, and its authoritative status, found contained in hadith, which in turn denotes both the individual items of reportage and the various literary collections of those. It could also be said that both hadith and Sunnah refer to content, at one level, with hadith referring mainly to the form, and Sunnah referring mainly to its authority. However, in much literature the terms are used interchangeably.

The significance of hadith and Sunnah for Islam reflect the central importance of Muhammad himself, both historically in respect to the inception of the Islamic community, and normatively in the ongoing formation and consolidation of Islamic identity through time. With the death of the Prophet there ended direct revelation. The closure of the Book, in that sense, signalled a rise in importance placed on whatever else may be derived from the life of the Prophet. Muhammad's actions thus served—and still serve—as ideals, or precedents for ongoing guidance; and his word itself emerged as law, his exemplary moral choices providing a system of personal and social virtue and ethics. Interest in their Prophet was and is intense.

---

[27] Siddiqi, *Hadith Literature, passim.*

In effect, Muhammad is himself the hermeneutical key for pious Muslims: knowledge of his deeds and words unlocks the mysteries of the Quranic utterances, making of the majestic divine recitation a way to living the mundane life of faithful obedience.

Within a century of the Prophet's death there were a vast number of hadiths—individual reports, sayings, exemplary illustrations and so on—in circulation. The material content of these included not only oral reports of the doings and sayings of the Prophet, but also references to 'the letters, laws and treaties, which were dictated to scribes by the Prophet himself'.[28] The second of the first four caliphs, Umar, was the first to consider the attempt to form a single grand collection of these hadith.

However, it was a caliph of the Umayyad dynasty at the end of the first century AH—Umar ibn Abd al-Aziz (Caliph, 717–19CE)—who was finally able to make the attempt, fearing that otherwise this source of inspiration and guidance might otherwise be lost.[29] Indeed he did so as part of his plan for the moral regeneration of the then Muslim community: he appointed teachers of the Qur'an and hadith and initiated the process of bringing together the vast quantity of hadith by now in circulation. He made contact with hadith scholars throughout the Islamic world but gave special attention to a great Traditionist (one Abu Bakr ibn Muhammad ibn Hazm) at Medina.

Early compilers of the written record of what had, like the Qur'an itself, first emerged as oral items 'were careful not to tamper with the texts as they received them from recognized specialists'. Indeed, the texts 'reflect their spoken origins' and the language of them is 'direct, conversational, active, often repetitive, with a characteristic use of formulaic expression'.[30] The early students and workers on hadith collections were followed by specialists in different parts of the world of Islam, notably at the cities of Mecca, Kufa and Medina. As a result there emerged, over time, significant and variant major collections. Many of these earliest collections have since been lost.

One early work which has survived, not itself a hadith although containing an authoritative collection of legally oriented hadiths, is the *Muwatta'* which was compiled by Imam Malik in the second century AH (eighth-century CE). This is mainly a discussion of law, ritual and religious practice with reference to the traditions of Medina. It was intended as a theoretical corrective, in respect of many things still in a state of flux, from the point of view of contemporary Islamic consensus and established Sunnah.

Hadith texts have been gathered into the various collections according to a range of classifications. Some collections may fit one or more classification. These include, in the first instance, two classifications based on temporal proximity to

---

[28] Ibid., 43.

[29] Ibid., 6.

[30] R. Marston Speight, 'Hadith' entry in John Esposito, ed., *The Oxford Encyclopedia of the Modern Islamic World*, 84.

Muhammad's lifetime. The classification *Sahifa* refers to texts—units of hadith—written down by one or other of the Companions during the Prophet's lifetime, so preserved in book or lecture-note form for the next generation.[31] Further, collections of such hadith passed on under the authority of a single individual who was either a Companion or one of the immediately succeeding generation forms the second classification (*Juz'*). Hadith may also be classified topically (*Risala*), either in respect of a collection relating to one particular topic from a list of eight, or else spanning all eight topics (*Jami*). The topics include belief; laws and rules; matters of piety; manners—to do with, for example, drinking, eating, and so on; historical and biographical items; end-time expectations of sedition and crisis; and finally items of virtue and defect in respect of peoples and places. A further classification is *Musannaf* and refers to comprehensive collections ranging over most, if not all, of these topics arranged into 'books' or 'chapters'.

Another classification, *Musnad*, originally referred to collections of hadith supported by a chain of transmission that clearly went back to the Prophet himself via a recognised Companion. It has come to mean, more broadly, collections that are reliable, reflecting an authoritative tradition; or, more specifically, collections whose material is organised according to the original named authority. In this case there is no arrangement according to subject matter. However, where such collections have arranged their subject matter simply in alphabetical order, this is the general classification of *Mu'jam*. But this term is also used more specifically for collections where the internal arrangement is according to the name of the Traditionist from whom the compiler himself received the text, rather than the name of the Companion who first reported it. Hadith collections that contain only legal-liturgical traditions, thereby omitting the larger body of spiritual, historical and other types of material, are known as *Sunan*.

The canonical hadith collections

We have seen above how texts and collections of hadith are classified; now we need to identify the hadith that have emerged as the six canonical collections. Undoubtedly the most important is the Musannaf work known as al-Jami al-Sahih of al-Bukhari. For many Muslims *al-Bukhari* is second only to the Qur'an in authority. The scholar Bukhari (AH194–256), after whom the collection is named, was of Persian extraction. Having finished his schooling he then spent most of his life travelling the Islamic world in the quest for knowledge. He is held in great esteem as a pious and rigorous scholar and is regarded as perhaps the greatest Traditionist of his time. Bukhari's scholarly aim was to collect only sound traditions, that is

---

[31] See for example, Siddiqi, *Hadith Literature*, 3.

traditions as were handed down to him from the Prophet on the authority of a well-known Companion, via a continuous chain of narrators who, according to his records, research and knowledge, had been unanimously accepted by honest and trustworthy traditionists as men and women of integrity, possessed of a retentive memory and firm faith, accepted on condition that their narrations were not contrary to what was related by the other reliable authorities, and were free from defects.[32]

Bukhari was a careful compiler, paying meticulous attention to the history of the traditions as reported and recorded. But his concern was not simply with the soundness or reliability of a tradition as such. He was effectively constructing an early work of Muslim law and theology, for he wanted his readers to grasp the contents, as well as be confident with the sources, and thereby discern the legal and doctrinal implications and conclusions that followed from such reliable and authoritative material. Thus the Sahih al-Bukhari was constructed, by its author, around thematic groupings of traditions embracing nearly 3500 chapters arranged into over 100 books. Numerous commentaries have been written on al-Bukhari, and the work has been subject to critical scrutiny from within Islamic scholarship. On the whole, however, the work and its author are accorded pride of place in the history of Muslim Traditionists.

At about the time that al-Bukhari was being compiled, another compilation of hadith by a scholar, *Imam Muslim*, was also in process. The end product also takes the name of its compiler. Muslim is deemed to be at least equal in stature to the Bukhari. Imam Muslim (AH202–61) travelled widely throughout the Islamic world in pursuit of knowledge. He wrote many works on hadith and other subjects and he utilised a threefold hadith classification according to reliability of both source and transmission. On this basis the first group, hadith of impeccable heritage, formed the substance of his collection; the second group, admitting of some critical query, was included only as corroboration to the content of the first. The third group, deemed unreliable, he rejected outright. As a result, the Muslim collection of hadith is not as comprehensive as that of Bukhari, but it is deemed more reliable overall and better in its arrangement of the traditions it contains.

The remaining four of the six canonical collections are all in the Sunan (legal-liturgical) category, which has been called the 'richest branch' of hadith literature.[33] Islamic Traditionists, in the interests of developing and undergirding the practice of religion, understandably placed greater significance on legal and doctrinal hadith than those of a more historical nature. The emphasis on practical topics and material useful to the daily life of Muslims increased from the third century. Collections of this kind of hadith are the Sunan type of which the *Abu Daud* leads the list. Abu Daud (AH203–75), after whom this collection is named, is said to have sifted through half a million texts in order to select the 4800 hadith he eventually

---

[32] Ibid., 56.
[33] Ibid., 61.

included in his work, a task that spanned some 20 years. Abu Daud won a high reputation as a principled scholar of photographic memory and encyclopaedic knowledge. He travelled often to Baghdad, but settled in Basra where he eventually died. In making his compilation he extended the parameters for determining the reliability of tradition governing what could be included, although still identifying any perceived defect. His overriding concern was with the subject matter, namely, legal hadith. Thus, as Siddiqi remarks:

> Containing all the legal traditions which may serve as foundations for Islamic rituals and
> law, and furnishing explicit notes on the authority and value of these traditions, Abu
> Daud's book has generally been accepted as the most important work of the *sunan*
> genre.[34]

The widespread acceptance and popularity of this collection is testified by its use within a wide variety of Islamic schools, especially in the Middle East and North Africa.

The second great Sunan work is the *al-Tirmidhi*. Al-Tirmidhi (AH206–79) was a Meccan of renowned retentive memory who became a well-travelled and widely respected scholar. He followed principles laid down by Abu Daud although his own work is more comprehensive. He included the great bulk of legal, dogmatic and historical hadith, which had by his time been accepted as the basis for Islamic law. One of the criteria for his inclusion of a text of hadith was that it had been established as authoritative by scholarly consensus. Further, he expanded Abu Daud's threefold classification into seven categories of reliability ranging from 'sound' to 'undetermined'. He identified intermediate grades of reliability that pertained to traditions that functioned as a source of law. This had the effect of both widening the base of authoritative text and undergirding the orthodox development of Islamic law codes.

The third Sunan work is that of *al-Nasa'i* (AH 214/5–303) who had settled in Egypt, travelled to Damascus, and become recognised as a leading Traditionist of his day. His initial work was very large, encompassing hadith traditions of dubious reliability. However, he produced a synopsis that reportedly contained only reliable traditions, and it is this that is referred to as being one of the six canonical collections of hadith. Whereas Tirmidhi focuses on specific issues and problems, and arranges his material accordingly, Nasa'i was concerned to establish the text of traditions and highlight the divergences between various versions of them. Thus against a content-focused work Nasa'i produced a work of significant importance in respect of textual-critical work.

Two Sunan works vie for the position of the fourth to be included in the canon of orthodox hadith. They are the Sunan of *al-Darimi* (AH181–255) and the Sunan of *Ibn Maja* (AH209–73). Both authors were well regarded, but both works contain

---

[34] Ibid., 63.

suspect hadith in terms of reliability. There are a number of other Sunan collections, but none attained the status of the above. As has been indicated, of the major collections of hadith, those deemed most reliable are al-Bukhari and Muslim. The four Sunan works closely follow in rank. Other classifications of mixed reliability and limited applicability are ranked below these six books, as also later collections of traditions that are not found in the earlier collections.

Postscript: Companions and forgeries

Differences of opinion, within the Islamic community, as to the criteria whereby someone is deemed a Companion ranged from the broad criterion of merely having seen the Prophet in the flesh, to more restrictive criteria having to do with the nature and length of association with Muhammad. In general the term 'Companion' (*al-sahaba*) denotes an adult Muslim who associated directly with Muhammad for any reasonable length of time: in effect, anyone who had associated long enough to be on 'speaking terms' as it were, and certainly including all family and close friends. No exact number can be given, but estimates range from an early Islamic census count of about 1500 to an encompassing reckoning in excess of 100 000.[35]

The importance of the Companions, as a group, is that they were in a position to report on what Muhammad said and did. The Companions, in so reporting, in effect generated the body of hadith material; they are the primary authorities from whom the next generation—the Successors—received the traditions so reported. It is in the initial transfer of information from the witnessing generation to the generation immediately following wherein the groundswell and impetus to generate a body of authoritative guiding reference material occurs. However, the possibility of a large number of Companions who in principle could provide hadith material, and the need to ensure authenticity of the received material, prompted the rise in early Islamic critical scholarship. As a result, it has been shown that the bulk of the received traditions that make up the corpus of hadith literature originate from less than 300 named Companions whose identified contribution range from less than 20 to over 5300 individual items.[36] Further, while it is clear that some reports of the Traditions of the Prophet had already been written down during his lifetime, many were conveyed orally, and, indeed, the question of orality versus literacy with respect to record and transmission of hadith was an early point of controversy within the Islamic community. Only over time did the need for amassing a written authoritative collection—a canon of hadith—gain universal acceptance.

These initial conveyors of hadith, the Companions of the Prophet, were followed by both those who lived at the same time but who were not Companions, as well as those in the next immediate generation of Muslims keen to maintain and

---

[35] Ibid., 14-15.
[36] Ibid., 15ff.

perpetuate the nascent traditions that were giving shape to the religion. However, enthusiasm in the absence of orthodox limits and guidelines bred excess and error. Hadith forgeries emerged alongside the authentic. Thus the task of identifying and excising forgery and fiction from the authentic and factual emerged as an early specific task of hadith scholarship, and contributed to the eventual emergence of the 'strong' or 'trustworthy' (*Sahih*) collections. Muslim scholarship identified forged traditions that have been attributed to four broad classifications of perpetuators.[37] First are the *heretics* who, being of alternative religious persuasion (for example, Manichean) and/or philosophical leaning (for example, dualist), sought to define Islam in their own way and influence the religious development of the Islamic Ummah by actively forging and disseminating inauthentic traditions of the Prophet. On the whole, however, their clear alternate agenda and identity meant such forgeries were readily identifiable and so quickly marginalised. The second group, whom we might call *heterodox*, were deemed to have been a more pervasive threat to the emergence of Islamic orthodoxy. This group consisted of certain pious and sectarian Muslims who were not averse to inventing traditions to suit their own agendas and desire for self-aggrandisement. They represent, in effect, Muslims at the margins of the emerging community, hence the denotation of heterodox to broadly distinguish them.

Next came a large group known as the *Qussas* or *storytellers*. Members of this group had no political status. They were the entertainers of the populace, and that meant, not unnaturally, being panderers to credulous common folk more interested in fabulous fables than sober guidance. However, whenever religious fervour and commonplace credulity meet, a seedbed for invention and a fount for the fanciful can be found. Such was the case in the early years of the Islamic community. The resultant fund of fictional traditions that earned the storytellers their entertainer's fee had to be subsequently identified and set aside by the serious Muslim scholar of hadith.

Finally, from among the most devout of the Traditionists came the most pernicious type of false hadith—the forged tradition that was undertaken for the highest of ideal, namely to honour the Prophet and promote Islam, but which, in being a forgery, risked disrepute and the dilution of genuine traditions. We might denote the group responsible for such hadith as *pious forgers* or the *religiously arrogant* who view themselves as having the right to determine tradition, rather than humbly submitting to the discipline of tradition. In all these cases it was the efforts of scrupulous scholars that identified and countered the effects of forged traditions within the emerging body of hadith literature.

---

[37] See Ibid., 33f.

Chapter 4

Islamic Community
Sunni, Shi'a, Sufi

Introduction

In the early days of Islam—as well as subsequently—there were many newcomers to the rapidly expanding Islamic world who had never seen or heard the Prophet, yet they were naturally keen to learn about him and his teachings. For practical purposes these people were disciples of the Companions, rather than of Muhammad himself, and became known by the title *al-Tabi'un*—'Successors' or 'Followers'. Divided into three classes in respect of the standing of the particular Companion to whom they were attached (namely, pre-Meccan conquest Muslim; post-Meccan conquest Muslim; and those who, at the death of the Prophet, were mature youths but not yet adult Muslims), the Successors are important as the first link in the post-Companion chain of transmission of hadith report. From them emerge those known as Traditionists, namely those who were keen to preserve and promote the Traditions of the Prophet of Islam and so Islam itself. The task of the Traditionists, collectively speaking, was to produce the parameters of Muslim orthodoxy, so far as it could then be determined. But the road they trod was no easy one.

As with the rise of any new religion, key determining moments wherein historical survival is assured or lost comes with the demise of the founder and, subsequently, the first generation of followers: will the baton of new religious identity be passed on? In the case of Islam the succession process in respect of both leadership and communal identity had begun during the lifetime of the Companions. The way was by no means smooth. Differences in leadership ideology emerged, as did tensions in respect to issues of Islamic identity. Spiritual idealism was quickly enmeshed with political power play and Islam early experienced a civil war, known as the *Fitnah*, which resulted in the change from the succession of elected Caliphs to that of rule by dynasty and the emergence of major divisions within the Islamic community—and all this within 30 years of the death of Muhammad.

So it was that, early in its historical development, Islam divided into three groups: *Sunni, Shi'a*, and *Khariji*. The first two have survived in the sense of denoting the two main branches of Islam, and the third survived by way of a 'tendency' or 'style' of Muslim identity that was given expression in and through a number of sectarian movements (being neither Sunni nor Shi'a). Its remnant is found in the North African *Ibadiyyah* movement that exists today in a few locations. The origins of these distinctions initially derive from a difference in respect to the question of the right line of succession from Muhammad, together with differing views on the nature of the Islamic community, and related issues of Muslim identity. Such issues are both religious and political.

Today the majority (approximately 85 per cent) of Muslims belong to the Sunni group, which traditionally holds that the successor to the Prophet is no more than an elected guardian of the prophetic legacy. After all, the Qur'an is the final and perfect revelation of the Divine Will and it declared Muhammad to be 'the Seal of the Prophets'. Therefore, any successor could only manifest a subordinate authority as leader of the believers, and consequently it would be by a process of consensus (*al-ijma*) that the community of believers would choose the successor. Initially the selection was from among the males of Muhammad's own tribe, the Quraysh. These early successors were deemed to have lived sufficiently close to the Prophet for their example to be ranked almost equal to that of the Sunnah of the Prophet himself. In general terms Sunnism can be summarised as follows: it accepts the first four Caliphs—the Rushidun—as legitimately appointed by the early Islamic community; it follows the Sunnah of the Prophet; it proceeds by consensus of the community through its scholars; and it contains within it four schools of law, that is, schools of differing interpretation and understanding (*Fiqh*) of the one Divine Law (*Shari'a*).

Shi'ism arose from the question of the rightful succession of leadership following the Prophet Muhammad. In consequence, the dissension produced the group favouring Ali (hence the 'party', or *Shi'a,* of Ali), the Prophet's cousin and son-in-law. It rejected the first three of the Rushidun, proclaiming that Ali was the rightful spiritual successor (*Imam*), and still follows its own variant of the Sunnah of the Prophet. It proceeds by way of following the guidance of the lineage of revered Imams and it has its own forms and schools of Shari'a. Although in terms of basic religious belief and the dynamics of the religious life there is, arguably, little fundamental difference between Sunnis and Shi'ites—other than the main issues of origins and ideological variance—differences in the detail of custom and practice have certainly evolved which mark one from the other. Shi'ism evolved its own forms of popular religion including religious observances undertaken at shrines, pilgrimages, and passion celebrations. Shi'ism tends to coalesce the five daily prayer times into three, for example, and it tends to be more lenient in respect to the dictates of the fast during the month of Ramadan. Akbar Ahmed notes also that differences include beliefs 'regarding folk or cultural practices around tombs of saints'.[1] Although there have been times when Sunnis indulged in various ritual practices around the tombs of saints and martyrs, Ahmed comments that nowadays

---

[1] Akbar S. Ahmed, *Living Islam* (London: BBC Books, 1993), 52.

Sunnis tend to be more ambivalent whereas Shi'ism incorporates the practice as integral to Islamic custom.

> The difference reflects a deeper philosophical position. For Sunnis, God and human beings have a direct relationship; saints and scholars cannot be intermediaries to God but are only formal interpreters of religion. Belief in shrines and saints was often viewed by the Sunni orthodox as heretical and even dangerous deviation from the true and singular worship of God.[2]

It would be fair to say, however, that many folk traditions persist within Sunnism, despite the objections of purists and the caveats of scholars. But, of course, that is true for all major religions. And it is often the case that such 'little' traditions blur the distinctions and demarcations that otherwise mark out the 'great' traditions. There will be many Sunnis who look to Muhammad to fulfil some form of spiritual intermediary role. However, Shi'ism holds that there is an integral role for the place of salvific intercession in the divine scheme of things, thus the stress on the role of the Imam as intermediary between the ordinary believer and Allah.

Differences of interpretation and application of what is, in essence, a common bedrock of religion have contributed towards a history of tension between these two streams of Islamic identity including even, at times—especially where Sunnis and Shi'ites live in close proximity to each other—violent outbursts between them. This has occurred in recent years in Pakistan, Afghanistan and also Iraq, for example. In much of the Arab world the predominance of Sunnism means Shi'ism tends to be on the defensive.

Out of nineteenth-century Shi'a Iran there arose two notable heterodox movements, Shaykhism and Babism, from which there subsequently emerged the *Baha'i* movement. This has since become itself a world religion, albeit a relatively small one. Such heterodox movements have been heavily persecuted within, and rejected by, Shi'a Islam. By contrast, the mystical Sufi movement within Islam, the ideology of which might be thought to pose an even greater threat, has actually informed and enhanced the Islamic identity of adherents to both Sunnism and Shi'ism. In this chapter I will discuss the idea and reality of the *ummah* before proceeding to a more detailed review of the emergence of Sunni Islam and the rise of Shi'a Islam and then concluding with a brief introduction to Sufism.

The Ummah: creating the Islamic community

When Muhammad took up the full reins of leadership in the city of Medina he not only created a new political identity, he also laid down the basis for Islamic religious belief and communal life. In the process, two developments occurred that

---

[2] Ibid.

were to determine the essential shape and dynamic of the religion: political consolidation, and religious practices that were to become the 'pillars' of Islam. As we saw above, migrants to Yathrib, and the population who received them, made up the nascent Muslim community. As Prophet, Muhammad was given wide-ranging powers over the city effectively dictating its total life, whilst at the same time evolving by decree and example a new religious culture. In response to his presence and impact the city changed its name to *Medina al-Nabi*, the city of the Prophet, or Medina for short. The net effect of all this was to form a theocracy, a community under God, the *Ummah*.

> The Ummah is a community based on a common faith, a community of prayer and worship as well as a community with its own government, economy, and military force. The basis of this Ummah is recorded in the Constitution of Medina, which states that any serious dispute between parties in Medina must be referred to God and the prophet Muhammad.[3]

Furthermore, the Constitution of Medina accepted the co-existence of Jews and Christians alongside the Muslims. Indeed, 'Muhammad discussed and debated with, and granted freedom of religious thought and practice to, the Jews and the Christians, setting a precedent for peaceful and cooperative interreligious relations'.[4] However, relations with the Jews, in particular, soured: the Jewish tribes would not co-operate to the satisfaction of the Arab Muslims and in the end were expelled from Medina. Of this reversal of an initial positive relation, Esposito has made a trenchant observation:

> This confrontation became part of the baggage of history and would continue to influence the attitudes of some Muslims in later centuries. Recently, this legacy can be seen in official statements from Hamas and Osama bin Laden. Both not only condemn Jews for Israeli occupation and policies in Palestine but also see the current conflict as just the most recent iteration of an age-old conflict dating back to the Jews' 'rejection and betrayal' of Islam and the Prophet's community at Medina.[5]

However, there were also continuing tensions among the Arab tribes, some of whom only superficially accepted the new Muslim identity.

With the Ummah consolidated in Medina, attention turned to Mecca and its unbelieving community. At first, of course, the Islamic community at Medina was at odds with the Meccans. A series of battles ensued: eventually Muslim forces began a series of assaults on Mecca. Muhammad's Islamic forces grew in strength—many tribes were joining his cause and converting to this faith—and in

---

[3] Theodore Ludwig, *The Sacred Paths* (New York: Macmillan, 1989), 194.

[4] John Esposito, *What Everyone Needs To Know About Islam* (New York: Oxford University Press, 2002), 73.

[5] Ibid., 81.

the year 630CE the Meccans surrendered in peace to an overwhelmingly superior Muslim force.

When Muhammad first instituted the religious practices of Islam, the direction of prayer for Muslims was not Mecca but Jerusalem. *Al Quds*—Jerusalem—is the holy city wherein there is found the patch of rock upon which, tradition held, Abraham had made his sacrifice; and at which Muhammad had, on his miraculous 'Night Journey' as recorded in the Qur'an, joined with Abraham, Moses and Jesus in prayer and then ascended into the presence of Allah. However, by the time of the capture of Mecca, Muhammad had long since fallen out with local Jewish tribes in Medina, and the direction of prayer had been changed: no longer Jerusalem, but Abraham's shrine—the Ka'ba in Mecca—had become the point of liturgical focus.

Mecca surrendered in 630CE. Muhammad had entered in peace and awarded a general amnesty. Then he went into the Ka'ba and destroyed all its idols with the proclamation: 'God is great! Truth has come. Falsehood has vanished'. Thus Muhammad 'Islamised' the Ka'ba. Henceforth the shrine was to be for Allah alone, an everlasting symbol of the final triumph of belief in One God over belief in many. This act of islamisation was important for two reasons. On the one hand it demonstrated the triumph of the belief in and the religion of the One True God over all rival idolatries and religions. On the other hand it provides an insight into the essential dynamics of Islam: the religion of submission has cause to ensure, impose, or enforce this submission in certain circumstances.

One of the distinctive features of Islam is that, with respect to its early years, expansion and development were rapid and extensive, to say the least. Soon after the death of Muhammad, Islam impacted vigorously on the surrounding countries of the Near Eastern world. Within a few short years Muslim expansion out of Arabia was well under way. During these decades the leadership of the Islamic community was in the hands of a series of caliphs, leaders who were the deputies of Muhammad, continuing all his functions except one, that of being the Prophet, the 'mouthpiece' of Allah. Muhammad had been the last of those. When Muhammad died in 632CE his right-hand man, Abu Bakr, was elected his successor: the first Muslim Caliph. Thus the leadership of the Ummah, in succession, through the four Righteous or Rightly Guided Caliphs beginning with Abu Bakr and ending with Ali, the cousin and son-in-law of Muhammad. But even as expansion and conquest continued and increased under these caliphs, there was much controversy surrounding them. *Abu Bakr* (632–4) strengthened the political unity of the Ummah; *Umar ibn al-Khattab* (634–44) was responsible for major expansions and conquests; *Uthman ibn Affan* (644–56) became embroiled in nepotism and power struggles; and *Ali ibn Abu Talib* (656–61) died a controversial figure. In the end he was deemed unfit by some to be the Caliph and so he was assassinated as, indeed, were his two predecessors. Indeed, it was disagreement over Ali's response to Uthman's assassination which led to increased dissent and the rise of a five-year civil war—*Fitnah*—which itself helped precipitate the dividing of the Islamic community into two blocs: Sunni and Shi'a. It was not long before Muslims were regarding the period of the first four Caliphs as an era when Islam had been ruled by devout men, who had been close to the Prophet, but had been brought low by evil-doers. The events of the first *fitnah* had become symbolic, and rival parties now drew upon these tragic incidents as they struggled to make sense of their Islamic vocation. ... The *ummah* seemed to be moving away from the world of the Prophet, and was in danger of losing its *raison d'être*.[6]

Following the period of the first caliphs, who ruled from Arabia, both the structure as well as the location of the leadership of the Ummah underwent radical change: a dynastic era, with power bases outside of Arabia, held sway for several centuries. Indeed, some 600 years after the commencement of the Islamic community the notion of a united Ummah was but an ideal: the political reality was one of diversity and difference.

Nonetheless, as noted above, in its earliest years the majority of Muslims concurred with the principle of electing the Caliph by consensus, which became a key mark of the praxis of Sunni Islam. However, another group argued that Muhammad himself had decreed a line of succession that should have started with Ali. These became the Shi'a Muslims, the party (*Shi'a*) of Ali. Thus began the first major division within Islam. The second division consisted of those who broke away from the nascent Shi'ite group. These became known as the Kharijites from the Arabic *kharaja*, meaning 'to go out, secede'. I will examine both these divisions and allied movements below. For the most part, the Islam of which we speak is the majority Sunni stream.

Muhammad had left both a religion and a state—a theocratic caliphate. Initially this caliphate was constituted on the lines of a federation of tribes and clans. As it grew and expanded it became, necessarily, more organised. Roving Arab tribes had long been in the habit of raiding their neighbours as a matter of economic necessity and nomadic tradition. Both Muhammad and his immediate successors realised they could not keep peace within the federation unless the raiding energies were channelled and given outlet and expression. Thus expeditions were organised with the aim of acquiring booty, especially domestic animals. This activity was viewed as an economic function, and stood alongside the religious function of challenging unbelievers, which was also a goad to expedition and expansion.

The initial raids from Medina were highly successful because there was a power vacuum in the region. The Byzantine (Roman Christian) and the Persian (Zoroastrian) empires had exhausted themselves after 50 years of constant warfare. The Muslim raiders quickly consolidated their advances, creating forward base camps to allow them to spread further afield. Thus, within a mere dozen years of Muhammad's death they had taken Egypt, Syria and Iraq. They were moving rapidly westwards into Libya, and eastwards into what is now Iran. Within a decade of the death of Muhammad, the armies of Islam captured Jerusalem. A Muslim

---

[6] Karen Armstrong, *Islam: A Short History* (London: Phoenix Press, 2001), 31.

shrine was later built over the patch of rock that features in Muhammad's Night Journey and upon which both Jews and Muslims believed Abraham had demonstrated his willingness to sacrifice his son as a demonstration of his perfect submission to the divine command. The shrine built over the rock is the famous 'Dome of the Rock'. It dominates the Jerusalem skyline to this day.

Wherever the Muslim forces conquered, the governors of the previously ruling empires fled and the Muslims made treaties with the locals granting them the status of 'protected minority' (*dhimmi*). Thus local communities were allowed to run themselves, politically and economically, but paid a tribute or tax to the Ummah through the Muslim governor. At the religious level the status of protected minority was granted only to those who were deemed People of the Book—that is, Jews, Christians and Zoroastrians, all of whom believed in one God and possessed a written scripture. For many centuries Jews and Christians enjoyed relatively peaceful lives under Muslim rulers, albeit as second-class citizens. Indeed, for the most part, Jews who lived under Muslim rule fared better than Jews living under Christian rule in the west.

During the first century of Islam, expansion of the community was as relentless as it was rapid. Factors involved in this early spread included not only military accomplishments but also the impact of traders and merchants and the good impressions made by teachers and holy men. To the west, Islam swept over North Africa as far as the Atlantic, crossed into Spain, and for a while occupied a portion of the south of France. Over the next few centuries the pace of expansion hardly seemed to slacken. To the north-east, Islam advanced as far as Constantinople (Istanbul) eventually pressing on through the Balkans and at one point threatening to take Vienna. To the east, Islam occupied the whole of Persia and Afghanistan, penetrated into Central Asia, and crossed the Indus River into North-west India (now Pakistan). For some five centuries the Islamic empire continued to expand and was ruled successively by two great dynasties. The first of these, the *Umayyad* dynasty, was based in Syria with Damascus as the capital. The second, the *Abbasid* dynasty, shifted the power base of Islam to Iraq with Baghdad as the capital. At its height the empire extended from the south of France in the west to China in the east. The Islamic empire, at that time, covered a territory which dwarfed that of the Roman empire.

Following the period of the four elected Rushidun, the burgeoning Islamic empire was ruled by the Umayyads from 661CE to c.750CE. The geographic extent of this era of governance was vast, and this very fact produced significant problems. The seeds of religious upheaval were sown and took root, contributing to the eventual downfall of this dynastic rule. It is worth noting that the treatment meted out to conquered peoples was on the whole fair and just. However, by contrast, it was sometimes the case that pagan Arab tribes were offered 'Islam or the sword' because, were they to remain non-Muslim, they would be viewed as a serious threat to the unity of the Ummah. At that stage the Ummah was predominantly an Arab phenomenon: most, but not all, other peoples were viewed as protected minorities and were well treated in that context. Muslim rulers looked upon treatment of such groups as a matter of honour. Nevertheless, very often non-Muslims felt themselves to be second-class citizens and this promoted a steady trickle of converts to Islam over the centuries. Thus Islam came, in the end, to predominate in countries that had previously been Christian. As for Persian Zoroastrianism, as it was already in rapid decline, the rise of Islam quickly and effectively, although not entirely, extinguished it.

The demise of the Umayyads led to a major shift in the power base governing Islam. A new dynasty with a new leading city emerged out of the struggle for control and the assertion of orthodoxy. The Abbasids ruled from Baghdad from c.750CE to 1250CE, a period which saw a gradual fracturing of ruling powers and the dissolution of a single theocracy into a number of kingdoms and empires. Factors pertinent to this period include significant cultural development, political decadence, and religious turmoil. For example, Spain and Spanish Islam remained independent of Baghdad, and eventually other outlying areas also seceded. Yet the first two centuries of this dynasty saw much in the way of political, cultural, social and religious consolidation. The study of Islamic law, or jurisprudence, became the core of higher education and many Greek works were translated into Arabic. There were also considerable advances made in the sciences, in literature, in the arts, as well as in the skills of government and administration.

In the middle of the thirteenth century Mongol invaders swept through from the east, overran much of the empire, and sacked Baghdad. The epoch of great dynastic rule came to an abrupt end. Initially it would have appeared the tide had turned: infidels had Islam on the run. Ironically, however, although the invaders triumphed militarily, they came under the sway of the Islamic faith and they, too, submitted to Allah: the Mongols became Muslim and hence gave rise to the Mogul (or Mughal) Empire that was to predominate the Indian sub-continent (1526–1858CE). The combination of this inroad into much, though by no means all, of Islamic territory, coupled with inherent political, ethnic and even religious diversity that was bubbling away, meant that the era of the single Islamic empire gave way to a succession of—sometimes competing—kingdoms and caliphates. All this had important consequences for the proclamation and effecting of the ideal of a united Ummah.

Following the Mongol invasions and the destruction of the dynastic caliphate, the intellectual flowering of Islam withered. Major schools of philosophy and theology declined, vanished, or resorted to a 'conservative' mode, simply maintaining a kind of status quo. One new influence, however, emerged in the period of the Middle Ages: Sufism and, allied to it, a resurgence of Neoplatonic philosophy. Meanwhile, in India, the grand period of Islamic power under the Mughal emperors, which lasted for many centuries, finally waned by the middle of the eighteenth century. But Islam had been a predominant political force in India for a thousand years, from its early incursions during the eighth century down to the arrival of the British in the middle of the eighteenth century. Religiously, Islam initially treated Hindus as also a 'People of the Book' on account of the Vedic scriptures and the fact that Hindu philosophers tend to be monotheistic. While there were some group conversions to Islam, most Indians remained Hindu.

From India, Islam spread through largely peaceful trading contacts into Southeast Asia as far as the Philippines. Muslim traders also took Islam further into Africa as well as eastwards from Central Asia into eastern China. Expansion thus continued over time through conversion and cultural adaptation—the receptor cultures by and large adapting to Muslim ways. This continued expansion gave further rise to a variety of kingdoms and rulers. However, in Spain Islam experienced a marked contraction. Military pressure from the Christian Holy Roman empire slowly reduced the area of Spain under Muslim rule until the final collapse in 1492CE. For a short time Muslims continued to live in Spain, but were then either driven out or executed by the Inquisition.

By about 1500CE the Turkish Ottomans had restored the caliphate in the west and went on to conquer much of south-east Europe and the southern coast of the Mediterranean. The Ottoman Caliphate, which can be traced back to the fourteenth century conquests of Osman I (from whom the term 'Ottoman' derives, although the term 'Osmanli' is more apt and is often found in relevant Muslim literature) emerged as one of the more prominent and dominating of the kingdoms and caliphates that followed the era of the great pan-Islamic dynasties. The Ottoman empire had its power base in Turkey and its predominance lasted until the early twentieth century, by which time post-Industrial Revolution Europe was making new sorts of profound impacts on the Islamic world. This, the last great Islamic Caliphate, was finally abolished in 1924. The only remaining expression of the ideal of Ummah had passed away; the stage was now set for new movements to arise to claim the mantle of 'Ummah', or at least proclaim themselves as the authentic promoters of the Islamic Ummah.

During the nineteenth and twentieth centuries many Muslim lands that were once ruled by vast and complex Muslim bureaucracies gave way to the emergence of the modern nation state. However, in the Middle East the concept of 'kingdom' still prevailed as a kind of overlay, to a greater or lesser degree. Nonetheless, today the Islamic community for the most part exists in the context of either the modern secular state or an Islamic nation state. As I have already noted, the ideal of the united Ummah is countered by the reality of geographic and political diversity: Islam exists in many different countries and within a variety of political arrangements. We will return to these themes later.

The emergence of Sunni Islam

Sunni Islam, representing the largest body of Muslims, was not a self-conscious term of identity for quite some time. The word 'Sunni' derives of course from 'Sunnah', and refers to the fact that Muslims, as such, are a people who follow the traditions (Sunnah or sometimes Sunna) of their Prophet (together with God's Word, the Qur'an, of course). Montgomery Watt notes that it was quite some time before the majority group of Muslims referred to themselves as 'Sunni', that is, as belonging to the 'people of the Sunna' (*Ahl as-Sunna*). Watt also notes that variations on this phrase were in use late in the ninth century, but the phrase itself 'was not in common use until the tenth century, and the adjective *sunni* seems to be first recorded towards the end of the tenth century'.[7]

In the development of Sunnism, as a distinct branch of Islam, a number of major issues and allied movements can be identified as playing key roles. In effect Sunnism began with the emergence of a major point of theological understanding. During the first (Umayyad) dynasty attention was given to defining the power of God to determine events. The key issue was the extent to which Allah is involved in human actions. The emerging Muslim view was oriented towards a concept of divine predestination: divine all-powerfulness means Allah is the source of power, the necessary and sufficient efficient cause behind all events. Thus humans act under the compulsion of the power of Allah. Among the early theological disputes and issues on points of faith, such as authority, leadership, and the identity and substance of the Ummah, the matter of faith and works—or the relation between simply believing in Allah and the performance of required actions—sharpened the differences between these first theologically distinguished groups. There are six in all, which I will identify and briefly comment upon.

The 'Separatists', or Kharijites, constituted an early sectarian movement that broke away from the nascent party of Ali (the Shi'a) between 656 and 661. Their name derives from the Arabic for those who 'exit' or 'depart' (*Khawarij*). This group, in effect, constituted the third stream of early Muslim identity. The question of Muslim self-definition was prominent for this group: what and who is a Muslim? They believed that the will of God is and should be expressed through the decisions of a whole community of believers, something that was akin to the emerging Sunni perspective. However, they also strongly resented moves towards laxity of conduct, which had begun to appear even in the early days of the Rushidun. As far as the Kharijites were concerned, an unjust ruler ought to be overthrown, and by force if needs be. And indeed, this did occur. On the issue of 'faith and works', they rejected the idea that a particularly bad sinner could remain a member of the community.

In many respects the Kharijite movement could be viewed as an early form of Islamic dissent and revivalism, tinged with the imposition of strict mores and interpretations of Qur'an and Sunnah, often with the consequence of a harsh application of Islamic values and judgements. Indeed, it was extremist Kharijites who assassinated Ali because he did not act decisively in the cause of God: he was too lax, he had departed from the strict ways of true Islam so far as these Kharajites were concerned. As one scholar has remarked, 'The Khawarij are noted for

---

[7] W. Montgomery Watt, *Islamic Philosophy and Theology* (Edinburgh: Edinburgh University Press, 1987), 21.

steadfastness and unwillingness to compromise'.[8] In time this movement fragmented into many sects and groups of which one, the Ibadiyyah, has survived to the present. However, it could be said that something of the values and perspectives of this particular early movement has continually resurfaced in other movements throughout the history of Islam and, indeed, are to found in some of the extremist and harshly assertive expressions of Islam in the contemporary world.

The 'Postponers', or *Murjiites*, constituted a second early movement, in this case representative of what we might call a comparatively 'liberal' or 'relaxed' tradition within emerging mainstream Sunnism. Rather than insisting on the application of harsh judgements in the present, the Murji'a view advocated belief in a 'delayed judgement', thus constituting a relatively liberal counter to the strict views of the Kharijites. Also, they were less severe in matters of ethical judgement. In contrast to the strictures of the Khawarij, the Murjiite perspective allowed for the inclusion of 'sinners' within the Muslim community. The Murjiite perspective was that the Last Judgement of Allah would be sufficient: serious sins don't necessarily preclude salvation, and it is certainly not the task of the human being to prefigure the mind of Allah. Indeed, God is merciful and if there is any case for mercy it would surely be given.

This more tolerant position followed logically from the belief that Allah was the supreme and sole source of salvation. But the Murjiite position was not just one of a relatively more liberal approach to ethical and related matters; this view also had a significant theological dimension. The general view about the structure of Islamic belief that was emerging within the wider community of Islamic scholars was that belief is comprised of three components. First, there is inward assent, 'avowal of truth by the heart' (*tasdiq*); then there is articulation, that is: 'verbal confession of the truth by the tongue' (*iqrar*); and finally the expression of belief in life, namely, 'acts of obedience or good works' (*'amal*).[9] Whereas a more strict viewpoint, such as that held by the Kharijites, would want to insist that professed belief is also evidenced in a godly, pious, and 'correct' life, the Murjiite viewpoint 'postpones' the matter of 'good works' or 'politically correct lifestyle' as we might say, to a secondary ranking. Inward motivation and the intention of faith are sufficient: the outcome can be left to the judgement of the merciful God.

A third group is the Freewill Party, called *Qadarites*, who took an even more radical stance in favour of human autonomy against the rising dominance of emerging Sunnism, which tended to subordinate human autonomy to the Will of Allah. In the dispute concerning human freewill versus divine predestination, the Qadariyya viewpoint emphasised freewill, holding that human beings have the power and capability to act of their own volition. Thus human beings are accountable and so are free to act as they choose. In other words, as a 'hard'

---

[8] John A. Williams, 'Khawarij', in John Esposito, ed., *The Oxford Encyclopedia of the Modern Islamic World* (Oxford: Oxford University Press, 1995), 419.

[9] See David Waines, *An Introduction to Islam* (Cambridge: Cambridge University Press, 1995), 106.

predestination would undercut human morality, and as moral culpability is essential to the operation of Shari'a (Law), then humans must be responsible for their own actions: human freewill is therefore essential. An early text expounding a Qadarite perspective is an epistle (*Risala*) written by one *al-Hasan al-Basri* (642–728CE) around the year 700 in response to a question about the power (*qadar*) exercised by a Caliph. At the time, the Umayyad Caliphs viewed themselves as Caliphs of Allah (rather than Caliphs of Muhammad, as was the case with the Rushidun). Accordingly, they saw their combined religious and political authority as having been ordained by the power of God. Clearly any response, whether supportive or critical of the Caliphal view that their exercise of power was in fact divine, or at least divinely sanctioned, was both theological and political.

Al-Hasan's response identified with the emerging Qadarite view that all exercise of human authority, action and power, was freely chosen and so accountable. Certainly there is divine involvement in human affairs. But, if the Qur'an is considered as a whole, then according to al-Hasan, 'the determination of human activity by God follows on some act of human choice and is a recompense for it'. Furthermore, 'Al-Hasan also maintained that God creates only good, and that men's [sic] evil acts are from themselves or from Satan; but he allowed that God's "guidance" ... contained an element of "succour" or "grace" (*tawfiq*)'.[10] Al-Hasan argued the illogicality of believing that God had sent a prophet to be obeyed, but then would prevent, or undermine, the free response of obedience. Rather the Qur'an itself indicates (Sura 74:37) that there is a God-given capacity (*qudrah*) whereby human beings are enabled to make genuinely free choices. 'Without choice there can be no morality in Allah's reward or punishment'.[11]

Although al-Hasan asserted human freewill in respect to moral behaviour and the religious life, in respect to the material fact of existence the all-determining power of Allah is supreme. While there is debate as to whether al-Hasan was himself a Qadarite as such, his writings were significant in contributing to the formulation of this particular Islamic theological perspective. Qadarism, as a distinctive philosophical-theological position, and the Qadarite group as a religio-political perspective, eventually lost out to the emerging mainstream of Sunni Islamic thought and politics. Watt asserts that by the eighth century there were no Qadarites as such and that some form of predestinarian belief emerged as triumphant even where room was made for moral effort.[12]

The Freewill movement became, in effect, the rather more philosophical *via media* perspective of the fourth group, known as *Mu'tazilites*. In the attempt to systematise Islamic thought they began the process of defining orthodoxy by virtue of being the first theological thinkers to challenge heretics and non-Muslim views. They promoted the way of reasoned defence and apologia, and premised their work

[10] Watt, *Islamic Philosophy*, 27.

[11] Waines, *Introduction to Islam*, 114.

[12] Watt, 28.

on the oneness or 'unity' (*tawhid*) of Allah and on the notion of justice (*'adl*).[13] Influenced by Greek philosophical thought, they objected to both the rigorism of the Kharijites and the laxity of the Murjiites and Qadarites. From a perspective that saw scripture as a support for theological reasoning (and not the other way around), the Mu'tazilites 'honed and refined an already existing technique of dialectical argument on matters of theological speculation which they employed in polemics against their opponents within the community, but also encounters with Christians'.[14]

Rejecting notions of predestination, the Mu'tazilites advanced the view of freewill and responsibility for one's actions. But they also rejected the notion of the eternity of the Qur'an and the literal reading of anthropomorphisms within it: in other words, the Mu'tazilite stance was one of a sophisticated, even in our terms modern, reading of religious texts. However, their views were eventually rejected by the emerging Sunnite orthodoxy, even though Sunni theologians often made use of Mu'tazilite ideas. In the end the Mu'tazilites fell into disfavour with the Abbasid court when the Ash'arites (see below) gained the ascendancy to become the dominant intellectual leaders. Nonetheless the Mu'tazilite group, and the work it undertook, is credited with instituting Islamic rational theology proper.

The Traditionalist dimension of Islam emerged as the fifth group, that is the *Hanbalite* school of both theology and law, named after its founder *ibn Hanbal* (780–855CE). Traditionalist groupings, representing the pious conservative dimension of early Islam, had grown out of opposition to the Mu'tazilites and eventually became identified with what we might refer to as 'ultra-orthodox' mainstream Sunni thought. Hanbal's shaping of hadith reinforced the place of the Sunnah of the Prophet as, perhaps, the key source of interpretative guidance, thus shoring the unique source of authority and substance against the encroachments of external dimensions such as Greek thought and 'free' thinking. For Hanbal, all that Islam needs is the Qur'an and the Sunnah. Shari'a, the Islamic Law derived principally from the Qur'an and Sunnah, is a total way of life. This is the position of conservative orthodoxy today and, indeed, many contemporary conservative revivalist and reform movements, as in Saudi Arabia for example, trace their spiritual heritage to ibn Hanbal.

One key theological debate around which these schools offered their different responses was that of the status of the Qur'an—what is it, exactly? Was it, itself, something created or uncreated? For Muslims, the question of the createdness of the Qur'an—not unlike the question of the createdness of Christ for Christians—emerged as a crucial theological issue. The Mu'tazilites argued that the Qur'an, as the record of God's revelation to Arabs, is something created. Against them, the Hanbalites argued that the Qur'an is the eternal uncreated Word of God. Theological and metaphysical issues were subtle and complex, but the political

---

[13] Cf. Waines, 117.
[14] Waines, 116.

ramifications were not: Hanbal's opponent, the Caliph al-Ma'mun, required a public declaration from his chief civil servants to the effect that the Qur'an was created. Hanbal himself chose imprisonment over subversion of religious conviction. The rounding up and conviction of dissenters from the doctrine of the Created Qur'an is known as the *mihna*, or inquisition.

Finally, another school of law and theology, the *Ash'arites*, is significant as it was the theologian al-Ash'ari (died c.935CE), and this school he founded, which brought about the defining Sunni response to the Mu'tazilites. Opposition to the Mu'tazilites had been from pious puritans who eschewed reliance upon Greek philosophy and the use of independent reason from which to interpret the Qur'an and Sunnah. The sole source of religious knowledge ought to be a literal reading of the Qur'an and the obedient acceptance of the authority of the Sunnah of the Prophet.

The stance of al-Ash'ari was to combine reason and revelation. Following ibn Hanbal, he set the scene for the 'orthodoxy of paradox', that is, believers are to accept the truth literally, 'without asking how': critical questioning was ruled out. The ways of Allah are not the ways of humankind: to regard the workings of God in human terms is to liken Allah to the human. This is a form of high blasphemy in Islam, known as *shirk*, the essential meaning of which is the association with God of that which is not divine. Thus human reasoning is always and necessarily subordinate to the primary religious response, which is obedient believing.

Al-Ash'ari and his school took the view that reason was certainly a legitimate tool to be applied in respect to *understanding the sources* of the faith, but *not* for *critical analysis* of those sources or what they contain. That is to say, reason can be used for defence and explanation of basic and popular beliefs, but not to subject these beliefs to searching rational and analytical criticism.

This approach effectively constitutes the basis of what today may be regarded as Islamic 'revivalism', or the re-assertion of the fundamentals of faith and practice supported by, but not directly subject to, the principles of reason. The relation between 'reason' and 'revelation' in the field of religious knowledge thus constitutes another key issue in early Islamic thought, and retains contemporary applicability.

Furthermore, the Ash'arite School propounded the concept of the Qur'an as itself eternal, that is, it was not created in time. This item of mainstream Sunni orthodoxy marks the radical distinction between, for example, Islamic and Christian views of scripture. The Qur'an is not, theologically speaking, the counterpart of the New Testament, but the Islamic equivalent of the Christian understanding of the eternal Word of God (Christ). Also, the Ash'arites held that although Allah causes all to happen—both good and bad things—yet Allah is beyond categories of evil and injustice when it comes to the attempt to fathom predeterminism, for example.

The rise of Shi'a Islam

Shi'ism, or Shi'ite Islam, holds that the principal religious figure for the ongoing community is the *Imam*, believed to be one invested with the qualities of inspired and infallible interpretation of the Qur'an, and who is in spiritual succession directly from Muhammad. Whereas the first Caliph was in fact appointed by popular consensus in Sunni tradition, Shi'ites (or Shi'is, those who belong to Shi'a Islam) believe Muhammad appointed an Imam, namely Ali, to be his successor and thereby instituted the lineage of legitimate succession. What was, and is, at stake is not just who should be the leader of the community after Muhammad, but involves profound differences of opinion concerning the nature and role of that leadership: Sunni Caliph versus Shi'ite Imam; decision of choice by a process of consensus versus the succession as determined by the existence of a pre-ordained dynasty.

There is a multiplicity of hagiographical traditions concerning Ali, some that are common to Sunnism and Shi'ism alike, and some peculiar to Shi'ism. As with many areas in the study of a religion, we must be alert to the distinction between 'loaded' or biased, often quasi-legendary, traditional history; and that which is the domain of authentic and critical scholarship. Both are important, yet often hard to distinguish. However, it is clear that Ali soon attracted the opprobrium of many Sunnites, eventually leading to open revolt by *Mu'awiya*, the death of Ali after a period of conflict, and then the establishment of the Umayyad dynasty with Mu'awiya its first Caliph. Shi'a identity and belief derive directly, of course, from the figure of Ali, the cousin and son-in-law to the Prophet Muhammad, indeed also the first male adult convert to Islam. Ali was appointed Caliph after the murder of Uthman. He is thus the fourth Muslim Caliph, but he is also the first Imam of Shi'ism. He is, however, revered in both Sunni and Shi'a traditions.

Ali had two sons, *al-Hasan* and *al-Husayn*. After the assassination of Ali, al-Hasan became the second Imam of the Shi'ites, but he abdicated under pressure from Mu'awiya. Al-Husayn replaced him as the third Imam, but he then died a martyr at the hands of the Umayyads. The year this happened was 680CE and the new Umayyad Caliph was *Yazid*, son of Mu'awiya, who ordered his army to suppress the nascent Shi'a community. At the town of *Karbala* (in what is now Iraq) al-Husayn made his last stand. He and his retinue faced overwhelming odds, but they refused the shame of surrender, choosing instead to fight for the truth of Islam, as they saw it, to the last man. Gradually his small force fell and in the end al-Husayn was himself executed. His martyr's death quickly formed a 'passion-point' for Shi'a Islam, and has provided the rationale and ethos sanctioning the virtue of Shi'ite martyrdom ever since. Indeed, the death of al-Husayn is commemorated annually as a religious/political rallying point for many Shi'ites. The Shi'a position is unequivocal: Ali should have been first Caliph, and his sons should have become Caliphs by succession after Ali's death. Nevertheless, there follows a succession of Imams through a dynastic line descended from Ali, but at points this is broken, and at each point there is precipitated a schismatic fragmentation of Shi'ism into sub-groups.

The fourth Imam was the eldest son of Husayn—*Ali ibn Husayn*—who was religiously pious and politically aloof. It appears he might have been murdered. Then *his* first son, *Muhammad ibn Ali*, became the fifth Imam. Like his father he was not a political activist, but he did have to face off a rival claimant to the leadership role. During his imamate the Shi'a movement began to take a more distinctively independent stance from the wider Sunni community on matters of ritual practices and law. Shi'ites who hold that the fifth Imam was in fact *Zayd*, and was the last of the line of Imams, are known as the 'Fivers' or *Zaydis*. This group constitutes the first major division within Shi'ism. *Ja'far*, eldest son of Muhammad ibn Ali, became the sixth Imam and was known as *al-Sadiq*, 'the truthful'. He led a relatively quiet life under the Umayyad rule of the wider Muslim community, but he was persecuted by the Baghdad-based successors, the Abbasids. The sixth Imam, who is also viewed as the effective founder of Shi'ite fiqh, was thus led to promulgate the Shi'a doctrine of 'prudent dissimulation' (*taqiyya*), that is, it is acceptable, even needful, to give apparent allegiance to one form of religious identity and authority structure (Sunni Abbasids, in this case) while covertly, but authentically, professing loyalty to another.

The seventh Imam was *Musa ibn Ja'far*, whose mother was a slave. However, he was not the eldest son and so his succession was disputed and this led to the second major division in the ranks of the Shi'ites. The eldest son, *Isma'il*, had died before his father; hence the line of succession went, in practical terms, to Musa. But some believed the true Imamate to have been passed on to Isma'il, and then to his son Muhammad ibn Isma'il, and it was this viewpoint that led to a split within the Shi'ite ranks so giving rise to a new Shi'ite group since known as the *Isma'ilis* or 'Seveners'. Meanwhile Musa, the Imam acknowledged as the true Imam by the majority Shi'a community, was constantly harassed by Abbasid authorities and eventually killed. The eldest son of Musa, *Ali*, was the eighth Imam and he was known as *al-Rida*, 'the Acceptable'. During his time the Abbasid caliphate itself split into two blocs, namely Arab and Persian. Much later Persia would become virtually completely Shi'a, and this gave rise to the great *Safavid* empire.

The ninth Imam, *Muhammad ibn Ali*, was aged only seven when he succeeded his father. His youth was a cause of controversy. Following him, a number of other sub-groups emerged. The tenth Imam, *Ali ibn Muhammad*, was also only seven years old when he succeeded his father. He lived into his forties whereupon his son, *Hasan*, became the eleventh Imam. But Hasan was to live out his imamate in a form of detention for just six years when he died, apparently of poisoning. The last of the line of Imams of what had now become the major Shi'a sectarian group is the twelfth, *Muhammad ibn Hasan*. However, in his case it is believed he did not die but was taken by God into 'occultation'; that is, he was spiritually transported into a hidden realm, from whence he will one day return.[15] Thus there emerged the

---

[15] 'In its simplest form, the doctrine of Occultation (*Ghayba*) declares that Muhammad ibn Hasan, the Twelfth Imam, did not die but has been concealed by God from the eyes of men. His life has been miraculously prolonged until the day when he will manifest himself again

belief in the return of the *Mahdi*, the hidden Imam, the one awaiting the proper time to return, or to be revealed. This major group is thus known as the 'Twelvers' or *Ithna Ashari* Shi'ites and constitutes the third major division within Shi'ism. The significance of the Imams for Shi'a is that they 'believe that the Divine Light which dwelt in Muhammad has passed from him to the Imam; and that the Imam is therefore both sinless and infallible'.[16]

In further distinction from the Sunnis, the Shi'ites have their own hadith and they reject the four Sunni law systems or schools. They believe instead that the infallible and hidden Imam guides them. Significant internal variations have led to the further development of main Shi'ite sects, many of which faded away, such as the *Nizari Isma'ilis*, whose particular form of violent opposition to the Abbasid rulers gave rise to the term 'Assassin'. However, some have persisted into the present, such as the contemporary non-violent form of the earlier Nizari Isma'ilis led by the *Agha Khan*. Fragmentation and diversification have been a feature of Shi'a history. Yet the political dimensions of the Shi'a movement were, and have been often since, very important. Like Sunnis, Shi'ites have been variously political in expression and orientation, inclined to shifting allegiances and emphases, and even having links, at least by some, to the Sunni Hanafi School despite being the main alternative movement to Sunnism.

There have also been significant religious innovations introduced into Islam through the activities of some Shi'a groups. For example, religious speculation, which introduced new ideas such as the transmigration of souls; occultation and return of the last Imam; the possibility and fact of the alteration of God's Will; and the idea of the imamate as divinely-inspired leadership. The Imams are those who, after the Prophet, give teachings which are sources of inspiration along with the Qur'an and the Sunnah; indeed, such teachings are viewed as being part of the Sunnah. The Isma'ili sect, for example, was especially assertive and enterprising in advocating its esoteric doctrines throughout the Abode of Islam (*dar-al-Islam*).

What was originally a breakaway, largely political, movement within the wider Muslim community emerges, during the time of the fifth and sixth Imams, as the main alternative sect within Islam. It evolved a distinctive jurisprudence; it resulted in the depoliticising of the Imamate; and it promoted doctrines of the divine designation, the sinlessness and infallibility, and the supreme exemplariness, of the Imam. It emerged with a set of distinctive beliefs, unique doctrinal developments, and a stress on the prominence of the community of scholarly religious leaders (*Ulema*). The Abbasid movement had begun as a manifestation of Shi'ism. The Abbasid court was more open to Shi'ism than the Umayyad, therefore allowing the

---

by God's permission. During his Lesser Occultation, he remained in contact with his followers through the four *Babs*. During the Greater Occultation, which extends to the present day, he is still in control of the affairs of men and is the Lord of the Age ... but there is no longer a direct route of communication.' Moojan Momen, *An Introduction to Shi'i Islam* (New Haven and London: Yale University Press, 1985), 165.

[16] D.A. Brown, *A Guide to Religions* (London: S.P.C.K., 1975), 217.

Shi'a to flourish more openly in the early centuries. But the Shi'ites constantly argued for Ali as the rightful heir to the Prophet, not the other three of the Sunni-acknowledged Rightly Guided Caliphs. Then, with the emergence of a clear proto-Sunnite identity, the Abbasids became anti-Shi'ite. Later, Sufism and the Mongol invasions of the thirteenth century impacted heavily upon Shi'ism.

The emergence of Sufism

Through the centuries Islam has contained within itself two broad divisions or groupings, Sunni and Shi'a, as we have seen. The interaction between Sunnism and Shi'ism, and the inherent tensions and diversities within each or these main divisions, have led to the formation of the many sectarian and other variant groups that can be found within the wider Ummah. However, a third dominant movement, with its own internal diversity, has impacted on both these major divisions. This movement—it is not really another major division as such—to which I refer is of course Sufism, and it has affected and contributed to both Sunnism and Shi'ism. It is not itself a division *of* the Ummah; rather it represents an experiential element or dimension within Islam itself. Martin Lings states simply, 'Sufism is nothing other than Islamic mysticism'.[17] He also remarks, 'Sufism is necessary because it is to Islam what the heart is to the body'.[18] And Ahmed remarks that Sufism is 'Islam's tolerant, mystical and universal philosophy'.[19] This inwardly spiritual dimension of Islam evolved in various ways and embraced different forms of personal piety and mystical expression. The Sufi movement originated in pious asceticism and cut across all social and religious divisions. In the emerging Sunni context it gave expression to mysticism and the contemplative ideal. It provided the counterpoint of inner experience to the external demands of a rigorous legalism. Sufism may be referred to as the foremost Islamic expression of the religion of the heart.

Unlike Shi'ism and the Kharijites, Sufism did not begin as an organised movement but rather as an expression of piety, a seeking of the experiential dimension of religion that went beyond the mere discharge of duty. To be sure it evinced its own demands: Sufism is, after all, a spiritual discipline, but what was in essence sought for was an immediacy of experience and direct knowledge of the Divine. Deep learning and intense devotion coupled with sensitivity to that spiritual dimension of religion, which transcends mundane expression and observance, were the hallmarks of this pious and mystical element. And so it touched all areas of the Islamic world.

Evolving from the early association of Muslim spiritual masters and their disciples, Sufism emerged as both religious sub-culture and as itself an institutional

---

[17] Martin Lings, *What is Sufism?* (Cambridge: The Islamic Texts Society, 1993), 15.
[18] *ibid*, 106.
[19] Ahmed, *op. cit.*, 55.

or structural component of Islam,. These associations were, by their nature, elitist and so limited in their appeal, at least initially. But as the need for 'felt religion'—that is, the need or desire to be engaged in the exercise of the experiential dimension of a faith—arose within the Islamic orbit, so more of the mass of Muslims were attracted to this development with the consequence that distinctive 'Orders' emerged. Each Order had its founder and a chain (*silsilah*) of authority. This 'chain' functioned in respect of the line of authority in somewhat similar fashion to the isnad of hadith transmission. Sufi silsilah thus guaranteed the transmission of the teachings and practice of the founding master of an Order. Regulations governing not only religious practice but even mundane matters established a wide diversity of Sufi experience and expression and delineated Orders from each other.

The first and most famous of the great Orders was the *Qadiriyya*, so named after its founder, *'Abd al-Qadir Jilani* (1078–1166CE). 'Abd al-Qadir was a Hanbalite based in Baghdad. The Order he founded had, by the fourteenth century (eighth century AH), spread to India and Pakistan and later found its way to Indonesia. It is also found in North West Africa as far as Morocco. A second great Order is the *Suhrawardiyya* named after the mystic *al-Suhrawardi* (1144–1234CE). This Order also featured strongly in India. A third was the *Shadhiliyya*, named after its founder *al-Shadhili* (1196–1258CE). This Order belonged to the *Maghrib*, the Islam of North West Africa, and was particularly strong in North Africa and Egypt, as well as in Arabia and even Syria. This Order had a particular focus on attaining purity of soul by way of utilising a process which had a wider coinage, namely that of gaining special knowledge or 'gnosis' (*ma'rifah*). Further, unlike some other Orders whose members were distinguished by way of dress codes, members of the Shadhiliyya remained indistinguishable from the rest of society.

The fourth of the great Orders of this era commenced in Turkey but was founded by a great Persian mystic, *Jalal al-Din Rumi* (d.1273). He was also called *Maulana*, and the Order was thus named the *Maulawiya*. In the Turkish context it is known as the *Mevleviya* and the followers *Mevlevi*. This Order came to prominence within the Ottoman Empire. It was this Order that produced the Whirling Dance form (Dervish) of devotional expression. A fifth major Order is the *Chishtiyya*. In this case, however, the name is not taken from the founder, *Mu'in al-Din* from Iran, but rather from the name of a town—*Chisht*—in Afghanistan where there was a group of Sufi seekers. Mu'in al-Din took the name of the town as his own and so bequeathed it to the Sufi Order of which he was Master. The Chishtiyya flourished in India by adopting and adapting certain Hindu meditative practices and generally echoing some of the values, such as religious tolerance, found in Hinduism. But it was also an Order that advocated a demanding form of devotionalism and asceticism. It remained important in India for several centuries, but never went beyond India into the wider Muslim world.

Sufi practice, or *tasawwuf*, has been defined in somewhat minimalist terms as 'Sufism is to possess nothing, and to be possessed by nothing'.[20] Self-examination and a rigorous attention to the structures of Muslim life—prayer, fasting, and so on—above and beyond the norm has through the centuries marked the Sufi individual as particularly pious and diligent. However, while there was often an ascetic undertone it did not lead to the development of a monastic tradition. As David Waines remarks:

> The ascetic's opposition to the world was psychologically felt, not physically dramatized by withdrawal from it. Scriptural sources did not condone the hermit's isolation or simple celibacy and they could not, therefore, become the norm in Islamic asceticism. Modesty, temperance, contentment with what the divine will offers, and the denial of luxuries were ascetic characteristics.[21]

Pious and ascetically inclined Muslims, in the early period of the emergence of Sufism, tended to eschew fine clothing in favour of a simple woollen garment. Thus they were known as wearers of wool (*suf*), hence the terms Sufi and Sufism. However, as Lings notes, the application of the term to a small group of ascetics and mystics did not mean that all who were deeply pious necessarily wore similar woollen garb. Rather, once coined, the term was soon widely used to denote the identity of this pietistic sub-group within the wider Muslim community.

The way of the Sufi is the way of contemplation and pious living out of the Islamic life. While, in one sense, this could refer simply to anyone who is a good and diligent Muslim, in practice it involves the intentional pursuit of a particular path (*tariqa*) of spiritual practice as determined by a Master or spiritual guide (*shaykh*). All Sufis would claim that their ultimate source and inspiration for their path is the Qur'an, together with the exemplary practice of the Prophet. But the particular path that is followed is nonetheless that usually prescribed by a Sufi Master.

> Sufi masters are central figures for their disciple in helping to unravel the mysteries and ideas of Sufism. The first and primary function of the Sufi master is what may be called ego-busting, that is to diminish the individual ego in order to establish the supremacy of God.[22]

There are many layers of meaning and symbolism involved within Sufism—hidden depths of meaning and cryptic allusions to be uncovered—all requiring the guidance of a Spiritual Master or shaykh.

---

[20] Cited in Waines, *Introduction to Islam*, 138. Waines also cites Sufi-authored maxims: 'Sufism means being at ease with Allah' and 'Sufism is not composed of practices and sciences, but it is morals', *passim.*

[21] Ibid., 136.

[22] Ahmed, *Living Islam*, 55.

In general, the path which a Sufi novice would tread involves progressing through a number of 'stations' (*maqam*) and attaining to certain 'states' (*hal*). This process begins with some form of repentance and conversion (*tawba*): that is, turning away from the former lifestyle and turning towards, and embracing, the new disciplined way of life. Inherent in this first step is a deep sense of humility and a deepening of the sense of both submission to, and dependence upon, Allah. Beyond this there are 'stations' such as striving earnestly (*mujahada*) for the mystical life; standing in awe (*taqwa*) of Allah; renunciation (*zuhd*) even of that which is permitted; humility (*tawadu*); gratitude (*shukr*); patience (*sabr*); trust (*tawakkul*) in Allah and satisfaction (*rida*) with one's lot. The ranking and order of these, and other, stations varies with the different ways or paths of the Sufi Masters. However, whatever the detail of the sequence, as one attains the stations, one undergoes changes in spiritual 'state'.

Ultimately the Sufi would reach the stations of love and esoteric knowledge and so be able to attain the state of 'annihilation' (*fana'*). This refers to a sense of the extinction of selfhood in the sense of an emptying of the ego into the being of Allah. The experience of this was deemed to be transformative in that those who attained it then returned to the mundane world no longer seeking for Allah but effectively subsisting in the Divine. Here Sufism gives expression to the mystic dimension of spirituality that finds echo in other religious traditions. To this extent it can be said there is evidence of Christian and even Buddhist influence upon the emergence of Sufism, and a suggestion of some Hindu elements as well as hints of Near Eastern Gnosticism also playing a part. There is a strongly inclusive and tolerant spirit underlying Sufism, inasmuch as the range of prophets acknowledged by Islam is incorporated within Sufi piety. Ahmed cites 'The Eight Qualities of the Sufi' as given by a renowned Sufi Master, according to which the Sufi has:

Liberality such as that of Abraham;
Acceptance of his lot, as Ismail accepted;
Patience, as possessed by Job;
Capacity to communicate by symbolism,
as in the case of Zachariah;
Estrangement from his own people,
which was the case with John;
Woollen garb like the shepherd's mantle of Moses;
Journeying, like the travelling of Jesus;
Humility, as Muhammad had humility of spirit.[23]

One further major feature of Sufi practice to be noted is the active remembrance (*dhikr*) of Allah, often expressed in the recounting of the many names of God. This is undertaken very often in groups and is associated with rhythmic breathing,

---

[23] Ibid., 56.

swaying, twisting or twirling. Such practices have become a feature of some of the Sufi Orders.

At times the pursuit of Sufism led to excesses of expression and action, with fatal results. For example, the pursuit of experiential, even ecstatic, being 'at-one' with the Divine was, by definition, an intoxicating event in the process of which one famous Sufi pronounced 'I am the Truth'. In so doing he identified himself with one of the names of Allah (*al-Haqq*—the Truth). But such a claim to association with the Divine was viewed as high blasphemy (*shirk*) and the hapless Sufi was summarily executed by the outraged authorities. The martyrdom of this Sufi, *al-Hallaj*, in 922CE has made a considerable impact on Islam down through the centuries. It has inspired a wide range of literary output and has been interpreted as the example of the stand of the pious Muslim against social and political injustices. However, this event—and the fact its occurrence lay in an effective misinterpretation of the Sufi intent—led to the writing of many Sufi manuals on doctrine, practice and terminology aimed at clarifying the understanding of Sufism and avoiding such extreme reaction and prejudice. For example, the Sufi notion of 'incarnation', which al-Hallaj was expressing, was not to be understood as an association or identification of human being with divine being, but rather as a particularly pious expression of 'entering into' or 'dwelling within' the qualities and attributes of God in the sense of divesting oneself of will and ego and submitting utterly to the Will and Nature of Allah. The 'self-extinction' or *fana'*, which this pious process entailed, referred to the surrender of the essence or sense of self in favour of the spiritual indwelling (*baqa'*) of the Divine within the life and experience of the Sufi supplicant.

The tendency to mystical excess has perhaps also been moderated by the more clearly spiritual motif of being 'friend of Allah' (*wali Allah*) 'in the sense of someone under the care of, or client of, Allah'.[24] The notion of piety articulated in terms of some understanding of 'friendship' with the Divine finds reference in the Qur'an (cf. Suras 10:62; 2:257). It is indicative of a relational approach and understanding that has infused Sufism down to the present. Waines draws attention to the fact that, despite anxieties at the dangers posed by Sufi excesses,

> the Islamic mystical tradition in general shared deep affinities with the piety of the Hanbali traditionists in their mutual emphasis upon Qur'anic meditation and adherence to the prophetic tradition that good works are the product of a pure heart. ... Furthermore, the respect of the common people was won by many Sufis by the virtues of dignity and purity they preached and mirrored in their own lives, together with the moral assistance they extended to all who brought their problems to them.[25]

---

[24] Waines, *Introduction to Islam*, 145.
[25] Ibid., 144.

If these early Sufis were 'of the people' in the sense indicated by Waines, they also had a tendency to 'spiritual elitism' and subjected the Qur'an to their own esoteric exposition and interpretation. Furthermore, Sufism allowed for metaphysical speculation and mystical experimentation. One such dimension, illuminationism, involved the symbolism of light and echoed more eastern practices.

> Illuminationism was infused with the symbolism of light, which had traditionally played an important role in Persian reflections on the nature of the divine. ... Neoplatonic philosophy ... conceived of the cosmos in gradations of being from the most perfect and abstract (God) to the material, corruptible realm of earthly existence.[26]

By the fourteenth century the impact of Sufism upon and across all regions of Islam was as assured as it was pervasive. As Waines remarks:

> Sufi ideas and idioms had penetrated all levels of society and every region where an Islamic presence had become established. Dissemination was facilitated by the institutionalization of Sufi beliefs and practices in the brotherhoods and the plethora of their offshoots.[27]

However, this development within Islam did not come without its problems and, in the end, was secured only as a result of considerable intellectual intervention.

Together with the many significant Orders of Sufism there emerged over time some important leaders and ideological contributors who promoted the Sufi way but did not themselves start yet another Order. One such was the Spanish-born *Ibn al-'Arabi*. His influence has been pervasive throughout Sufism to the present day. He died in Damascus in 1240CE (AH638) after a life of considerable travels and prolific writing. His philosophical views were not uncontroversial and have remained a challenge. He was himself denounced for these views by a famous Hanbali philosopher and theologian, *Ibn Taymiyyah*. However, as Waines notes, 'Ibn al-'Arabi's ideas found favour in the Shadhiliyya brotherhood and in its later sub-groups down to the present century'.[28]

The Sufi claim that the ideal of union with God placed them beyond the ritual requirements of the Shari'a led to criticisms from Sunni theologians of moral laxity among the Sufis. Against the claims of the Sunni *Ulema* (community of scholars) to speak with authority on matters of practice and faith, the appeal of the Sufi brotherhoods and Orders widened during the so-called 'dark ages' (thirteenth to eighteenth centuries CE). In the end, the impact of Sufism upon Sunni Islam was moderated. As an experiential dimension it was integrated into mainstream Sunni life largely through the efforts of scholars such as *al-Ghazali*, a philosophically

---

[26] Richard C. Martin, *Islam: a cultural perspective,* (New Jersey: Prentice-Hall, 1982), 102.

[27] Waines, *Introduction to Islam,* 153.

[28] Ibid.

trained jurist and theologian who had himself become dissatisfied with the legalism and rationalism of theology and had turned to the way of the Sufis, only to find excesses there which he eventually moderated.

Al-Ghazali sought to repudiate the theoretical and scholastic theology that had come to dominate Sunni orthodoxy. He set out to reject Greek philosophical ideas with which Islamic intellectualism had become infused, especially where they were deemed to be inconsistent with orthodox Sunni interpretation of the Qur'an. At the same time, he sought to check the more extravagant claims of Sufism. The resulting synthesis concluded the establishment of Islamic (Sunni) orthodoxy. Al-Ghazali melded the experiential and the legal dimensions of the religion thereby forming the intellectual groundwork that has continued into the modern era. At the same time Sufism found an acceptable place within the life of the Ummah and has continued, in terms of its continuing Orders, to be the primary locus of experiential piety. And in terms of its pervasive stimulus to the expression of piety and sincerity in matters spiritual, it has secured its place as a prime experiential focus for the practice of Islam.

Finally, it is worth noting that the very nature of Sufism meant that Sufi Orders have played an important role in the expansion and spread of Islam. Sufis have been the gentle missionaries of Islam.

> Their tendency to adopt and adapt to local non-Islamic customs and practices in new places and their strong devotional and emotional practices helped them to become a popular mass movement ... Sufism became integral to popular religious practices and spirituality in Islam.[29]

However, there was a down side. Sufi adaptability, including a 'willingness to embrace local traditions', which ironically helped with the spread of Islam, 'also left them open to criticism by the conservative religious establishment for being unfaithful to the tenets of Islam'.[30] Nevertheless, Sufism has thrived, and remains today an integral part of the life of many Muslims.

---

[29] John Esposito, *What Everyone Needs To Know About Islam*, 58.
[30] Ibid.

Chapter 5

Belief, Practice, and Law
Being Muslim

Introduction

Islam shares with Christianity a stress on 'right belief' as a hallmark of true religion. A Muslim is first and foremost a believer. What is believed is the message of Allah as given through the Prophet Muhammad. This is recorded in the Qur'an. It is embellished in the Sunnah of the Prophet. It is lived out through law. Belief is not a matter of simple intellectual assent: it also has to do with living by certain principles, with the application of a perceived divine intention in respect to the business of mundane life. The Way of Allah is given expression in Islam by *Shari'a*, the Divine Law articulated through the principles and regulations of Islamic *Fiqh* (jurisprudence). This is much like *Torah*, the Way of God given in ancient times to Moses as Divine Law, with its concrete expression through the many *mitzvot* (commandments) of the Levitical codes later expanded by the work of rabbinical schools. In keeping with its theological heritage, many of the beliefs of Islam have to do with ways in which human beings are to live in accordance to the Will of Allah.

All major religions, especially in their early formative years and in times of reforming upheavals and change, produce thinkers who shape the expression and self-understanding of their faith. This involves articulation of the religion's world view and related matters in belief, creed or other modes of proclamation. These thinkers are the intellectual movers and shakers whose work contributes to the forging of religious identity and the life of the religious community. They are the leaders who determine a religion's 'orthodoxy': that is, they are the conservators of the emerging tradition or religious ethos against 'heterodox' innovators and 'heretical' combatants. What finally emerges as the orthodox, or normative, tradition does so in the context, usually, of a process whereby a position is determined over against active detractors and critics, or against novel and innovative deviations or departures from the emerging normative position. Out of this process comes a definition of what is orthodox and, in relation thereto, who are the 'conservatives': the protectors and conservators of the now identified orthodox tradition.

This intellectual activity has to do with the cognitive dimension of the religious life and is denoted differently across various religions. For Christianity, for example, it is known as 'theology' from the Greek *Theos* (God) and *Logos* (reason, word). Thus, as with other '*-logy*' terms (psychology, biology, geology, and so on), theology is the term used to refer to the cognitive dimension of this religion which can be thought of as 'God-talk' or 'God-reason', the process of rational, intellectual 'thinking about' Christian faith. The term 'theology' is often used to refer to similar intellectual endeavours in other religions, but this is not always appropriate, even where the other religion is, like Christianity, theistic; that is, where the ultimate focus is 'God'. The reason is that the term, 'theology', does not just refer to an ultimate focus of cognitive concern, or to a common intellectual process: the manner, structure, style and rational processes used can be quite different. All we can say is that there are some common issues and parallel processes. However, the distinctive differences in modes of thought and intellectual discourse should not be ignored, which may happen if terms appropriate for one religion are unthinkingly applied to another.

For Islam the term that has come to be the rough equivalent to the Christian term 'theology' is *kalam*. It denotes a particular way, a certain methodological style, of religious thinking. In its developed form it may be thought of as the attempt, through rational argument, to demonstrate and prove the validity of Islamic dogmas and beliefs. This intellectual activity draws from the two key documentary sources of Islam, the Qur'an and the Sunnah. Revelation is regarded as the prior, and primary, category. Reason is the subordinate process. The purpose of theological endeavour is to define and defend 'orthodox' or 'normative' faith. Although, as a specific development, kalam came into the picture from around the ninth century, appropriate and relevant intellectual processes, or 'theological thinking', had certainly been vigorously underway during the preceding two hundred years of Islam.

Islamic theology: early developments

The stress in Islam upon belief meant that, from early on, questions arose as to who was a 'believer': that is, who could be rightly considered a member of this community of believers, and who excluded? What would be the grounds? What does the community do with someone deemed a 'great sinner' (*fasiq*) or an infidel (*kafir*)? Is it enough that someone professes faith (*iman*) inwardly such that the outward life of morals and behaviour are of secondary or limited importance? What weight is to be given to the practice of good works or duty (*ihsan*)? These and other issues quickly provided a blueprint for intellectual engagement and the production of a cognitive map or maps (theologies) for the religion of Islam in its early history.

In common with all monotheistic religions, the problem of evil was one issue that commanded early attention in Islam: given the nature of God as good and all-powerful, why is there evil and suffering? Is there another source for this outside of Allah? But if Allah is the source of all, for what purpose does God send or allow evil and suffering? An underlying issue in respect of such questions concerned matters of power and accountability: does Allah pre-ordain events? Not only is the issue of the nature of deity implicit in the question, but so also is the nature of human being. It is, accordingly, the problem of *predeterminism* that received much early attention. Those who opted in favour of a concept of God that implied divine predetermination as an expression of divine power, constituted a sort of 'predestination perspective' within nascent Islam, for example the Hanbalites and the Ash'arites as discussed above. In their view, divine all-powerfulness meant that Allah was the *source* of power—the efficient cause, to use a philosophical phrase—behind all events. Thus it is that humans act under the compulsion of the power of Allah. On the other hand, viewpoints in favour of a greater measure of human autonomy and accountability gave rise to a 'freewill' point of view, such as found with the Qadarites and the Mu'tazilites.

It is to be noted that historical and political factors often also contribute to the context of any theological, or religio-ideological, debate. In the case of Islam it was in the interests of the ruling elite to uphold predeterminism on the grounds that their rule is divinely decreed as, for example, with the Umayyad caliphs. Added to that, the interests of pious submission and the religious desire for a right ordering of things inclines conservative elements to endorse predestination and accept the divine right of rulers to rule regardless: so the predominant view of the early Ummah. However, reformers and free thinkers will ever charge that even rulers are human beings accountable for their actions. Thus, in the Umayyad Age, the Qadarites were acting politically as well as theologically in being opposed to the emerging mainstream of thought.

Furthermore, there is an ambiguity with respect to relying on scriptural source and authority for the determining of theological orthodoxy: in the end it is theology that determines the reading of the source, even as the source is read supposedly to inform and verify the theology. In the case of Islam, there are many Quranic passages which state or imply that God decides if a person shall be a polytheist or unbeliever or whatever: there is nothing that person can do. Here, Islamic theology comes close to variants of Christian Protestant theology, especially the double predestinarianism of Calvinism. Yet other passages in the Qur'an appear to say that humankind is to be held accountable for its sins on the Last Day. Thus, there is an obvious implication that 'human beings are masters of their own acts'.[1]

The Mu'tazilite school is of particular significance here in that it propounded five fundamental principles which quickly came to constitute the basic subdivisions of most early works of Islamic theology, namely God, theodicy, eschatology, political theology, and mission. This fivefold classification can be briefly described as follows:

1) Allah: *Divine Unity*. This refers to the oneness (*al-tawhid*) of God, and especially that Allah cannot be conceived of, or talked about, in human

---

[1] Richard C. Martin, *Islam: a cultural perspective* (New Jersey: Prentice-Hall, 1982), 98.

terms. The Mu'tazilite school de-anthropomorphised the idea of Allah. It argued that Quranic references to Allah were to be interpreted allegorically. Intellectually, it also countered Zoroastrian and Manichaean notions of duality of the Godhead. The Mu'tazilites thus challenged early Islamic literalists.

2) Theodicy: *Divine Justice (al-adl)*. The issue of theodicy (justifying or reconciling the existence of evil with the existence of God) was resolved by the argument of the moral nature of the Divine Being. This holds that God, being just, must do what is best for God's creation. Even though all-powerful, Allah cannot (or better 'does not') do evil, nor will Allah require human beings to do what is evil. Therefore whatever God does is, by definition, good and just. Evil as such is not of God's doing; rather a 'bad outcome' from a human perspective is simply to be accepted as the exercise of Divine Justice. It is the Will of God.

3) Eschatology: *'The Promise and the Threat'*. This phrase—in Arabic *'al-wad wa-l-wa'id'*—expresses the stark eschatology of Islam. Beliefs about the Last Day are couched in the language of both 'Divine promise'—the expectation of heavenly reward—and 'Divine threat', or the prospect of being cast into hell as a consequence of Divine judgement.

4) Political Theology: *An Intermediate Position*. This refers to a *via media* or the 'position between two positions' in respect of what is called 'political theology'. Specifically it referred to the position of taking the middle ground over any issues of debate and contention. In the context of the time it denoted the principle of middle ground between the extremes of the Kharijites and the Murjiites, on a number of issues.

5) Mission: *Commanding the Right and Forbidding the Wrong*. This has to do with the missionary and educative outreach of Islam, referred to by the Arabic term *da'wah*. It refers to the Islamic injunction to spread the faith, to make the command and the demands of God known by way of informing, educating, and inviting a response to God's 'call'.[2]

Islamic belief – *'Aqida*

The work of early theological development resulted in the consolidation of the basic Islamic belief system. Beliefs which are fundamental to Islam include, in particular, the *tawhid,* or unity, of Allah; the prophethood of Muhammad; the

---

[2] For a substantial discussion of this last category, see Michael Cook, *Commanding Right and Forbidding Wrong in Islamic Thought* (Cambridge: Cambridge University Press, 2000).

finality of the Qur'an; the existence of a spiritual realm; eschatology, or ultimate destiny; the servanthood of humankind; and the particularity and proper applicability of *jihad,* the struggle to maintain and advance the faith and, allied to that, the struggle of belief against unbelief. These will be briefly discussed in turn. Some, of course, have already been dealt with more fully in preceding chapters.

The tawhid *of Allah*

The Islamic doctrine of *tawhid* is the assertion that God is One, a Unity of Divine Self-Being. It is expressed in the first part of the fundamental creed of Islam, the *Shahada*: 'There is no deity but God'—*La ilaha illal lah*. Yet it is more than a statement that only one God exists, one 'al-lah', so to say. It implies and signifies that God is an ontological unity, or single Reality. Contrary to apparent Christian ideas, there are no subdivisions within the Divine Reality. God is unique, wholly different from all else. This is a perspective echoed by both Judaism and Christianity although both, in slightly different ways, admit of some measure of identity of God with the world. Islam opposes any such thoughts. Nothing may resemble Allah, no thing or person can be associated with Allah, or is equal, or in any way alike, to Allah. Any such suggestion amounts to *shirk*, the high blasphemy of associating anything with the being of God, thereby compromising or disrupting the singleness or 'unicity' of the Divine Being. Indeed within the Qur'an is found a stark warning:

> God does not forgive anyone for associating something with Him, while He does forgive whomever He wishes to for anything else. Anyone who gives God associates (or partners) has invented an awful sin.[3]

Allah is utterly different from the realm of creation. The idea of *tawhid* signifies the transcendental reality of God. But the underlying motif of 'oneness' also finds ideological expression elsewhere in Islam: the oneness of deity issues in unicity or singularity of identity as paradigmatic to Islamic thought and understanding. Hence, for example, the importance of the idea of a single community—the Ummah—under God, that lies at the heart of Muslim communal identity.

Muslim theologians sought arguments, both from scripture and through reason, to make persuasive the fundamental oneness and unity of Allah to the exclusion of other lesser gods, or plural implications of a 'godhead', that threatened that unity. Muslim mystics evolved the practice of special meditations or modes of remembrance that focused the consciousness upon God, for in their view God is the only Reality: the singularity of God becomes the sole unified Reality. One very important dimension of Islamic belief in the One God has to do with the notion of the Will of Allah, a stress on a concept of a controlling God, a God in command of

---

[3] Sura 4:48.

all things, who works within and upon creation through the Divine Will. Allah is omnipotent and omniscient: all things exist by the Will of Allah; Allah can do anything and knows all. Indeed, as one scholar has commented:

> The omnipotence of Allah was so strongly stressed in the Qur'an that not only did Allah guide the faithful to the truth, but in some sense also he led the wicked astray ... a matter of letting people lose their way ... it was ultimately the will of Allah which controlled (human) destiny.[4]

Allah is the 'Master of the Worlds' (*rabb al-'alamin*). The Islamic account of creation follows the biblical six days, but there is no seventh day of rest, for that would suggest divine weariness. Rather, the idea here is that once creation is effected Allah continues as the direct and active ruler or regulator of all that occurs.

So, in a broad sense, the oneness of God is the centre point for existence and in Islamic life the name Allah is much pronounced, often used in greeting and blessing. For example, 'Praise to Allah' (*alhamdu-illah*); 'If Allah wills' (*insha-allah*); 'In the name of Allah' (*bismillah*); and the perhaps more widely known 'God is most great' (*Allah-hu-akbar*). Subsidiary beliefs that flesh out the stark monotheism of tawhid include belief in the many attributes of God—Allah is eternal, without beginning or end; Allah is independent of the universe. Allah hears all and sees all. Allah gives guidance—through the world of nature and history; through the intermediary activity of angels (spiritual messengers and 'unseen workers'); also through the Scriptures (including all forms or expressions of 'the Book of God'); and through the Prophets, including all those of Judaism and Christianity. Allah is present to the world and is full of mercy. Allah, the all-merciful, expresses the Islamic notion of divine immanence as the counter to the otherwise overwhelming stress on the utter transcendence of the Divine Being.

The prophethood of Muhammad

The second part of the fundamental creed of Islam, the Shahada, declares that Muhammad is the Prophet, or Messenger, of Allah (*Muhammad al rasul ul-lah*). That is, Muhammad is the last or the 'Seal' of the Prophets: after Muhammad there will be no more such messengers of Allah. Muhammad is not himself divine; he is but an ordinary human being, a mere man. Nonetheless, the tendencies of Islamic piety have resulted in the natural elevation of his character and the veneration—but *not* the worship—of Muhammad as a special person. Legendary embellishment surrounds historical record.

Certainly, it would seem Muhammad understood himself to be the last in a line of prophets. In him the revelation of Allah reached finality. This has meant that belief in Muhammad's prophethood necessitated that the Qur'an be read as infallible, for it is there that the prophethood of Muhammad is defined and

---

[4] Ninian Smart, *The Religious Experience of Mankind* (London: Fontana, 1969), 488.

declared. The life of Muhammad, his prophethood, and ongoing significance have already been discussed in more detail above.

The finality of the Holy Qur'an

The Qur'an is not simply a piece of 'holy writ'. Whatever its literary categorisation, it is believed by Muslims to be itself the copy, as it were, of the eternally existing Divine Word, or Book (*al-Kitab*) of Allah. As we have seen, only the language of Arabic is believed to be the accurate and true rendition of this Book: the language of Allah is necessarily Arabic in this regard. Jewish and Christian heritage is variously affirmed and criticised in the Qur'an and in Muslim thinking. In essence, Muhammad's recitations are believed to be the complete and final revelation of the word of God—the 'mother of the Book'—against which all previous revealed books are believed to have become distorted and corrupted versions requiring Quranic correction.

The spiritual realm

Below Allah, orthodox Muslim belief holds that there exists a range of angelic beings, or spiritual intermediary messengers, who carry out the Divine behest. They actively and directly execute the Divine Will. But these angels, as with traditional Christian belief, are deemed to be creatures. They are not divine beings in their own right. The devil, called *Shaitan* or *Iblis*, is a fallen angel, much as is the case in Christian mythology. The devil and his agents often obstruct the work of the faithful, albeit within the limits laid down by Allah. Together with belief in a range of lesser devils, there is also belief in other spirits and, particularly in the Arabian context, in creatures called *jinn*, from which is derived the English term *genie*.

Eschatology

The term *eschatology* derives from the Greek *eschaton*, which means 'the last things'. It therefore refers to notions about a final purpose, ultimate destiny, or consummation of existence in accordance with the Will of God. Islamic belief in a last judgement, involving the concepts of Heaven and Hell as the locations of divine reward and punishment, is vividly expressed in the Qur'an.

The idea of a Last Day involves the notion of a general resurrection. On that day, the angels will bring everyone for judgement. Each individual's deeds will be weighed in the scales of divine justice. Those who pass the test will be admitted to Paradise; those who fail will be sent to Hell.

This eschatology reinforced the insistence on serving Allah through righteous and just behaviour. It was also an important factor in the faith and courage that animated the warriors of Islam. Death would be rewarded by something more splendid than plunder and power. Disloyalty would be punished by something worse than earthly torture and execution.[5]

A natural concern for many Muslims is how to ameliorate, if not completely avoid, the Day of Judgement, called also the 'Day of Doom'. In keeping with the pervasive and defining theme of submission, there is little one can do except await the Divine outcome in accordance with the requirements of the Divine Will but, hopefully, tempered by Divine Mercy.

However, if one were to die the death of a martyr, that is, be killed in the act of defending the faith, then the Day of Doom is by passed and immediate entry into Paradise is guaranteed. Hence within Islamic eschatology there is found a powerful element that has coloured and influenced the conduct of Islamic politics through the centuries: a martyr's death in the cause of true religion has ever been a powerful attraction for the fanatically faithful.

Human beings

Allah has appointed humans as his agents—or caliphs—on earth, giving to them the earth with all its resources.[6] A human being is the servant of God (*'abd-ullah*). It is natural, therefore, to submit to God as the servant submits to the master. But it is this very submission that confers the highest possible dignity: one could say the 'caliphate' of being human is most naturally in being 'the servant (*'abd*) of God'.

Thus, in contrast to notions of fallenness and original sin as the hallmarks of the human being from a traditional Christian perspective, Islam views human beings as, by nature, '*muslim*': as a matter of fact born under—so already and naturally in submission to—God's law. However, humans are yet predisposed, individually and collectively, to negligent forgetfulness, which is the root of unbelief. As the scholar Theodore Ludwig has commented:

> Though humans were created as God's caliph and though they made a covenant with God to accept the divine trust, they are always forgetting who they really are and neglecting the natural law of submission to God as the way of fulfilling their true nature.[7]

Thus someone who, by virtue of neglect and forgetfulness, or by outright rejection, denies Allah is a *kafir*, an 'unbeliever'.

---

[5] Ibid., 489.

[6] Sura 43.10–14.

[7] Theodore Ludwig, *The Sacred Paths* (New York: Macmillan, 1989), 221.

Jihad

Often misunderstood as a religious or holy war, the root meaning of *jihad* is one of struggle, primarily the struggle against sin and unbelief from within oneself; and secondarily with unbelievers—especially those who directly challenge or deny the Islamic faith—from without. It has been said that the war with an army is but a minor jihad: the real struggle is against the encroachments of doubt and unbelief in the mind and heart of a believer. Unbelief is a matter of neglect and forgetfulness: the intentional or unintentional falling from true belief. More specifically, sin is a matter of either doing what God has prohibited, or not doing what God has commanded. Acts considered major sins, usually liable for severe punishment, include:

1.   To believe there are partners of God.
2.   To disbelieve in God, God's prophets, or God's books, or to deny
      any of the fundamental principles of Islam.
3.   To lie.
4.   To commit adultery or other illegal sex.
5.   To steal.
6.   To cheat or deceive anyone.
7.   To bear false witness.
8.   To bring a false charge against anyone.

More broadly, jihad refers to an overarching obligation for Muslims, both individually and communally, to be actively engaged in the realisation of the Will of Allah by leading virtuous and upright lives, and by extending the realm and influence of Islam through the activities of *da'wah*: education and outreach. Thus jihad signifies that belief is an activity, not just a matter of ideas.

Religious Duty – *Arkan*

Clearly, Islam is not just about belief alone: it is also very much a religion of action. Religious life is given visible and daily concrete expression by way of the obligations to fulfil the requirements of piety. This active life of faith is summed up in the five pillars of religious duty (*arkan*) as laid down by the Prophet Muhammad at the very formation of the Islamic community. These five include a creedal profession of basic belief, the obligation of daily prayer; the giving of alms, an annual period of fasting, and the requirement to make pilgrimage to Mecca.

Profession of faith: Shahada

This two-part creedal statement, or testimony to the faith, says: 'I testify that there is no God except Allah, and that Muhammad is the Messenger of Allah.' To utter this with sincerity in front of adult witnesses is effectively to declare oneself to be Muslim. Thus this 'creed' both affirms the Oneness of God—tawhid, the unique Islamic monotheism—and the identity of the speaker as one who is a believer and, as such, is one who submits to the Will of this God. To take up the remaining four pillars is to live the life of a Muslim in accordance with that Will.

Prayer: Salat

The prayer act consists of obligatory prayers performed five times per day within the Sunni world. The actual occasions of prayer are announced by a special call in Arabic proclaimed by the *muezzin* (the one who makes the public call to prayer) from a minaret (a tower) that is part of a mosque. In many places, especially larger towns in Muslim countries, this call may be broadcast through speaker systems within a mosque and often to the world outside. The call to prayer (*adhzan*) includes the uttering of the shahada within it.

> God is most great (*Allahu Akbar*) [repeated three times];
> I witness that there is no god but God (Allah) [repeated];
> I witness that Muhammad is His messenger [repeated].
> Come to prayer, come to prayer. Come to prosperity, come to prosperity.
> God is most great. God is most great. There is no god but Allah.

The first prayer (*al-Fajr*, the Dawn Prayer) takes place at first light and is to be completed by sunrise. It is conducted most usually within the home. The second (*al-Zuhr*, the Noon Prayer) occurs around the middle of the day, taking place sometime from noon to the early afternoon, whereas the third (*al-'Asr*, the Afternoon Prayer) occurs during the latter part of the day and before sunset. The fourth (*al-Maghrib*, the Sunset Prayer) takes place during the period from after sunset to the end of evening twilight, and the fifth and final prayer of the day (*al-Isha*, the Night Prayer) takes place at some stage during the hours of darkness, most normally around mid-evening, or some two hours after sunset.

Because the time frames for each prayer occurrence are broadly denoted, and the point of reference is the shifting daylight hours, each Islamic community will publish a schedule of official times for the performance of *salat*, thus indicating when these activities take place in the mosque. But the individual Muslim may nonetheless legitimately perform the prayers within the time zone allotted. Shi'ites coalesce the middle and last pairs to give a three times per day pattern.

The performance of salat is preceded by ritual ablutions (*wudu*) involving the thrice cleansing of hands, mouth, face, and feet. Each salat consists of two or four rounds of prayers and prostrations, depending on the time of day, and uses standard formulas and excerpts from the Qur'an, including the uttering of 'God is most great' (*Allahu Akbar*) and the opening short one-verse (*aya*) chapter (*sura*) of the Qur'an. Salat involves a combination of mental concentration, vocal utterance, and bodily or postural expression of submission. The purpose of salat is to maintain the constant focus upon God as the centre point of life. The prayer itself can be said anywhere: the mosque is the communal meeting area primarily, but not solely, for the purpose of prayer.

Salat itself is something to be done: the location is secondary. However the direction faced during prayer is most significant. Prayer is performed facing Mecca, the foremost holy city, which is the geographic and spiritual centre of Islam. Thus the Ummah is physically united in prayer by way of a universal focusing upon this central orienting reference point. And this symbolic union is effectively constant: with the continuous shift in time zones as the globe turns, there are likely to be Muslims facing Mecca for one or other prayer, with perhaps morning coinciding with night on opposite sides of the planet, at any given moment. The idea of unity is the underlying motif: here it is given concrete temporal geo-physical expression by virtue of the incessant 'remembering of God' through the ritual of prayer.

Prayer is expressive of piety and it reinforces religious identity. The Muslim at prayer is ever reminded of belonging to the worldwide community of Islam. The Friday noon prayer (*al-Jumma*) replaces the usual Noon Prayer (*al-Zuhr*) and is the designated congregational prayer to which faithful Muslims make every effort to attend. Women are not obliged to attend the mosque for prayer as are men, but they may do so. However, as with other times of attendance, women pray apart in another room or screened-off area. Prayers in mosques are led at all times by the prayer-leader (*imam*) who stands in front of a wall-niche or marker (*mihrab*) that indicates the direction (*qibla*) of Mecca. At the Friday prayer there is the addition of a sermon (*khutba*) preached, or read, by an imam standing on a pulpit (*minbar*).

Almsgiving: Zakat

Almsgiving is a form of annual taxation, generally calculated at 2.5 per cent of net wealth, and is used as a form of welfare tax to assist the poor and needy. It is an expression of communal support and an element of communal responsibility reinforcing identity and belonging. As a religious act, it gives expression to the service of God and submission to the Divine Will. It is a practical act of social welfare. Modes of collection and disbursement vary among Islamic countries. In some cases they are independent of governmental agencies, while in other cases Islamic governments might assume the right and responsibility to collect and utilise the tax. However it is discharged, the universal obligation is clear: Muslims are to share their wealth with the less fortunate in society. This obligation can also have a corporate dimension. For some Muslims, this obligation can be said to apply to wealthy Muslim nations as well as all Muslim individuals.

Annual fast: Sawm

This is a daytime fast that takes place during *Ramadan*, the ninth month of the Muslim calendar. The Fast comprises physical abstentions—which are symbolic of the inner purification of character—but all prohibitions are relaxed during the hours of darkness. All adult Muslims are enjoined to participate, health permitting. Fasting involves the complete abstaining from food and drink and any form of sexual activity. Although physically rigorous, the month of fasting is also profoundly spiritual. It is a customary act of piety to read a portion of the Qur'an each night so as to have traversed the entire Qur'an during this holy month. Breaking of the fast in the evening can be a joyous affair and, indeed, in many Muslim communities the rigours of daylight abstentions are ameliorated by nights of compensatory enjoyment, as well as by acts of piety. Many will visit their mosque for the evening prayers, which are special to this month, or perhaps engage in forms of Sufi chanting. Muslim families will rise well before dawn to eat a meal that must then sustain them until nightfall.

The Fast may be broken by a number of violations, in which case they should be made up during the next month. Such violations include, for example, intentional swallowing of foodstuff; intentional vomiting; and engaging in sex during daylight hours. Fasting in Islam has high spiritual values. As one Muslim has put it:

> It is not only the physical part of abstaining from food, drink and other desires. It means that if for the sake of his creator a human being can give up the good things in life which otherwise are permissible, how can he not give up the bad things? Fasting also enables a rich person to experience the pangs of hunger which makes him more considerate toward the poor.[8]

The end of the fast is marked by a festival, a special day of celebration called *Eid-ul-Fitr*. The actual day is determined by the sighting of the new moon, which marks the end of the month of Ramadan. The celebration involves worship and much feasting, rejoicing, and the exchange of gifts. This activity marking the end of the Fast is one of the two occasions eagerly awaited by all Muslims; men and women, young and old, rich and poor alike. The other occurs during the month of the Hajj.

The Great Pilgrimage: al Hajj

The major pilgrimage to Mecca is the final pillar of religious duty. It takes place during the last month of the Islamic calendar, *Dhu al-Hijja*, between the eighth day and the twelfth or thirteenth days. All Muslims are meant to go on this pilgrimage at least once in their lifetime, health and wealth permitting. However, the logistical realities required to enable millions to attend this event have meant, in fact, that nowadays the Saudi authorities allocate most countries a quota of pilgrims based on their Muslim population. Humility and equality are engendered by the requirement of ritual purification whereby all are clothed in plain white garments,

---

[8] Mohammad Afiz, *Press Release*, Waikato/Bay of Plenty Muslim Association, Hamilton, New Zealand, 1990.

or else are dressed in very simple national costume. All take special vows in respect of promoting pious behaviour and decorum. Attention focuses on the activities of the pilgrimage and on its devotional dimensions.

> The pilgrimage epitomizes the ritual duty of Muslims. It is a dramatic connection to the sacred story, walking in the footsteps of Abraham, Ishmael, and Muhammad. It is an intensely individual experience, and at the same time a moving communal experience ... one human race standing together in submission to the one God.[9]

Hajj rituals begin with the circling (*Tawaf*) of the Ka'ba seven times, an act that symbolically makes the house of God the centre of one's life, and then running seven times between two small hills (*al-Safa* and *al-Marwa*, 1247 feet apart and enclosed within the precincts of the Great Mosque) in an action of identifying with Hagar's frantic search for water for her son Ishmael after both had been expelled from the house of Abraham.

On the following day all pilgrims stand together on the Plain of *'Arafat* as an act of remembrance of what Muhammad himself once did there. This is an essential component of the pilgrimage, the omission of which invalidates the Hajj. It is both an act of communal solidarity, symbolically with Muhammad as well as, in real time, with one's fellow pilgrims. But in particular the ritual focus is the remembering of Muhammad who, standing upon a small hill, delivered his final sermon to his followers gathered on this plain. Prayers are said while the pilgrims are gathered there and they also listen to a sermon.

Then there comes the stoning of the 'devil-posts', an act of ritual catharsis, and the concluding feast of sacrifice, the *Eid-ul-adha*, on the third day of the pilgrimage—or the tenth of the month—in which an animal is purchased and slaughtered. The sacrificial *Eid* constitutes a high point. The sacrificial act is done in commemoration of Abraham's example of obedient submission, and the responding mercy of God, wherein the sacrifice of an animal occurred in place of Abraham's son.

This feast takes place towards the conclusion of the Hajj both at Mecca and throughout the Islamic world: it is thus another rite expressing both identity and solidarity of the Ummah. And meat from the sacrificial animals is distributed to the poor and needy, an echo of zakat. As well as the major Hajj there is also a lesser hajj, or devotional pilgrimage, with its own rituals. This minor hajj is called, in Arabic, *'umra* (visitation) and can take place at any time other than in the month of the greater Hajj. It involves the visiting of holy places, both those included in the greater Hajj as well as other important sites such as Muhammad's mosque at Medina.

---

[9] Ludwig, *Sacred Paths*, 232.

The governance of law—Shari'a

For Muslims all of life is structured according to Shari'a, the Divine Law, which is guidance given by God. All of life, both in terms of morals and in religious duty, is a matter of service to ('ibadat), and worship of, God. The primary goal of human existence is this submission in the service of Allah. A way needed to be delineated, beyond the prescription of religious duties we have already examined, to give substance to this submission. The term Shari'a means 'that which is prescribed' or 'the Path to be followed'. It is given by Allah for the guidance of His creatures: it is only Shari'a that liberates humanity 'from servitude to other than Allah'.[10] The specific detail of Islamic law in its concrete application is the responsibility of religious scholars.

> Throughout history Islamic law has remained central to Muslim identity and practice, for it constitutes the ideal social blueprint for the believer who asks, 'What should I do?' ... The law's comprehensive coverage, including regulations ranging from religious rituals to marriage, divorce and inheritance to setting standards for penal and international law, provided a common code of behaviour and connection for all Muslim societies.[11]

Shari'a is based on legalistic suras of the Qur'an that are believed to represent Allah's revelation of the law in its entirety. It is Quranic injunctions that command the doing of justice, and it is by way of Shari'a that 'the doing' is spelt out. I shall examine below the principles and sources of Shari'a, then undertake a similar examination of the notion of *fiqh* or jurisprudence that will include a review of two areas of Shari'a: relationship law and punishment law. I have chosen these simply because they are the areas of Islamic law that most obviously impact on social life and, in relation to that, at times come to the attention of the wider world, very often because of controversial enactments of such law. But first a word concerning the distinction between Sunni and Shi'a in regards to Shari'a.

Early in the history of Islam Sunni and Shi'a Muslims developed their respective systems of interpretation and application of Shari'a. Law provides for an overarching community cohesion that can nonetheless allow for some variety. Yet with all things there is submission to Allah. The development of Shari'a emerged out of the belief that everything is governed by the decrees of Allah. Law is given by God: it is the task of the community of scholars, by a process of consensus, to work out and systematise the detailed content of this law in terms of both its principles and its application in daily life.

---

[10] Abdur Rahman I. Doi, Shari'ah: The Islamic Law (Kuala Lumpur and London: A. S. Nordeen, 1989), 2.

[11] John Esposito, What Everyone Needs To Know About Islam (New York: Oxford University Press, 2002), 139.

The examples, or traditions (Sunnah), of the Prophet Muhammad, as collected in the various hadith, provide the primary sources for interpreting the Qur'an and developing the systems of law. Islamic scholars expended much time and effort in striving (*ijtihad*) to work out applications to all areas of life. The different geographic locations where this occurred led, eventually, to the emergence of the four Sunni 'schools of law' or, more correctly, schools of jurisprudence wherein law is interpreted, applied, and developed—*Hanafi, Hanbali, Maliki* and *Shafi'i*. More about these will be discussed below. Within two hundred years or so of the inception of Islam the process of establishing the essential system was fixed; for Sunnis, the 'gate of ijtihad' was then closed. No further novel interpretation or development of principle could occur: the task has since been to pass on the law and simply update its practical application.

However, Shi'a, with their concept of divine guidance through the Imam, generally do not consider the gate of ijtihad to be closed: the process of developing principles and rethinking fundamentals continues more vigorously in the Shi'a world. The Shi'a have two major schools, the *Jafari* and the *Zaydis*, and also developed others such as the *Imami* and *Ibadi* schools. All are based on different hadith sources to that relied upon by Sunni Muslims.

Principles of Shari'a

Shari'a, in terms of human legal systems, is the temporal application of divine justice. The underlying principle is not that of blind obedience to rules as such, but the active outworking of God's demands for justice. Thus the exercise of Shari'a implies a number of related principles or factors. Justice must be done equally to all and sundry: the exercise of judicial partiality is improper. As all human beings are servants of Allah, all must be judged according to the Book of Allah. Furthermore, from the Muslim perspective, Islamic justice is something 'higher' and more humane than, for example, the formal justice of Roman law or any other human law. Shari'a is based on mutual respect of human persons; it promotes the priority of human welfare over human liberty; it is a matter of justice exercised with a view to equity, 'even to the benefit of an enemy and to the detriment of a relative'.[12]

The entire Muslim community lives under the Shari'a. Every member submits to the law under the sovereignty of Allah. As the Islamic legal scholar Abdur Rahman Doi has commented: 'The laws of Islam are firmly based upon the Shari'a and are, therefore, in the interest of the people as a whole. They are not the work of warring politicians, but of sober jurists'.[13] Indeed the Ummah as a whole is collectively responsible for the administration of justice, and to judge justly is as much a religious and devotional act as it is a judicial one. Hence, the leading

---

[12] Doi, *Shari'ah*, 10.
[13] Ibid., 6.

scholars and religious leaders of Islam, as previously noted, are not just theologians but are also jurists: the essence of Islam is conveyed in both belief *and* law. There is not one without the other.

According to Doi, the basic principles of Shari'a may be summarised as follows:

(a) The larger interest of society takes precedence over the interest of the individual.

(b) Although 'relieving hardship' and 'promoting benefit' are both among the prime objectives of the Shari'a the former takes precedence over the latter.

(c) A bigger loss cannot be inflicted to relieve a smaller loss or a bigger benefit cannot be sacrificed for a smaller one. Conversely, a smaller harm can be inflicted to avoid a bigger harm or a smaller benefit can be sacrificed for a larger benefit.[14]

Sources of Shari'a

There are two primary sources and three secondary sources from which is derived the substance of Shari'a. The first primary source is, of course, the Qur'an. Viewed, as we have seen, as the final revelation of God, it provides a code of conduct in terms of both commandment and warrant. Islamic scholars have delineated four categories of legal injunctions within the Qur'an. *Concise Injunctions* are precise commandments of principle, but the details as to specific application are not included. Instead, they are elaborated in hadith. The *Concise-cum-Detailed Injunctions* provide some detail, but still much is left to reliance on hadith and the working of scholarly logic when it comes to practical application. The classification of *Detailed Injunctions* concerns those where the Qur'an gives complete detail. Here there is no room for ijtihad, the process of rational scholarly logic, to work out the implications. Finally, there are the *'fundamental principles'* of guidance derived from injunctions—norms rather than clear-cut definitions—requiring due process of rational deliberation (ijtihad) for their outworking in daily life. Such normative and general principles include freedom, justice, consultation, public interest, equality, and so on.

The second principal source of Shari'a is the sunnah of the Prophet as collected in hadith. Units of sunnah comprise three broad categories, namely:

i)   Thrice repeated verbal teaching or instruction of the Prophet on matters of importance, as remembered by the Companions—his close followers and disciples—and which were even checked out by the Prophet to ensure the teachings were properly memorised.

ii) Teachings given by way of letters (in similar fashion to the epistles of the Christian New Testament) sent by Muhammad to kings, rulers, chieftains,

---

[14] Ibid., 11.

Muslim governors, and so on, in connection with matters of faith and practice.

iii) Teaching by way of practical demonstration, for example, showing by example how to perform pre-worship ablution (wudu); demonstrating how to perform prayers (salat), and explaining how to correctly observe the pilgrimage (hajj), as well as how to properly observe the fast (sawm) and so on.

As Doi remarks:

> After the death of the Prophet, every case that came up for a decision had to be referred either to the Holy Qur'an or to some judgement or saying of the Holy Prophet, which judgements or sayings therefore, obtained a wide reputation. ... The Hadith Literature, as we now have it, provides us with apostolic precept and example covering the whole duty of man; it is the basis of that developed system of law, theology and custom which is Islam. Muslim law is so very comprehensive that all the minute acts of a Muslim are guarded by it.[15]

Qur'an and Sunnah together constitute the primary sources of Shari'a. The secondary sources are legal consensus (*al-ijma*), analogy (*al-qiyas*), and logical reasoning (*al-ijtihad*), to which we now turn.

Al-ijma, or 'legal consensus', refers, in the first instance, to the consensus of opinion of the Companions of the Prophet and the agreement reached on the decisions taken by the learned Muftis, Mullahs, Ayatollahs and so on—the various titles given to the Muslim Scholar-Jurists—in respect to various Islamic matters. The scholarly processes of consultation (*shura*) and the use of rational argument (*ijtihad*) are normal methods used for obtaining or arriving at a binding *ijma*. Thus the term al-ijma refers to a particular process, as well as a type of outcome, in the matter of framing laws based on agreement between learned jurists. Ideally it denotes total unanimity; in practice it often means the rule of the majority.

Al-qiyas means 'analogy' and refers to a particular process of reasoning adopted where there is no clear-cut directive in either the Qur'an or the hadith, but where there are parallelisms or analogous instances. Thus novel situations and innovations can be accommodated. For example, the Quranic prohibition against wine is extended, through application of al-qiyas, to all alcoholic beverages. Technically this is analogical deduction, thus al-qiyas is a legal principle introduced in order to arrive at a logical conclusion pertaining to the extension and application of the law. This method was not always well received or highly regarded in some Islamic circles. Historically there were both 'for' and 'against' lobbies in respect to the issues of application and extension of law, each relying on

---

15 Ibid., 50.

Quranic support. In the end, conditions were laid down for the application of al-qiyas, namely, it should apply only when there is no solution in the Qur'an or hadith; its usage must not go against the principles of Islam, neither must it go against the contents of the Qur'an; and it must be a 'strict *qiyas*', that is, one based upon the Qur'an, or the hadith, or arrived at by the due process of al-ijma.

The final source of Shari'a is the process of 'legal reasoning', or legal logic, called al-ijtihad. This is the matter of intellectual effort or exercise to arrive at a point of clear judgement. It refers, most widely, to the use of reason in the elaboration and explanation of law, covering a variety of intellectual processes, including especially the notion of innovative thinking and argumentation. Indeed, al-qiyas is one such form of reasoning and al-ijma is one process of reasoning. It is part of the individual's inner struggle to live congruently with the theme of submission to the Will of Allah: what does it mean, how does it apply? Al-ijtihad may be viewed as the positive struggle for faith, in contrast to jihad, which is the defensive struggle against unbelief. However, certain proscriptions apply. Al-ijtihad must not be used in regards to the existence of Allah. Nor may it be exercised in respect of the truths imparted by the prophets; neither can it be applied to questioning the very existence of God's prophets. And it can never be used to question the authenticity of the Holy Qur'an. Those who undertake ijtihad in the proper way are called *al-Mujtihad*.

The result of the application of these secondary sources—consensus, analogy, legal reasoning—leads to an extension of law beyond that which is found directly in the Qur'an and the Sunnah. For example, the type of punishment for drinking alcohol is not specifically prescribed in the Qur'an. But the reported early consensus was: 'He who drinks, gets drunk; he who gets drunk, raves; he who raves, accuses people falsely; and he who accuses people falsely should be given eighty strokes of the cane according to the injunction of the Holy Qur'an.' By the application of al-qiyas, then, the drunkard is to be given eighty strokes: law is extended by analogy by way of consensus through a reasoning process.

Islamic jurisprudence – *Fiqh*

Jurisprudence is the science and philosophy of law. Known as *fiqh* in Islam, it is the process whereby Shari'a is extended through the application of extrapolated principles. Within Sunni Islam four schools of law, or Schools of Fiqh, emerged over time and have consolidated into a predominantly quasi-regionalised differentiation of Islamic practice.

The *Hanafi* School derived from the *Imam Abu Hanifa* (AH80–150). It developed from ancient legal systems in Iraq and is today found mostly in the wider Arab world of the Middle East and also South Asia, especially the Indian subcontinent. The *Maliki* School, derived from the *Imam Malik ibn Anas* (AH 93–179), was responsible for codifying the Medinan fiqh. This means that, as the then current centre of learning was Medina (the City of the Prophet), the content of this fiqh was derived directly from Muhammad himself and the succession of early teachers there. However, as with the Hanafi School, the Malikis recognised other sources of law and developed accordingly. The Maliki School is strong today in North, West and Central Africa.

The *Shafi'i* School, from the *Imam Muhammad Idris al Shafi'i* (AH150–204), who is sometimes called the 'Father of Islamic Jurisprudence',[16] expanded upon the early work of the first two schools. This school is prominent in East Africa, Southeast Asia, and also Southern Arabia (for example, Yemen). The last school to emerge, the *Hanbali*, derives from *Imam Ahmad ibn Muhammad ibn Hanbal* (AH164–241). This is the most rigorous of the Sunni schools of law. It is the official School of Saudi Arabia and one of the foundational components of the Saudi Wahhabi movement. As with the other schools, while there is a geographical correlation in terms of predominance, it is by no means restricted to the region in which it predominates. Differences in adherence to the schools contributes to local variations and 'flavours' within the wider Islamic community, thus contributing to vigorous internal debate, at times even conflict.

While there are variations between the schools on points of particular interpretation and application, they usually recognise each other as valid expressions of normative Shari'a and they each subscribe to overall principles, such as, for example, the division of human behaviour into the following five categories:

i) *Haram*, or that which is *forbidden*. This covers any action the commission of which is punishable by law; as well as anything stated as unlawful in either the Qur'an or the Torah of Judaism. Such forbidden behaviour is both sinful and criminal: the drinking of alcohol is an example. The opposite of haram is *halal*, meaning 'that which is permitted'. The haram/halal distinction is most commonly applied to foodstuffs such as meat.

ii) *Makruh*, which means that which is *discouraged*. This comprises actions disapproved by Shari'a, but which do not carry any specific penalty. However, makruh behaviour, while not sinful, may be criminal and therefore punishable by a Shari'a court where such exists. Definitions of what specific acts constitute makruh vary across the different schools of law.

iii) *Mubah* refers to actions that are permissible yet legally indifferent. It represents the neutral dimension of Islamic social life; it is simply descriptive of that which is the case, as in 'This is how we've always done it'

iv) *Mustahab*, meaning that which is actively *recommended*, comprises actions that are positively rewarded, but for which their omission is not punishable.

---

16 Ian Netton, *A Popular Dictionary of Islam* (London: Curzon Press, 1992), 229.

Mustahab equates roughly with civil law. It governs customs, manners, protocols, and so on, such as marriage, family life, and funeral rites. Reciting additional prayers or visiting Medina following the Hajj at Mecca would be examples of the mustahab category.

   v) *Fard*, which means that which is *obligatory*. It concerns compulsory duties the omission of which is punishable. Fulfilling the obligations of the Five Pillars of religious duty falls into this category. Sometimes this category is referred to as halal, but this term seems to connote a more active sense of permission rather than strict obligation.

Principles of law give rise to detailed legislation. As in all systems of law, there are broad categories, or areas, of focus. As already indicated, I will briefly examine two areas that often feature, one way or another, in the public image of Islam, namely personal relationship law, which focuses on the position of women in Islam, and punishment law, which is often taken as a mark of a society's degree of civilisation and human rights.

Relationship law

There are four principal items dealt with by relationship law: the status of women; marriage; polygamy; and divorce. The legal status of women in Islam is generally governed by the concept of necessary gender-differentiated roles. A woman has equality of value with a man, but difference in role and function, and therefore a difference in status. There is an expectation for the obedience of a woman, first to her father and then to her husband. She is not, however, required to obey where this would conflict with something else in Shari'a. Obedience is not meant to be blind or oppressive, but rather in accord with the Will of Allah, which means women are meant to receive the respect and care which is their due. Nonetheless, the Qur'an asserts that men are 'above' women. Thus the wilful disobedience of a wife, for example, may be punishable by 'beating'. In fact, however, this is tempered by injunctions to self-restraint on the part of the male, and the development within Shari'a of a process of admonition, ranging from verbal reprimand, to the withholding of sexual relations, then to administering a 'light' or symbolic beating.[17]

   Women are enjoined to keep the Five Pillars, but the Friday *jumma* prayer is largely a male affair. No woman may lead prayer. By and large there is a strong menstrual taboo, in some Muslim countries expressed as *purdah*—total confinement for the duration of menstrual discharge. However, the origins of this are more cultural than Quranic. It is the process of ideological as well as legal extension by al-qiyas that has led to requirements for women, in some Islamic societies at least, to be totally covered in the presence of non-family males. The

---

[17] Cf. Doi, *Shari'ah*, 130.

extent to which this is applied, and the detail of governing law, is variable and also culturally influenced. So, too, with the practice of clitoridectomy (female circumcision) which is suppressed in many Muslim countries, but which is widespread in Arabia and Africa, albeit frowned upon by State authorities. Muslim women are, however, guaranteed property rights—indeed they had these ownership rights centuries before Christian women, for example—and mostly they enjoy full political participation. They also have the right to sue for divorce themselves. In summary, and at least in theory, Muslim women do have full separate legal identity and, relative to men, equal standing before the law, albeit within certain constraints and parameters.

Second, marriage in Islam is prized, indeed assumed. Celibacy is not valued, and extra-marital relations are forbidden. The family is seen as the primary social institution. Thus marriage is encouraged, expected, and of central value and importance. Heterosexual partnership is viewed as the norm of creation: it is of the Will of Allah, the Creator. In terms of the hierarchical structure of jurisprudential values, marriage is generally viewed as at least 'recommended'. It may also be applied as 'compulsory', by way of being a counter to the temptation to fornicate, for example, or as 'obligatory', to be undertaken simply because it is of the Will of Allah.

The marriage-act is a simple contract specifying obligations and duties. It requires two special rites, proposal and acceptance, incorporated usually into the one ceremony. The bride has the right to negotiate the value of the dowry (an endowment of property which is hers to keep, not a bride-price paid to a family for her), and whether or not she will allow polygamy to occur. In practice most Muslim marriages are arranged and the bride has little say in the matter. Her only effective resistance is to reject outright the marriage contract put to her. Regional variants occur over the woman's right to make their own contract of marriage: Indonesia, Malaysia, North Africa and Saudi Arabia deny it; other Islamic countries and communities largely permit it. All versions of Shari'a prevent a Muslim girl from marrying a non-Muslim male. But a Muslim male may marry a non-Muslim woman, provided she is both virginal and one of the recognised 'People of the Book'.

The third item, polygamy, at least initially, was an institution legalised and regulated in Islam for the purpose of taking care of the widows of Muslim warriors killed in battle. Equality of treatment to all wives (to a maximum, normally, of four) is commanded in the Qur'an. Monogamy is the widespread practice. Where a second wife is taken it is usually for reasons of the first wife's infertility. In many Muslim countries polygamy requires also the permission of the State (for example, Syria, Iraq, Pakistan). In others polygamy has been abolished and in some (for example, Morocco) there is a law allowing the first wife to sue for divorce if she objects to a second or subsequent marriage of her husband. Islamic rulers often bent the rules for political purposes.

Fourth, divorce may occur under any one of three forms. *Talaq* is the simple and unilateral renunciation of marriage by way of a public declaration by the husband, provided the husband who does this is not insane, is not speaking in jest or attempts to do this while drunk. The wife so divorced is entitled to keep her dowry and the divorcing husband must provide for the children by way of a maintenance payment to the mother, at least for a short period. In practice this form is rare and has been abolished by some Muslim countries.

The form of *Khul* is divorce by mutual consent and is much more widespread. It is the mutual legal renunciation of the original contract. *Faskh*, or female divorce— that is, divorce at the request of a wife—is usually on the grounds that the original contract has been broken by the husband. In this case she must usually repay her dowry. Granted to all Muslim women in theory, in practice its availability varies. Relatively more liberal conditions are found in much of Eastern European Islam, and in Egypt; the most restrictive conditions apply to Saudi Arabia, Iran and the Gulf States. However, apostasy, or the renunciation of belief, leads to immediate judicial dissolution of the marriage.

Punishment law

Islamic penal codes do not make allowance for the rehabilitation of the offender: punishment is the meting out of punitive response to offensive behaviour.

> Society, in the religion of Islam, takes preference over an individual, and hence it is the interest of society that over-rides the individual and not vice-versa. It is because of this reason that any crime committed against the peace and well-being of the society will be deemed as the crime against the Creator Himself.[18]

The key principle is *Qisas*, meaning 'retaliation', or the principle of community redress. It relates to the notion of *Qasas*, the law of equality. Retaliation on behalf of the community derives from the ancient Hebraic notion of 'an eye for an eye', a principle that is enshrined in scripture as revealed by Allah to Moses.

Two key modes govern the exercise of punishment. *Tazir* means 'shaming', or putting the accused to shame or disgrace, in respect of an act committed against another member of society and thus society as such. Deemed a light punishment, the actual penalty is left up to the Shari'a Judge (*Qadi*). The form of punishment known as *hadd,* on the other hand, refers to 'limitation', or the assertion of the community's boundaries. This constitutes a form of severe punishment and is given when there is a violation of the people's rights. Penalties prescribed in the Qur'an apply to murder, theft, robbery, fornication and adultery, false accusation or slander, blasphemy and apostasy. Penalties include beheading, stoning to death, amputation, and severe flogging. However, both Qur'an and hadith give several warnings against wrongful application of hadd: it should be applied sparingly, and only when there are four eyewitnesses of impeccable character to the crime, or if the accused has confessed.

---

[18] Ibid., 219.

Four broad categories of punishment are delineated, including physical punishment; restriction of freedom (that is, imprisonment or exile); the imposition of fines; and a warning given by a Qadi. However, in all cases, legal liability does not apply to a person insane until the return of sanity, a person before and until the age of puberty, or a sleeping person till they awake.[19] Acts considered major sins, usually liable for severe punishment, include believing there are partners of God, that is, committing *shirk*; actively disbelieving in God, God's prophets, or God's books, or denying any of the fundamental principles of Islam; lying; committing adultery or indulging in other illegal (*haram*) sex; stealing; cheating or deceiving anyone; bearing false witness; bringing a false charge against anyone.

It needs to be noted that the cultural context for the original conception of the above was, of course, a pagan and violent Arabia in which dispute, feud, and blood revenge dragged on through generations. This had to change for the sake of the nascent Ummah. The unity of the growing Islamic community could not withstand the fragmenting forces of feuding clans and tribes. Muhammad replaced interminable feuding with swift and exacting qisas. Retaliation was immediate, punitive, and to the point. And, when warranted, it included the invoking of hadd; which, by its nature, decisively limits the wrong and so ends feuding. Better one amputation, one death, than a feud embroiling whole tribes and eventually killing dozens, was the logic of the day.

The reintroduction in the late twentieth century of hadd punishments in countries such as Pakistan, Iran and elsewhere may be seen as part of a general desire, which has emerged after the gaining of political independence, to return to Islamic fundamentals. It is a moot point whether there has been any impact on crime rates as a result, and it would appear little heed is being taken of the warnings to use hadd sparingly: contemporary politics is playing a part in some situations at least. So far as Islamic virtues and values are concerned, the ideal of 'turning the other cheek' as a response to offence is deemed weak and ineffectual.[20]

Being Muslim is both something simple and something complex. The simplicity lies in straightforward basic—'fundamental'—beliefs and the clear obligations of duty; the complexity lies in the subtleties of theology and jurisprudential interpretation and application. If there is an appeal in that which is straightforward, it is the complex dimensions that make for the richness and depth of Islamic identity and life. This has been so throughout the history of Islam. It is no less the case—perhaps, in truth, one should say it is even the more so—in terms of being Muslim in the contemporary world, a theme to which we shall return below.

---

[19] Cf. *ibid*, 226.
[20] *ibid*, 223.

PART II
ENCOUNTERING ISLAM
PARADIGMS AND CONTEXTS

Chapter 6

Christian–Muslim Encounters
History and Prospect

The religions of Islam and Christianity are pre-eminently religions of belief. Each has struggled to define its own orthodoxy against variant heterodoxies and heresies from within, and each has a history of self-proclamation as universal truth over against any other claimant from without. So it is little wonder that these two religions have a history of mutual competition, to put it mildly. Charles Kimball asks:

> Why have these two communities clashed so vigorously through the centuries? What informs the sense of mistrust that pervades the history of Christian–Muslim relations and skews attempts to relate more constructively today?[1]

In this chapter I shall attempt to sketch an answer and point to the possibilities of going beyond the impasses of the past.

The issues arising out of the history of Christian–Muslim interfaith encounter are complex. Here I shall simply present an overview of the course of Christian–Muslim encounter, suggesting a set of overarching hermeneutical perceptions concerning this complex relationship and history. On the way we shall note some of the particular dialogical options that have been utilised with varying degrees of success. More significantly, they lay the groundwork for reflection upon the nature of, and prospects for, dialogue now.

Jean-Marie Gaudeul has offered a useful review of the history of the relationship between Islam and Christianity in which the mutual challenge and response that has engaged the attentions of each may be tracked through broad ages or epochs.[2] I will use his outline, but re-interpret the historical process it yields in terms of a series of identifying epochs. Furthermore, these 'epochs', which I denote, for heuristic and hermeneutical purposes, as *expansion, equilibrium, exhortation, enmity,* and *emancipation and exploration*, do not just arbitrarily mark out historical eras. Rather they serve to delineate the ebb and flow of a relationship

---

[1] Charles Kimball, *Striving Together: A Way Forward in Christian–Muslim Relations* (New York: Orbis Books, 1991), 37.

[2] Jean-Marie Gaudeul, *Encounters and Clashes: Islam and Christianity in History* (Rome: Pontifico Instituto di Studi Arabi e Islamici, 1990).

of encounter, particularly that of intellectual engagement. But as well as indicating the state of play in the relationship between Islam and Christianity at particular times in history, these terms also indicate modes of relationship and interaction *per se*. While each may have dominated a particular historical period, it could be argued that they are always part of the wider picture of interreligious encounter. They certainly persist into the present day so far as the interaction between Islam and Christianity are concerned. So, we shall follow Gaudeul's overview, but cast a fresh perspective upon it, in order to paint the broad picture of Christian–Muslim relations and focus on some key themes and issues pertinent to dialogue. Unless otherwise stated, all reference to time is in terms of Common Era (CE) denotation.

Relations in an epoch of *Expansion* [*7th–10th centuries*]

When Islam commenced, historically speaking, Christianity was relatively settled. By the early seventh century its grounding theological terminology and worldview concepts had been articulated. That is to say, creedal orthodoxy had been decreed; internal ecclesial demarcations and divisions were well identified: the orthodox knew who they were, and who their heterodox opponents were. Rival Christian communities had staked their claims. Arianism, Nestorianism, and Monophysitism represented variant heterodoxies relative to the triumphs of orthodox Christianity in regard to the outcomes of the great councils of Nicea, Ephesus and Chalcedon. Christianity, a religion that espoused unity, nonetheless embraced wide diversity, and this not only in belief and theology, in church structure and liturgy, but also in linguistic diversity. Christian imperial cultures exuded an air of sophistication and erudition.

Into this context there erupted a brash and bold new religious movement, apparently proclaiming the same monotheism but vehemently eschewing the Christocentrism of the faith into whose territories and communities its early expansion made dramatic inroads. The context of Islam, at least initially, was that of a single language, Arabic; a unified politico-military community and sense of purposefulness; simplicity of learning; and the strong conviction of a straightforward and comparatively simple, or at least relatively uncomplicated, faith. This contrasted with the diversity of language and the breadth of learning that marked the context of Christianity at the time.

At first, in the earliest days of Islamic expansion, under the first four Caliphs (Rushidun), the focus of the Islamic community was in respect to seeing itself as carrying out a divine mission within and to Arabia. In the fervour of rightness and the confirmation of conquest there was little room to consider the religiously other as anything approximating a dialogue partner. But the cultural contrasts soon became apparent and, although Islam remained religiously confident, it quickly saw the need to redress a relativity of intellectual inferiority. This began with the Umayyad dynasty (c.660–750CE) with the flow of ideas gained from the work of translating Greek literary and philosophical texts into Arabic. Under the Abbasid dynasty (c.750–1250CE) the flow amplified at first, then ebbed during the ninth century as tendencies to reactionary reformism set in. It flourished again in the later half of the Abbasid era as interest in things Hellenic impacted on theology and stirred up philosophy within the Islamic world, only to wane once more as reaction to, and rejection of, foreign influences and ideas resurfaced within the body of Islam. However, as an overall assessment of this era, Gaudeul comments that there can be seen

> the eagerness of Muslims to discover the Greek culture, their efforts to learn, and at the same time the later realisation that Philosophy could present dangers for Faith, Reason could doubt Revelation, and Dialogue might be a threat to Islam.[3]

The epoch of expansion was an age in which Islam became a politico-military force and a religious, even theological, factor to be reckoned with seriously so far as Christianity was concerned. During this period an intellectual engagement, if not actual dialogue, began to take place in either of two modes: *direct* (as in the East) and *indirect* (as was the case in the West).

The term 'direct engagement' refers to the situation of interaction and relationship that occurred in regard to Christian communities living under Muslim rule. It was dominated by the Islamic concept of *dhimma*, or *dhimmi* community: the protected minority, specifically the 'People of the Book' (meaning those who believe in and worship one God, but who are not Muslims as such) who are to be afforded protection and the right to exist and maintain their religious observances, provided a special tax or levy (*jizya*) was paid to the regional ruling Muslim authorities. Thus, as a 'protected people' under the dhimma rubric, Christians were granted 'the right to exist and practise their religion provided they paid the jizya and remained submissive in front of the Muslim community'.[4] While this set the legal context for daily contact, socio-psychologically speaking, mutual suspicion and antagonism tended to prevail. So, we might say that the 'decrees of dhimma', together with concomitant beliefs and faith-attitude, predetermined the parameters of relationship from the Muslim point of view. It really could not have been otherwise.

The Christian response to the contextual parameters being set by Muslims may be seen in such early writers as St John of Damascus (675–753CE). Living within the Islamic Ummah, yet writing to present Christianity to Christians, John treated Islam as false belief: Christianity may regard Islam as simply another heresy against which orthodox faith is to defend itself. John attacked Islam with a variety of *reductio ad absurdum* arguments, turning the tables on Muslims who argued against Christian belief. Through his work can be seen the contours of early Christian theological dynamics. On the one hand, as in his *De Haeresibus* (Latin—

---

[3] Ibid., 25.

[4] Ibid., 27. Note: jizya refers to the special tax applied to dhimmi communities in lieu of military service and recognition of the protection afforded by the Muslim authorities.

False Beliefs), which is the second section of his book *The Fount of Knowledge*, Islam is subsumed under a more general discussion of matters pertinent to Christian life and faith. On the other hand, in a manual written in Greek, he directly addresses issues of interreligious encounter by way of providing Christians with answers to the kinds of questions that Muslims are likely to ask.

Although there is some element of superiority threading through John's work, it contains neither the negativity, nor the polemical aggression, toward Islam that was to emerge in later centuries. At this time the dominant sense is of Christians having something to offer Muslims as they seek to understand their own faith in the broader context. Gaudeul remarks that such work 'may be one of the earliest instances of Christian theology offering its help to other believers without any ulterior motive'.[5]

In the event, the form of early intellectual engagement in the east was effectively fixed in the work of the Nestorian patriarch Timothy (728–823CE):[6] Christians would be preoccupied with stating and re-stating received orthodoxy in clear terms and in a determined style. Creedal faith, as promulgated by conciliar and episcopal decree, would simply be proclaimed. The text of Timothy's *Apology*, his main work which was used by many generations of Christians, derives directly from dialogical engagement with the Muslim Caliph, *al-Mahdi*. Questions are put by the Muslim to the Christian. The response is a statement of faith: there is no attempt at bridging the divide between Muslim and Christian worlds of discourse; no advance in mutual understanding is made, nor is it possible. Such 'dialogue' is really a variant of parallel monologue. But this was the pattern that was to hold in respect of Christian–Muslim engagement over many centuries.

Meanwhile, there was evidence of a developing sophistication of Islamic argument. A Muslim retort to early Christian critiques was given by *al-Tabari* (ninth century CE), a former Nestorian Christian who wrote, as a convert to Islam, his *Refutation of Christianity*. However, Gaudeul argues that in the work of al-Tabari can be seen 'an attempt made by a convert to find peace of mind through achieving a synthesis between his former faith and his new belief. ... This would be similar to the Christian way of reading the Old Testament'.[7] Nonetheless al-Tabari did raise seven 'embarrassing questions' for Christians which typify the nature of issues raised in the dialogical encounter, for example: can God undergo suffering and death? Is Christ God or man? Is Christ the creator or a creature? Furthermore, he focused on the criteria of true religion, asking if the criteria used against Islam could not be used equally against Christianity. This applied particularly to the issue of prophethood and the charge by Christians that Muhammad did not fit the bill as a prophet.

---

[5] Ibid., 30.

[6] Patriarch from 780CE, Timothy was head of a missionary church (with missions to both India and China). He was active with Church reform and the education of his clergy. Fluent in Greek, Syriac and Arabic, he moved to Baghdad so that, as head and spokesperson for his Church, he would have direct access to the Caliph of the Islamic empire.

[7] Gaudeul, *Encounters*, 42.

Al-Tabari drew together the Quranic texts which set the rules for dialogical encounter so far as Islamic scriptural warrant is concerned: belief in the previous revelations from the one and the same God; belief in the veracity of the revelation through Muhammad without distinction; the utter oneness of God who only is the Lord to be served, and who will not guide his people into error.

By way of stylistic contrast, another early paradigm of direct engagement is that of the correspondence that took place between a Christian and a Muslim scholar, for example the purported Muslim letter of *al-Hashimi* and the Christian response of *al-Kindi* during the ninth century. This is probably a sole-authored work, most likely by a Christian, who uses symbolic names and the mode of an apparent interchange of letters to present a debate. Al-Hashimi, in a letter of some 37 pages, presents Islam and argues anti-Christian polemics; al-Kindi, in a 230-page retort, gives a Christian apologetic together with a critique of Islam. This work, Gaudeul notes, 'represents the state of Christian–Muslim dialogue as it was taking place daily among civil servants and educated people'[8] at that time. It is very important for the history of Christian-Muslim encounter. This is because most Muslim writers in later periods attempted in one way or another to answer al-Kindi and, for many generations, Christians—especially in the West—only knew Islam through the description given by these letters, which were translated into Latin from the twelfth century onwards. At the time of al-Hashimi and al-Kindi the key issues to have emerged were undoubtedly the question of the veracity and status of the doctrine of the Trinity on the one hand and the legitimacy and integrity of the Qur'an on the other. Each proponent accused the other of falsity and credulity in regards to these two respective foundational elements of faith.

Intellectual engagement with Islam by Christians under Muslim rule took place in many forms, both oral and written. Such encounter was rooted in lived experiential engagement and relationship. And if the tone of exchange was initially courteous and calm, politics soon brought about a shift from tolerance to intolerance, and so 'dialogue' gradually became an arena for hostile engagement rather than an exercise in friendly encounter. Indeed, Islam had effectively produced a set of limiting conventions to the game-play of dialogical encounter: there could be no direct criticism of Islam, the Qur'an or Muhammad. From the Christian point of view, reference to the scriptures became less acceptable and useful: Muslims were inclined to modify scriptural meaning in the service of Islam (so al-Tabari) or reject the scriptures outright as falsified (so al-Hashimi).

The context and experience of direct engagement was not the only mode of encounter between Muslim and Christian, however. In the West a different sort of intellectual engagement, 'indirect engagement', was pursued. In marked contrast to the East, the Western Christian Empire did not have a direct Muislim 'partner', as it were, residing within its borders. Thus Christians within the Western empire addressed Islam and Muslims indirectly, from a distance, and also across a

---

[8] Ibid., 52.

language barrier; writers of Greek, Armenian, Georgian, and Latin addressed Arabic writing and speaking Muslims. As a result, occasions of dialogical encounter were indirect and mediate. Also, such engagement served another purpose than actual interreligious dialogue such as we might think of it today. For the indirect mode was not self-reflexive: it did not raise the question of 'dialogical attitude' in modes of engagement with a dialogical partner, or in respect to the internal intellectual task as such. Rather, in speaking about the religiously 'other', ostensibly to that other, but in fact to their own, 'dialogue' is subordinated to internal apologetics. The 'other' is debated indirectly in order to bolster one's own view and perspective. Thus, as Gaudeul observes,

> Protected as they are by political or linguistic borders, the authors are prone to throw insults at Islam, Muhammad and Muslims ... (with) in the background all the resentment of the Byzantines or of other populations who have suffered defeat at the hands of the Muslims. It is often the militant tone of War literature.[9]

Examples from representative Christian writers indicate there was a wide range of issues involved in the defence of Christianity and attacks on Islam. For instance, some argued that Muhammad was an epileptic and a charlatan, that the doctrines of Islam were borrowed distortions from Judaism and Christianity, and that Islam teaches idolatry. It is not difficult to demonstrate that indirect dialogue in the early epoch of Islamic expansion was more a matter of diatribe and invective than dispassionate engagement in mutual understanding and critical self-reflection.

On the other hand there is a significant example of dialogical engagement by correspondence, conducted in the names of the Byzantine emperor Leo III (717–41CE) and the Umayyad Caliph Umar II (717–20CE), but actually compiled in the closing years of the ninth century. There is no particular originality in these documents. Nevertheless, they provide a good example of the typical intellectual encounter of the era. The Muslim letter argues that Jews and Christians adulterated the scriptures, that Jesus is not God, that Christian salvation is problematic and indeed that Christian practices were misleading. It then goes on to give answer to the Christian critique of Islam, to assert Muhammad as prophet, and to affirm that Islam is validated by its success. The Christian letter retorts with the witness of scripture that Jesus is the Word of God, that there is in fact an undergirding unity of all Christians, and that the Qur'an is falsified. It goes on to argue in favour of the Trinity, assert the divinity of Christ, and offer a defence of Christian practices. It ends with an attack on Islamic practices and discussions of sundry other items.

Gaudeul notes that, with this exchange, 'we reach the end of the first period of Christian–Muslim dialogue: a period of clumsy efforts on either side to try and define their own position in front of the 'other', and to formulate the relevant objections to

---

[9] Ibid., 62.

the other doctrine'.[10] Although more used as rhetorical devices for self-promotion, the dialogical encounters thus far noted reveal that the pattern of style and content, if not the form and argumentative substance, had emerged, and it had become quite fixed.

Relations in an epoch of *Equilibrium* [*11th–12th centuries*]

Gaudeul refers to the eleventh and twelfth centuries as a time of stalemate and balance of power. The earlier and dramatic expansion of the Islamic dynastic empire was checked; political fragmentation and relative weakness ensued. This was the time when Christianity made an aggressive comeback. Crusades to recover the Holy Land from the infidel were inaugurated, spurred on by the Spanish *Reconquista* and the emergence of the new European civilisation out of Europe's Dark Age. Islam had known nearly four centuries of untrammelled development and growth, with military success and political and cultural achievement a confirmation of divine sanction. Indeed, Islam had been militarily on the winning side and had found pride in its victories, while Christians had seemed destined for the losing side. But, after 1050CE 'the trend had stopped and Christians and Muslims met on the battlefield on equal terms. Military success could no longer be invoked as a sign of God's approval'.[11]

Even in the economic sphere the winds of change were blowing in favour of the West: ownership of the most prosperous trading vessels, entrepreneurial initiative, and the profits and power that went with that shifted westward. At the same time there was a growing mutual militancy and intolerance: each was inclined to invoke the idea of the Holy War against the other side. In the Christian West this made for resurgence and renewal in spiritual matters, which, coupled with growth in material prosperity, stimulated a new self-awareness and self-confidence. Europe 'idealised the figure of the Pilgrim and Knight defending Christendom against its enemies'.[12] But the world-view clash that existed between Christian and Muslim, fuelled by a wholly negative view of Islam as given out in sermons and writings, also pertained to the clash between Christian West and Christian Byzantine East: this was the age of the Great Schism in Christianity and the initial aftermath of mutual Christian anathema and animosity. And within and among the Muslim community jihad was exalted in books and poems; regulations concerning the dhimmi communities proliferated and intensified in humiliation; and the rise of both anti-Christian and anti-Jewish polemics spawned concomitant riots and massacres.

On the one hand this was an age of intense antagonism and a see-saw of violent outburst: neither side exactly had the upper hand. On the other it saw a mutual cultural exchange, which also gave a sense of balancing counterpoint. As Gaudeul again reminds us:

---

[10] Ibid., 74.

[11] Ibid., 81.

[12] Ibid., 82.

It was at this time that Islamic thought reached its zenith under the continued influence of Hellenism. The greatest thinkers of Islam lived during that period. ... Europe received from the Islamic world—through Spain—the treasures of Greek philosophy and science.[13]

Islamic intellectual greatness flowered during this age on three fronts: in theology, philosophy, and mysticism. Furthermore, the 'pendular movement of Christian zeal expressing itself in turn through the sword and the word' marked a re-invigorated Christian mission to Muslims that accompanied the age of the Crusades (1095–1270CE).[14] Gradually, the zeal for evangelical conversion tempered the zest for military conquest.

It was during this epoch of relative equilibrium that each religion looked to its own inner consolidation. In the development of orthodoxy within Islam, and the promulgation of defining criteria, principles, and methods, Islamic scholars tended towards theological options that offered protection against 'Christian contamination'. But Christians were no less adept at producing their own discrediting diatribes against Islam that also have persisted since. Both sides consolidated their paradigms of prejudice. For example, the Bible's multiple human authorship was taken by Muslims to mean that the text of Christian scripture was in some way falsified (*tahrif*), or that it had suffered textual substitution (*tabdil*). The argument used for the latter was: alteration could have happened; the existence of textual discrepancies, inconsistencies and contradictions prove it did happen. Thus Christian doctrine was condemned as false. The Trinity was regularly attacked as an invention and indeed self-contradictory: how can three things be one? The incarnation was constantly criticised as impossible and also an absurdity: if God becomes man, he is no longer God; if a man becomes God, he is no longer man; if Christ is composed of both, he is neither God nor man.

One critical Islamic anti-Christian polemic of this period worth noting is the book *Excellent Refutation* attributed to the famous Muslim scholar al-Ghazali (1059–1111CE) wherein, on the basis of the acceptance of both the truth of Islam and the authenticity of the Christian scriptures, an Islamic hermeneutic is applied to the Christian scripture. Thus texts implying the divinity of Jesus are read allegorically; texts implying his humanity are read literally. A detailed Islamic rebuttal of Christian claims, together with an Islamic explication of Christian phenomena, then follows and the whole forms a somewhat new departure, an approach that eclipses the pattern of this era. It remained little used until recent times.

Meanwhile, from the Christian side, we find a dialogical treatise in an apologetical style, written in the early eleventh century in a climate of considerable mutual respect and openness, between Muslim and Christian, conducted by a

---

[13] Ibid., 83.

[14] Ibid., 84.

Nestorian bishop, *Elias al-Nasibi* (975–1046CE), who became Metropolitan of Nisibis (on the border of present-day Turkey and Syria). An attempt is made to explain the Trinity by using universal philosophical categories; the need to search for a common language about God is advocated: 'no human language about God can avoid being analogical or metaphorical'.[15] The eirenical work of persons such as Elias notwithstanding, the epoch of which he is part is more an age of enhanced missionary motivation than polite and erudite inquiry. Nevertheless, the spirit of eirenical engagement was furthered by none other than Pope Gregory VII (1020–1085CE).

Despite a variety of battles that took place between Muslims and Christians during his time as Pontiff, Pope Gregory continued to stress peaceful missionary outreach and, in 1076CE, wrote a letter to *al-Nazir,* a Muslim leader, in response to the latter's request that the Pope ordain a bishop for the Christians under his rule.[16] The Pope's letter is notable in that he avoids any antagonistic statements—he neither deprecates Islam nor elevates Christianity over it—and, indeed, he stresses common elements of faith and the working of God in both religions.

A Christian letter and its Muslim reply, written around the middle of the twelfth century, succinctly encapsulate the issues of the day.[17] The Christian says: Christ is God and Saviour; Christian prayer is efficacious and excellent; Christian morality is better than Muslim law; the Bible is most excellent, and is superior to the Qur'an; miracles are performed by Christians. The letter also raises objections to the Muslim notion of paradise and the spread of Islam by the sword. The Muslim reply includes an attack on key Christian dogmas (Trinity, Incarnation, and Redemption) as but inventions of Constantine; a defence of Islam as embracing a better law; arguing the veracity of Muhammad's prophethood; attacking the Bible with the theory of falsification; giving an answer to the objections of the Christian; and dismissing Christian miracles as tricks and lies. Christianity, it concludes, is the worst enemy of Islam. Clearly, this correspondence represents a clash, or combative-type encounter, wherein mutual hostility prevails. It reflects a socio-political context of military engagement and loss, coupled with missionary endeavour and corresponding loss of members to the missionising faith, and the pressing need for that to be resisted.

However, a new Christian paradigm emerged with the work of Peter the Venerable (1094–1156CE), in particular with his *A Refutation of Islam.* Gaudeul has analysed its reasoning as follows: (1) The Muslims are obliged by the Qur'an to regard the books of the Bible as revealed by God. (2) Owing to inconsistencies between Qur'an and Bible, one of the two books must be rejected. (3) The Bible cannot be rejected: that would be against the Qur'an. But the reverse is possible. (4) It can be proved from both Bible and Qur'an that: (i) The Qur'an was not

---

[15] Ibid., 102.

[16] See ibid., 104f.

[17] Cf. ibid., 114.

revealed by God, and (ii) Muhammad was not a prophet (according to the Biblical meaning of the term).[18]

Peter represents the responsive Christian intellectual challenge: Islam had to be answered. Of his own efforts he said 'it would be proper to have a really suitable reply as a Christian armoury against this pestilence'.[19] Yet he wrote to Muslims seeking to redress military approaches (attack and destroy) with missionary ones (persuade and convert), thus: 'I do not attack you—Muslims—as our people often do, by arms, but by words; not by force, but by reason, not in hatred, but in love'.[20] Peter was not attempting genuine dialogue, of course: he learnt about Islam in order to provide Christians with an 'armoury'; his concern was to prove the other wrong, which does not allow for any real exchange of thought and idea. Of course, Peter's style reflected the emergence of scholasticism in the Christian West as the predominant method of religious discourse and reflection.

Relationships in an epoch of *Exhortation* [*13th–14th centuries*]

The thirteenth and fourteenth centuries may be viewed, as Gaudeul suggests, as a time of two worlds at war. We might call it an age of hortatory hubris, or an epoch of *exhortation*. The worlds of both Islam and Christianity underwent great change. The Crusader states steadily declined and fizzled: under the Mamluks of Egypt, Islam regained much of what it had formerly lost to the Christians. Then there came the Mongol invasions, which disrupted and changed forever the shape of *dar-al-Islam*. The seeds of the Ottoman ascendancy were also sown. A new Europe was emerging, signalling new cultural development; new prosperity and growing self-confidence coupled with both a spiritual renewal and a revitalised militaristic outlook. The emergence of this new Europe dominated the encounter between Islam and Christianity. The Christian West worked to eliminate Islamic rule from Europe (cf. the Spanish Reconquista). But, at the same time, Islam sought to rid itself of Christian rule out of Asia (taking the Byzantine and Crusader states, for example).

The warring clash between these two worlds was as much psychological as physically militaristic. Self-image and the image of the 'other' were important dimensions, as Gaudeul notes:

> Europe had discovered its existence as 'Christendom' at the time of the first Crusade ... It was now exploring its roots (Greek and Latin cultures) as well as bearing new fruits (new structures and nations). A great need was felt for the integration of all these elements in a Christian synthesis.[21]

---

[18] Ibid., 118.

[19] Cited ibid., 119.

[20] Ibid.

[21] Ibid., 129.

At the same time, 'The Muslim world had been torn by strife and threatened in its very existence by the Mongol invasion. The aftermath ... was marked by a return to as orthodox a way of thinking and of living as could be achieved'.[22]

The Christian negative image of Islam that had emerged as the virtual standard perspective saw this religious 'other' as a falsehood and a deliberate perversion of truth; a religion of violence, spread by the sword; a way of self-indulgence and licentiousness; inspired by Satan and founded by the Antichrist, who was identified, of course, as Muhammad. Muslims could, and did, hold much the same kind of image of Christianity. Under Muslim rule, the situation of the dhimmi communities deteriorated further. But so too did the state of religious minorities, especially Jews, in the Christian West. Humiliation and degradation of the other was the order of the day.

Image is a function of imagination. The religious imagination, fuelled by hatred and prejudice, resulted in a dehumanising image of each by the other. The West's hortatory inclinations issued in new and vigorous missionary enterprises, notably those of the nascent mendicant religious Orders, the Dominicans and the Franciscans. In the process, Islam was perceived by many as the antithesis of Christianity. Christ was proclaimed over and against all falsehoods and idolatries, of which Islam was the most potent and threatening. This was the age of Thomas Aquinas (1225–74CE), whose great work, *Summa Contra Gentiles* (1259–64), was written to help with missionary efforts in respect of non-Christians in general and Muslims in particular. Here was a high-water mark of the shaping of the Christian negative image of the other now given intellectual respectability and reasoned perspective. Incidentally, Aquinas, and before him his teacher Albert the Great (1200–1280CE), had rediscovered Aristotelian logic and metaphysics by way of the work of Muslim philosophers. This opened to the West new ways of thinking and new approaches to the understanding of reality which were much more favourable to scientific empirical inquiry than had previously been the case.

In respect of theological reflection, both in general and with regard to interreligious encounters, St Thomas' method was to maximise the use of reason and draw on scripture for illustration. As faith includes supra-rational mystery that is beyond reason—being apprehensible only as revelation—therefore arguments from reason cannot prove faith nor convince the unbeliever. But argument can answer argument, showing up insufficiency and logical weakness. Aquinas' reasonable assumption was that the Christian could meet both the Jewish and Muslim co-religionist at intellectual depth because there is a common need for, and ability to grasp, the truth. Furthermore, it was possible to do this because the categories of such discourse, derived from Greek philosophy, were held in common.[23] Thus the overriding task is to seek the common faith experience and a common language to talk about it, a goal still relevant today.

---

[22] Ibid.

[23] Cf. ibid., 143.

The Oxford theologian, John Wycliff (1320–84CE), while accepting the general Western perception of Islam in his day, determined that the real conflict was not between Christian and Muslim *per se*, but between the spirit of the Gospel (meaning poverty, detachment, self-sacrifice) and the spirit of Islam (meaning worldly power, rule, and self-aggrandisement).[24] And the Spaniard, Raymond Lull (1235–1315CE), following a conversion experience in 1256, undertook a missionising dialogue with Jews and Muslims on the grounds of the commonality of reason.[25] Of such Christian scholars who tried to relate positively to Islam during this epoch, Nazir-Ali comments that 'Raymond Lull advocated a peaceful approach to Islam instead of the Crusades; Francis of Assisi actually visited Saladin during the Crusades, and John Wycliffe refused to deny the beatific vision to Muslims'.[26] It was not all a matter of hostility and war; intimations of *salaam* occurred in the midst of the hortatory animosity.

Relations in an epoch of *Enmity* [*15th–18th centuries*]

Gaudeul refers to the period of the fifteenth through the eighteenth centuries as a time of hostile indifference, an age of aggressive clashes rather than heuristic engagement *per se*. Some contextual considerations need to be noted. This was the time of the four centuries of Ottoman predominance. Christian–Muslim wars ebbed and flowed throughout Spain, North Africa, Ethiopia, East Africa, and Southeast Asia. It was a time that saw dramatic geographic expansion of the Christian West's Old World into the New World. It saw the emergence of Europe into modern nation states. Thus, 'Christian–Muslim dialogue was affected by this change since there would no longer be encounters between "Muslims" and "Christians", but encounters between "Turks" (or "Moors") and "Frenchmen", "Spaniards", or "Germans".'[27] It was also the time of the European wars of religion and the Reformation within the Church in Western Europe. Christianity, at least in the West, was absorbed with its own internal problems, its own encounters and clashes, which resulted in a relative indifference towards Islam. The inclination was to see Islam as 'just another heresy that had to be eradicated, by violence if need be'.[28] Behind the enmity there lay an increasing divergence of fundamental aspects of world view. The Renaissance and humanism, the roots of western secularisation, had emerged to drive the wedge deeper between Christian and Muslim grounding perspectives. For example, whereas

---

[24] Cf. ibid., 131.
[25] Cf. ibid., 158f.
[26] Michael Nazir-Ali, *Frontiers in Muslim–Christian Encounter* (*Oxford*: Regnum Books, 1991), 18.
[27] Gaudeul, *Encounters*, 188.
[28] Ibid., 189.

European thinking started from Human Rights, Islamic thinking was based on God's Law, or God's Right to Man's obedience. In the 13th century, Christian and Muslim scholars spoke the same language; in the 18th century their philosophical views had become incompatible.[29]

At the same time the Muslim world spread globally and diversified culturally throughout India, Africa and Asia, with concomitant problems and issues for the Islamic Ummah. The Ottoman rule in traditionally Muslim lands of the Middle East, North Africa, Egypt and so on, made for a greater emphasis on law and order, with a return to doctrinal orthodoxy, rigid control over scholars and writers, and domestication of Sufi Brotherhoods.

Attitudes of Islam to Christianity oscillated between indifference and hostility. Gaudeul comments that, in effect, both Islam and Christianity

> shared the same planet but mentally they lived in two worlds, and, as time went on, the mental universe of each society grew more impervious to the thinking, the values and motivations, and indeed the whole mental universe of the other.[30]

For the Christian West the pressing reality of the Ottoman empire provoked various attempts at a response to Islam, even, from some quarters, a call to Christians to renounce the responses of militarism and have recourse, instead, to ways of peaceful engagement with this religious 'other'. A dream of the essential unity of all religions was abroad, a dream given expression by Nicholas of Cusa (1401–64CE): *Una religio in rituum varietate* ('One Religion in a variety of rites'). Nicholas wrote an imaginary dialogue between members of different faiths in which he sought to expose the 'fundamental unity in religion even though each community worships God by different rites and under different names'.[31] This was, in effect, an early attempt to articulate a religious pluralism in order to deal constructively with the reality of religious plurality.

But the Reformation and the rise of the Ottoman empire reinforced the notion that, for Christianity, Islam was an inherent threat to be resisted. Martin Luther (1483–1546CE) and Dante (1265–1321CE) gave colourful and vehement expression to this perspective, as Kimball comments. 'This bias, rooted in inaccurate and invidious caricature, is a firm fixture in the cultural heritage bequeathed to contemporary Western civilization'.[32] Nonetheless, people such as Nicholas of Cusa attempted a Christian exegesis of the texts of the Qur'an to show that, deep down, the Qur'an agrees with Christianity. But then they would go on to prove the superiority of Christianity over Islam. Openness has its limits after all.

---

[29] Ibid.

[30] Ibid., 191.

[31] Kimball, *Striving Together*, 44.

[32] Ibid.

Following a period when the breeze of goodwill and optimism brushed the combatants engaged in hostile religious encounter, the main thrust of Christianity's perspective on Islam hardened again from the late fifteenth century. For example, a French bishop decreed 'Islam was the enemy of the Christians. To violence the only answer was violence. Discussion could only weaken the purpose of Christian armies'.[33] Although there were in the West some who were open to interfaith discussions with Muslims in a way that prefigures the modern approach to dialogue, such openness was, in effect, 'based on an illusion about the true extent of the differences between Islam and Christianity'.[34] Furthermore, the real underlying motive for interfaith discussion 'was the desire to return to a more evangelical attitude in spreading the Gospel'.[35]

In the end this openness was short-lived: the optimism based on discerned commonalities gave way to the despair of incontrovertible distinctive differences, as Gaudeul wryly notes. 'The formation received by these scholars was that of combative apologetics; it soon re-asserted itself when they began to study Islam more closely'. Furthermore, they 'could conceive of the possibility of "Religious Unity in a variety of rites", but not "Mutual Acceptance in a variety of Doctrines": all their thinking required that Islam be another form of Christianity for any religious negotiations to take place'.[36] Meanwhile, so far as the majority of Church leaders and Christians in general were concerned, there was a fundamental hostility toward Islam *and* to Muslims. It was as much Christendom as Christianity that stood opposed to Islam. And uppermost in the European consciousness was the threatening reality of the Turks: 'The Ottoman expansion and aggressive spirit turned everybody's attention away from the religious plane and fixed it on military confrontation. Dialogue with Islam could not be envisaged in those conditions'.[37]

In the end, Christian military triumphs resulted in decrees giving Muslims the choice of 'conversion' or expulsion as, for example, was the case in Spain. Those who converted remained ever suspect and fed the insatiable appetite of the Inquisition, ever on the lookout for the backslider and idolater to purge. Muslim reaction included resistance, adaptation, and compromise as possible options in response to attempts at enforced conversion to Christianity. All could be well, provided one's heart is set on Islam. In other words, a distinction was made between outward behaviour and inner intention. In this context a *fatwa* was issued allowing the maintenance of mental reservations while publicly professing Christian faith. Double allegiance or 'bi-confessionalism' was deemed allowable, although the criticism of this encouraging the evil of syncretism nonetheless prevailed.

---

[33] Gaudeul, *Encounters*, 198.

[34] Ibid., 199.

[35] Ibid.

[36] Ibid.

[37] Ibid., 200.

Out of this epoch we can discern a set of themes of Muslim anti-Christian polemics. The Trinity was attacked through rational argument and scriptural scrutiny as well as from the Qur'an; Christ was treated as being not divine, rather as being the same in human status as other prophets. His death and salvific role were challenged if not actively negated. Muhammad was affirmed as superior to Jesus. Church ideology, structures, and practices were criticised and attacked; Islam was propounded as a pure doctrine without superstition, having a pure scripture and being victorious. It is worth noting that many Muslims used, against Christianity as a whole, arguments that Protestants were using against Catholics. As a consequence it has been said that

> more than ever, Christians and Muslims are vaccinated against one another's religion. There is no sudden change, for most of the ideas ... were expressed by other polemicists long before. But there was certainly a trend towards more hostility, and yet, as the years went by, both communities, living on opposite shores of the Mediterranean, returned to their own concerns and became indifferent to the preoccupations of the 'others'.[38]

On the other hand, a surprisingly modern-sounding approach from this epoch emerged from the seventeenth-century Christian scholar Ludovico Marraci (1612–1700CE). Marraci critiqued the Qur'an for Christians, yet, at the same time he advocated an approach to Islam in terms of identifying three different modes of encounter. These were a scientific approach which sought knowledge of Islam from Muslim sources; theological reflection on this whereby an attempt is made to find a certain coherence between Christian belief and the information about Islam; and the missionary response which promotes a particular dialogue with Muslims wherein care is taken not to give offence, and pains are taken to render the Christian message intelligible to Muslims.

By way of conclusion we may say that on the whole, during this epoch of enmity, effective dialogical engagement was virtually non-existent: any 'encounters' were for the purposes of mutual refutation, the challenge of combative controversy, or else the attempt at missionary conversion.

Relations in an epoch of *Emancipation and Exploration* [*19th–20th centuries*]

Gaudeul refers to the nineteenth and twentieth centuries as an age of old quarrels and new perspectives. The nineteenth century saw the European Industrial Revolution with its various socio-political *sequae*, colonial expansion and consolidation. This period witnessed the decline of the Ottoman empire and the emancipation from Islamic rule of Christian countries such as Greece, Serbia and Rumania, together with accompanying reactionary massacres of Christians by

---

[38] Ibid., 213.

Muslims, such as occurred with Lebanese and Syrian Christians and the Armenians. It was the time of the rise of the modern missionary movement so far as the Christian West is concerned. All of this resulted in the humiliation of Islam: non-Muslims were seen to be usurping the Islamic heritage. Internal laxity was viewed as a contributing factor in the eyes of many Muslims. Islam was being judged by its abuses and its temporal weaknesses, and defined in terms of backwardness, fatalism, and fanaticism. The inevitable response was forthcoming in a resurgence of reform and revivalism, encompassing the theological, spiritual, political and social dimensions of Islam.

Throughout the twentieth century there was a continuing Western hegemony that rose to new heights in the aftermath of the first World War with the final collapse of the Ottoman empire and caliphate; and then, post-World War II, the complex Palestine/Israel issue which was followed by the shifting sands of Middle East allegiances. As Gaudeul has remarked: 'For centuries, Christians had been humiliated by Muslims, while for the past 200 years it is the Muslims who have suffered and been humiliated at the hands of "Christian' nations".'[39] Nowadays, of course, we see the aftermath of this in terms of the various struggles by many modern Muslim nation states to effect full post-colonial emancipation.

This epoch is also an age of mutual mission: Christian evangelism and Islamic *da'wah*. In response both to the efforts and methods of Christian missionaries, and in fulfilment of its own missionary calling, Islamic efforts to actively promote the faith and seek conversions have emerged since the late nineteenth century. Today, for example, the Muslim World League, formed in 1962, promotes the true faith in both Muslim and non-Muslim countries. 'It seeks to explain Islamic teachings and principles ... and to confront those trying to attack Islam or to convert Muslims'.[40] The underlying mutual perspective in this period would seem to be that neither side, on the whole, can conceive of a proclamation of truth without a concomitant denunciation and deprecation of the other's viewpoint. However, it has been argued that

> the real opposition is not between Islam and Christianity, but between a militant conception of mission and a more liberal approach, both trends being represented in each of the two communities, though in different proportions; the liberal trend seems to gain in importance among Christian missionaries, while it still remains marginal, almost non-existent among Muslims on account of the present mounting wave of militant Islam.[41]

Nevertheless, dialogue in the latter half of the twentieth century assumed a new level of importance and invited new prospects for mutual *exploration* as the positive sequel to political, social and religious emancipation. This is the hopeful

---

[39] Ibid., 252.
[40] Ibid., 275.
[41] Ibid., 283.

legacy bequeathed to the twenty-first century. The contrary would be a collapse back into old enmities by pursuing the new imperialisms of hegemonic globalisation and globalised terrorisms. In the twenty-first century of the Common Era, the invitation to dialogue and the finding of common ground between the great religions of revelation grows ever more urgent.

Conclusion

As was demonstrated above, the epochs of Christian–Muslim encounter may be denoted by themes of *expansion, equilibrium, exhortation, enmity*, and *emancipation*, with the future, hopefully, poised to develop the cause of mutual *exploration*. The interpretive terms I have chosen not only denote historical phases; they also represent aspects of the ongoing and contemporary relationship between Christianity and Islam. Expansion stands for the expansiveness of self-confidence, embracing self-righteousness on the one hand and magnanimity on the other. Religion in the expansion mode is determined and assertive. This can be seen today in both Islam and Christianity. But there is also more than a hint of equilibrium that shows through in the hesitancy to be overly self-assertive: an inclination to humility that properly counterpoints self-righteousness; a measure of openness that marks a balanced approach to the religious 'other'. Again we could say this is a feature of both religions to some degree in the present age. So, too, do we see evidence today of mutual exhortation, the proclamation and witness which, in its more extreme forms, seeks to declare an exclusive truth and engages with the 'other' in order to win. And, as well, there is evidence aplenty of enmity, of dismissive, derogatory and deprecatory prejudice that makes of the religious other an enemy to be fought and vanquished. At the same time, the cultural and socio-political expressions of, and concomitant realities in respect to, the religions of Islam and Christianity, are ever engaged in the quest for emancipation: that quest for self-determination and finding a rightful place in the affairs of the day, of finding and asserting meaningful identity as communities, and for the individuals who comprise those communities; of seeking socio-economic justice, and of sustaining unique ways of life and cultural expressions.

So then, all these elements and interpretive perspectives on the past notwithstanding, perhaps we might say that the underpinning feature of the present age—the early twenty-first century of the Common Era—to emerge out of the late twentieth century, and that holds these dynamics together in some sort of creative tension, is the motif of exploration. For, despite evidence of resistance and instances of opposition, there seems to be abroad in the world today intimations of a spirit of sincere, tentative, open and honest questing to know the religious other—for Christian to know Muslim, and for Muslim to know Christian for instance—and to do so in a climate of mutual recognition of integrity and validity, even as there is recognition of real difference and diversity. To the extent this perception is accurate it reflects, I suggest, the positive face of an age not just of the acceptance of plurality, but an embrace of pluralism and a desire to forge a future premised on that, rather than on combative mutual exclusivisms.

Rollin Armour reminds us that Islam is not just a religion in any narrow sense, but truly a total civilisation, one which, of course, cannot be ignored.

> In its first century the Islamic movement captured great pieces of Christendom, later the entire Byzantine empire, and then threatened the very heartland of Europe. During the early Middle Ages, when western Europe was little more than a backwater area, overrun and disrupted by barbarian invaders, Islamic civilization led the world in science and culture ... No problem would vex medieval thinkers more than Islam, as a religious movement to be interpreted and understood, as a cultural rival, and as a political and military adversary to defend against.[42]

It seems little has changed. Islam in the twenty-first century is as much a puzzle, problematic, and challenge as ever it was. Military-political encounters of one sort or another dominate the news headlines; the intellectual-theological encounter remains a challenge yet to be adequately taken up, despite a chequered history of attempts to do so.

In respect to the vexing issue of relations between Christians and Muslims, or more broadly speaking between the West and Islam, and the prospects for the ongoing dialogue between the two faiths, we might agree with Charles Kimball that

> For many people in both communities the basic theological issues constitute the primary agenda for Christian–Muslim dialogue. Understanding different orientations is an important step, but it does not resolve the seemingly inherent conflicts. Thoughtful, creative, and persevering efforts are required in order to bridge some of the real and perceived differences in foundational theological understandings. ... Although we all carry the cumulative baggage provided by our deep-rooted heritage, developments in the past 150 years have challenged traditional assumptions and prompted the vexing questions confronting people of faith today.[43]

By pursuing the challenge of dialogue we seek to comprehend better the respective faiths in which we live, and move, and have our being.

---

[42] Rollin Amour, Sr., *Islam, Christianity, and the West: A Troubled History* (Maryknoll, New York: Orbis Books), 2.

[43] Kimball, *Striving Together*, 48.

Chapter 7

Jewish–Muslim Relations
Islamic Paradigms

In the preceding chapter I explored some of the salient contours of the history of Christian–Muslim interaction and relations. Both Islam and Christianity between them account for the religious identity, at least nominally, of the majority of the earth's population. The relationship between them—or more particularly, between their adherents—has been historically significant and will be critical for the future of humanity. However, it is also the case that the relationship between Islam and Judaism—likewise, of course, between Jews and Muslims, practically speaking— is deeply significant, historically speaking, and of crucial importance in terms of current international relations and global stability. Whereas the encounter between Islam and Christianity, particularly in some quarters of the world (Indonesia, Nigeria, the Sudan, for example), is deeply problematic, generally it is a relatively localised issue when such interfaith relations turn sour. But the issue of the relationship between Islam and Judaism is another matter. What at first glance may appear a relatively local issue—Israel is no continent, for instance—actually has taken on the mantle of a global phenomenon: Muslims from around the world, with no first-hand encounter with Jews, are caught up in a profoundly concerning negativity.

Paradoxically, on the one hand there is, theologically speaking, much less of a prima-facie problem between Judaism and Islam than there is between Islam and Christianity. Indeed, when it comes to the business of day-to-day communal existence as religious persons, there is a high level of compatibility, and this is not only in terms of religious life,[1] it has also been borne out through much of the history of Islam. Yet, on the other hand, there is a deep vein of negativity towards Jews, Judaism, and Israel that is manifest throughout the world of Islam and which impacts on many areas of international affairs. It is as if there is a profound antipathy between Islam and Judaism that eclipses any posturing against Christianity and even the oft-expressed negativity toward the West in general.

---

[1] See for example, Jacob Neusner and Tamara Sonn, *Comparing Religions Through Law: Judaism and Islam* (London: Routledge, 1999); also Jacob Neusner, Tamara Sonn and Jonathan E. Brockopp, *Judaism and Islam in Practice: A Sourcebook* (London: Routledge, 2000).

In this chapter I attempt to identify and discuss some leading Islamic ideological leitmotifs that, I suggest, have been determinative for the history of Jewish–Muslim relations and which, furthermore, remain critically important in respect to the way in which, broadly speaking, the Islamic world of today perceives and relates to Jews and Judaism. It is my contention that we need a critical understanding of Islamic views and ideological stances in respect to Judaism in general and, *inter alia*, Islamic perspectives on Israel and Jews, especially as they are entertained and expressed in the contemporary world where Islamic rhetoric and ideological values are increasingly impacting. At the very least, this is necessary in order to seek ways of addressing salient and pressing inter-communal and interreligious issues, most notably those that impinge on the contemporary *sitz im Leben* of Israel and the overall situation of the Middle East, together with, in *dar-al-Islam* (the abode or house of Islam), the continual linking of Jews and Judaism to a prejudiced notion of Zionism and a concomitant presupposition of economic and social imperialism.

If the founding of the State of Israel could in any sense be said to be the legacy of the relationship of Judaism to Christianity, as outworked historically into the modern age then, I suggest, the deeper issue to the vexed question of Israel and the Middle East today has to do with the trajectory of the relationship between Judaism and Islam, as it has been historically developed and is now lived out in the modern world. Understanding this trajectory poses a very particular challenge, one which requires careful analysis and reflection. There are many scholars who have been working away at various aspects of the relationship between Judaism and Islam. I have drawn on the work of some, and I have attempted to make a start for myself by identifying a schema of paradigms that would seem both to reflect the historical variants and developments of the relationship between Islam and Judaism, and to offer a hermeneutical framework for thinking through the contemporary situation and prospects for future Jewish–Muslim inter-relationship.

A paradigm schema

The term 'Islam' can carry a variety of meanings.[2] Ideologically, from the Muslim perspective, it can denote the notion of original monotheistic religion as such, that religion which finds its genesis in the exemplary submission to the will of God of the patriarch Abraham. Historically, the term 'Islam' can—and indeed most often does—simply denote an historical religion which has arisen out of a particular religious and linguistic milieu and developed over time. Third, there is a socio-cultural use of the term that sees it denoting a whole civilisation which has likewise evolved through time. Depending on the sense used, the discussion of Islam with respect to other religions, especially Islam and Jews, or Islam and Judaism, varies.

---

[2] Bernard Lewis, *The Jews of Islam* (London: Routledge Kegan Paul, 1984). See pp. 4ff.

I suggest that, today, the three senses are very often intertwined in terms of Islamic discourse about, and perceptions of, Jews and Judaism. However, although we need to pay attention to the historical sense, my primary concern here is ideological for, I contend, this is what drives much of the contemporary prejudicial attitudes that seem to be both widespread throughout, and deeply embedded within, the Islamic world. So, in seeking to discern the paradigms concerning relations with Jews that are operative in Islam, we need to begin at the beginning, with the life and times of Muhammad himself. I will look primarily at this category, which I call 'originating paradigms', then go on to discuss two other categories: historico-legal paradigms, which treats of dhimmitude, or rules and protocols governing the so-called 'Peoples of the Book', the dhimmi communities; and contemporary paradigms, which highlights what I can only describe as Islamic neo-antisemitism. Thus my overall schema is as follows.

- Originating Paradigms: *Medina and the Qur'an*
- Historico-legal Paradigms: *Dhimmi regulations*
- Contemporary Paradigms: *Islamic Neo-antisemitism*

Originating paradigms: Medina and the Qur'an

As we saw in Chapters 2 and 4 above, although Muhammad was born in Mecca in the year 570CE, received his calling and began his preaching task there, his founding of the Islamic community proper—the Ummah—occurred after the flight (al-hijra) in 622CE from Mecca to the northern city of Yathrib. This city was renamed Medina (in full, Medina-al-Nabi, the 'City of the Prophet') in honour of the presence of Muhammad and the rights granted to him to undertake sweeping social and political reforms. The town's leaders and people desired strong political and religious leadership in order that internal dissension and disputes might be resolved. So, Medina is the place where the structures, policies and ideology of the Islamic theocracy were inaugurated. In the process, two developments occurred that were to determine the essential shape and dynamic of the religion: political consolidation that provided the power base and religious practices that were to become the 'pillars' of Islam. The mandate for this development was given in a treaty document, the Constitution of Medina. Significantly, when it was first promulgated, it accepted and upheld the peaceful co-existence of three religious communities: Muslims, Jews, and Christians. Indeed, as Esposito remarks, 'Muhammad discussed and debated with, and granted freedom of religious thought and practice to, the Jews and the Christians, setting a precedent for peaceful and cooperative interreligious relations'.[3]

As the new community developed, alliances with the local Jews and neighbouring pagan Arabs for the purposes of defence and security within Medina

---

[3] John Esposito, *What Everyone Needs To Know About Islam* (New York: Oxford University Press, 2002), 73.

were secured, for the city of the Prophet was by no means made up wholly of Muslim Arabs. Furthermore, the Muslims of Medina were themselves by no means a single homogeneous group. In fact, Medina comprised, on the one hand, Arabs who were Muslims as well as non-believers together with, on the other hand, three major tribes of Jews and some Christians. Arab Muslims were either immigrants from Mecca (the Muhajirun) or those who originated from the former Yathrib (called the Ansar, or 'helpers'). These had previously converted and so assisted the Meccan Muslims at the time of the hijra. But it was only the Arabs who had invited Muhammad to Medina. Jews were not party to the negotiations, even though it was the Jews—who together actually comprised the majority of the original populace at Yathrib—who displayed considerable internal sectarian rivalries.

The Jews of Medina were, like the Arabs, tribal peoples. In fact, there were three main tribal groups of Jews in Medina. Muhammad, as we have learned, had initially been asked to arbitrate in a bitter feud between the two main Arab tribes. But soon tensions arose between the original Meccan Muslims and those originally of Yathrib, as well as between some of the Jews and the Muslim newcomers.[4] The socio-political context in which Islam came to birth was decidedly diverse. But in this context the founding Islamic attitudes toward religious plurality were positive. Significantly, as one Muslim commentator has noted of the situation at Medina, it 'was absolutely necessary that the Muslim, the Jew, and the Christian have an equal opportunity in their exercise of religious freedom as well as in their freedom to hold different opinions and to preach their own faiths'.[5]

However, to achieve the aims of an Islamic theocracy nothing less than a total socio-political upheaval was required. This involved, at least on the part of Arab converts, the relinquishing of the ways of old and *becoming* 'muslim', that is, subscribing and submitting to a political and social order which was 'carefully established and observed in the here and now as a road to the afterworld'.[6] Arabic personal and societal identities were to undergo an immense upheaval. Of course, this was not possible for everyone to undertake, and certainly not for the three Jewish communities initially resident in Medina. By the time of Muhammad there were certainly considerable numbers of Jews in Arabia who were, by and large, well integrated into the life and culture of the peninsula.[7] They 'spoke Arabic, were organized into clans and tribes, and had assimilated many of the values of desert

---

[4] Fred M. Donner, 'Muhammad and the Caliphate: Political History of the Islamic Empire up to the Mongol Conquest' in John L. Esposito, ed., *The Oxford History of Islam* (Oxford: Oxford University Press, 1999), 9.

[5] Husein Haykal, *The Life of Muhammad*, trans. Ismail Raji al-Faruqi (Kuala Lumpur: Islamic Book Trust, 1993), 175.

[6] Abd al-Rahman Azzam, *The Eternal Message of Muhammad* (Leicester: The Islamic Texts Society, 1993), 22.

[7] Cf. Bernard Lewis, *The Middle East: 2000 years of History from the Rise of Christianity to the Present Day* (London: Weidenfield and Nicolson, 1995), 47. See also Lewis, *The Jews of Islam, passim.*

society. They formed alliances and participated in intertribal feuds'.[8] Yet, even though there was a relatively high degree of assimilation into Arabian society, 'Jews were still viewed as a separate group with their own peculiar customs and characteristics'.[9]

Although, in the early days of Islam, the Constitution of Medina granted to the Jews who were members of the Medinese community certain rights and responsibilities, this status was granted 'only as long as the Jews did not act wrongfully'.[10] It is thus suggested that the very 'vagueness of this qualification was to provide Muhammad with a legal avenue for changing their status at a later date'.[11] Learned Jews were certainly not impressed by Muhammad and his claims. Nevertheless, as Muhammad held 'with an unshakable religious certainty that his revelations were true, he came to the logical conclusion that whatever the Jews were citing to contradict him must be false'.[12]

As it happened, when in 624CE Muhammad first moved against one of the Jewish tribes, evicting it from Medina after a short siege, the others offered no assistance.[13] At this stage, the precipitating issues were tribal, not religious or in any sense 'ethnic'. In the following year, when a second Jewish tribe failed to support Muhammad in battle (the fight took place on the Jewish Sabbath and the Muslim forces were at this time defeated), Muhammad moved decisively against them. That Jewish tribe fled to a nearby oasis that was subsequently overrun by Muhammad's forces. As was customary in these situations, all the men were killed and the women and children taken into captivity.

When Medina was besieged by the Meccans in 627CE, the last remaining significant Jewish tribe assisted with the erection of defensive fortifications but then vacillated about active participation in aiding the Muslims against the Meccans. In essence they trusted neither side. However, after Muhammad defeated the Meccans he turned on these Jews for their lack of direct support. Following their surrender, after a 25-day siege, once again the men were killed and the women and children taken into slavery.[14] Any Jews remaining in Medina were effectively forced to leave.

Elsewhere, as Arabia came under Muslim rule, Jews and Christians both paid the jizya, initially a tribute then later, from 632CE, a poll tax. This taxation supposedly received divine sanction in 630CE with the revelation of Sura 9:29. It speaks of both the payment and the humility of the one paying, laying the

---

[8]   Norman A. Stillman, *The Jews of Arab Lands: A History and Source Book* (Philadelphia: The Jewish Publication Society of America, 1979), 4.

[9]   Ibid., 4.

[10]   Ibid., 11.

[11]   Ibid.

[12]   Ibid., 12.

[13]   See ibid., 13.

[14]   Ibid., 15.

groundwork for a perspective of divine legitimacy for the Muslim humiliation of Jews.

> The injunction was clear and unequivocal ... The non-Muslim was to be subjugated. He was made to be a tribute bearer, and he was to be humbled. Just how he was to be humbled was to be more explicitly defined as time went on. But the basis for his position in Muslim Arab society was permanently established by the eternal word of Allah.[15]

A close and detailed geographic and literary analysis of the evidence of Medina and its Jewish inhabitants on the eve of the Islamic era and during the early days of Islam, such as that undertaken by Michael Lecker,[16] yields critical insight not only into the detailed subtleties of life in Medina but also of the complex relationship between Muhammad, the Muslims of Medina and the Jews of Medina. Equally, a careful exegetical and hermeneutical reading of the Qur'an, especially in the light of the biography of Muhammad, indicates an early Medinan period in which Judaic and Christian elements and issues loomed large, albeit generally in a favourable light. The emerging Muslim faith seems to have been viewed as relating positively to these forebears. For Muslims, Jews and Christians were to be honoured as co-equally 'People of the Book', even though, from an Islamic theological point of view, Jews and Christians may have gone somewhat astray.

But there is also evidence of a late Medinan period, in which there is a noticeable hardening of attitude to Judaism and Christianity, and a series of proclamations of the final triumph of a distinct teaching, namely that which Muhammad had been commissioned by God to convey. The late Medinan suras in the Qur'an are also marked by a pronounced legislative tone. They are generally longer than the early chapters. They are less combative and often convey a sense of dominating authoritative pronouncement. A careful exegesis gives the clue, as Bernard Lewis, for example, indicates:

> The political problem posed by the relations between Muslim and non-Muslim was already clear in the lifetime of the Prophet, and the principles for its solution are contained in the Qur'an. As chief magistrate and later ruler of the community of Medina, the Prophet had Jewish subjects; as sovereign of the Islamic state he had relations with both Christian and Jewish neighbours in other parts of Arabia.[17]

If the problem was evident during the lifetime of the Prophet, what are the clues to the Quranic solution that Bernard Lewis refers to? What, indeed, can we say are the paradigms of Islamic attitude toward, and relationship with, Jews and Judaism

---

[15] Ibid., 20.

[16] See Michael Lecker, *Muslims, Jews and Pagans: Studies in Early Islamic Medina* (Leiden: E. J. Brill, 1995).

[17] Lewis, *The Jews of Islam*, 11.

that have been bequeathed to Islam from out of the Medinan context and the resulting formulation of the Qur'an?

Robert Wistrich points out that the Qur'an clearly echoes Muhammad's own interaction with Jews wherein he 'brands the Jews as enemies of Islam or depicts them as possessing a malevolent, rebellious spirit'.[18] Wistrich clearly sees that the main archetype derived from the negative Quranic portrayal 'is that Jews have rejected Allah's truth and always persecuted His prophets, including Mohammed who had been given the perfected version of their own revelation'.[19] A selection of verses, which provide the later Quranic overview that the Israelites attracted divine wrath for their unbelief, thus contribute to the Muslim conclusion that God's anger and curse toward Jews is simply *because* they are Jews. Furthermore, as Bruce Feiler comments, 'Islamic midrash, known as *tafsir*, is considered harsher toward Jews than toward Christians, largely because of the political circumstances during the prophet's lifetime'; thus he avers that 'Muslims prefer Christians to Jews because the latter actively opposed the prophet in Medina'.[20]

More, of course, could be said concerning the idea of 'originating' paradigms of Islamic relations to Jews and Judaism, upon which the base for a profound prejudicial attitude had been laid. And we need to remember that from out of the early Quranic material and the Constitution of Medina there are paradigms of positive predisposition and relationship. Historically, however, it would seem that such positive originating paradigms have been for the most part eclipsed by the negative, which then have tended to be regarded, it appears, as the normative originating paradigms. From the context of origins we move to the realm of socio-historical development and ask, what of Muslim treatment of Jewish communities within their midst?

Historico-legal paradigms: dhimmi regulations

Muhammad was a political and military leader on a divinely sanctioned mission. At least that is the Islamic perspective. Certainly, 'Muhammad became a statesman in order to accomplish his mission as a prophet, not vice versa, and it is clear that the more strictly religious aspect of these relationships was also a prime concern'.[21] In the course of discharging his mission the prime task, given the context of religious plurality of the day, was to assert the dominance of the one true religion over all others such that 'political classification was between those who had been conquered or who had submitted themselves to the power of Islam and those who had not'.[22]

---

[18] Robert S. Wistrich, *Anti-Semitism: The Longest Hatred* (London: Mandarin, 1992), 199.

[19] Ibid., 200.

[20] Bruce Feiler, *Abraham: A Journey to the Heart of Three Faiths* (New York: William Morrow, 2002), 174.

[21] Lewis, *The Jews of Islam*, 12.

[22] Ibid., 21.

From out of this context there arose, in connection with those religions that were deemed to stand within the religious lineage of Islam—namely other religions of the Book such as Christianity and Judaism—the regulations of protection, submission and deference that applied to the communities of followers of these religions, the so-called *dhimmi* communities. The Quranic injunction to honour co-religionists was tempered by the motif of submission. In this regard Lewis notes that Muslim discrimination against Jews, albeit profound enough, nonetheless 'never reached the levels of Christian hostility to Jews' rather, by contrast to deep Christian antipathy towards Jews, 'the Muslim attitude toward non-Muslims is one not of hate or fear or envy but simply of contempt'.[23] Yet, even by the ninth century, as Feiler remarks, both 'Christians and Jews in Baghdad were obliged to wear yellow emblems on their clothes, the origin of the yellow badge later used by the Nazis against Jews'.[24] Muslim superiority to both Jews and Christians was being asserted in overt political terms, and variations on this would continue within the world of Islam down to the modern era.

However, Judaism is not simply one among a number of religions of the Book. Although, together with Christianity, there is a distinctive influence upon Islam that can be traced to Judaism, the historical and prophetic lineage of the religion of the Jews clearly meant it ranked as the primary 'other' over against which Islam, in its formative years, had to distinguish itself. Furthermore, linguistic affinity meant that some Jewish terms and concepts crossed over into the speech of Arabs. Similarly, religious ideas, ethical notions, and the like were disseminated among Arabs who came into close contact with Jews.[25]

So, in the very process of determining its own identity and points of reference, Islam found itself drawing upon various types of literature which Muslim scholars attributed primarily to Jewish sources. The Islamic term for this literary source is *Isra'iliyyat*, in respect of which Ronald Nettler has made the following observation.

> Probably the most prominent type of this literature was the 'stories of the prophets' (*qisas al-anbiya'*) genre. Classical Islam in its main Sunni traditions typically dealt with this 'alien' material through the general principle that whatever was not contrary to Islam would be acceptable, and that which was contrary would be rejected. This allowed a large amount of *Isra'iliyyat* material to be absorbed and assimilated within Islamic 'canonical' textual traditions.[26]

---

[23] Ibid., 33.
[24] Feiler, *Abraham*, 177.
[25] See Lewis, *The Jews of Islam, passim.*
[26] Ronald L. Nettler, 'Early Islam, Modern Islam and Judaism: The Isra'iliyyat in Modern Islamic Thought' in Ronald L. Nettler and Suha Taji-Farouki, eds, *Muslim–Jewish Encounters: Intellectual Traditions and Modern Politics* (Amsterdam: Harwood Academic Publishers, 1998), 3.

Nettler concludes that the 'presence of the *Isra'iliyyat* within Islam constitutes an important example of traditional Islamic–Jewish cultural interaction and symbiosis which implicitly overrode the built-in monotheistic exclusivism on both sides ...'.[27] This gives a clue to one dimension of Muslim–Jewish relations, namely that of positive cultural interaction.

During the reign of the Caliph Umar (634–44CE) a theoretical treaty between the People of the Book and the Muslim state was enacted. It is known as the 'Pact of Umar'. It was

> a writ of protection (*amaan* or *dhimma*) extended by Allah's community to their protégés (*ahl al-dhimma* or *dhimmis*). In return for the safeguarding of life and property and the right to worship unmolested according to their conscience, the *dhimmis* had to pay the *jizya* (poll-tax) and the *kharaj* (land-tax). They were to conduct themselves with the demeanour and comportment befitting a subject population.[28]

Many of the provisions and restrictions of the pact were only elaborated with the passage of time. It is clear that terms imposed upon the conquered peoples varied greatly, and this variation depended upon the conditions surrounding their surrender. However, Norman Stillman remarks that the Jews

> were psychologically better able to adapt to the new facts of life created by the Arab's conquest than were either the Christians or Zoroastrians. They had already been a subject people for over five centuries. The rabbis had given them a concept of Jewishness that was independent of physical territory or political sovereignty. Their God was still the God of history, and they were still His chosen people. They were in *galut* (exile), and it was simply not yet over.[29]

Clearly the Islamic authorities were concerned that taxes be paid and that dhimmi subjects acknowledge in a variety of ways, some more and some less humiliating, the dominion of Islam. 'As long as the non-Muslims complied, they were accorded a good measure of internal self-rule. However, even in the conduct of their own communal affairs, they were not entirely free of government supervision and, at times, downright interference'.[30] At best Jews, as with other dhimmi communities, would enjoy considerable communal autonomy 'precisely because the state did not care what they did so long as they paid their taxes, kept the peace, and remained in their place'.[31] Nonetheless, the scene was set for a problematic history of interaction. A lot would depend on local circumstances. Clearly, a paradigmatic line is set: limits

---

[27] Ibid.

[28] Stillman, *The Jews of Arab Lands*, 25.

[29] Ibid., 27.

[30] Ibid., 38.

[31] Ibid., 39.

to dhimmi autonomy would be determined down the centuries of Islamic rule by Islamic expectations. Non-Muslims would know themselves to be a people submitted to those who themselves live in submission to Allah.

Examples of positive interaction certainly abound in the history of Islam and Jewish encounter. But it is also the case that negative perceptions, arising from the first close encounter in Medina, and developed throughout the variegated history of the application and interpretation of dhimmi regulations, also predominate. Nettler notes that, recently, 'in official "establishment" Islamic circles, such as al-Azhar, the equation between the misbehaviour of ancient Jews (particularly in Medina) and the modern misbehaviour of Zionist Jews in Palestine became an intellectual paradigm for some'.[32] Originating paradigms have remained, even through a history of relationships with the Peoples of the Book, including Jews, by way of the paradigms of dhimmi rules and regulations. Once again, much more can be said—and probably needs to be said—in order to gain a fuller understanding of this dimension of the relationship between Judaism and Islam, or more particularly, between the Islamic ummah and communities of Jews. For our purposes here, however, it is simply a case of being reminded of a legacy of negative perspective of, and so relationship with, Jews and Judaism so far as Islam is concerned. It is a feature of Islamic life that is embedded in its origins and has been proscribed by the particular paradigm of dhimmitude. With this in mind we turn to the contemporary context and my contention as to where the origins and history of Muslim–Jewish relations has headed during the nineteenth and twentieth centuries. It is this that constitutes the vexing legacy that must be addressed, with care and with urgency, in the opening years of the twenty-first century of the Common Era.

Contemporary paradigms: Islamic neo-antisemitism

Late in the twentieth century, a Muslim scholar reviewed two pieces of literature that appeared in the latter 1960s, a time characterized in the Arab world by the politics of Pan-Arabism and confrontation with Israel. Such writings represent a response to the Arab defeat in Palestine and the creation and consolidation of the state of Israel, and an effort to make sense out of this within the broader experience of colonialist intrusion into Muslim lands. The author of the review, Suha Taji-Farouki, notes that these writings adopt an essentialist approach, attributing to Jews 'an unchanging nature, which persists across the centuries'.[33] Thus is given, from a Muslim perspective,

> a convincing explanation for current Zionist successes and abuses in Palestine, and for
> perceived Jewish political and economic entrenchment and domination in other parts of

---

[32] Nettler, 'Early Islam', 11.

[33] Suha Taji-Farouki, 'A Contemporary Construction of the Jews in the Qur'an: A Review of Muhammad Sayyid Tantawi's Banu Isra'il fi al-Qur'an wa al-Sunna and 'Afif 'Abd al-Fattah Tabbara's Al-yahud fi al-Qur'an', in Nettler and Taji-Farouki, *Muslim–Jewish Encounters*, 15.

the world. To confirm the timeless and unpleasant Jewish character they uphold, these writings also recruit observations on Jewish nature emanating from sources extraneous to the Islamic (and Arab) traditions.[34]

An Israeli scholar, Ilan Pappe, published conjointly with the Muslim, notes a new categorisation of Palestinian political attitudes towards Jews, Zionism or Israel that emerged in the late twentieth century, namely, 'a spectrum between militancy and maximalism on the one hand, and pragmatism, moderation, and mainstream politics, on the other'.[35] However, Taji-Farouki makes a telling comment:

> While changing political circumstances may have raised awareness of the question of contextualizing Qur'anic verses depicting the Jews in a negative light, it should not be forgotten that the issue remains part of a broader modern internal Islamic debate concerning the correct hermeneutical approach to Islamic scripture. An unjust regional settlement and the emergence of an inequitable new order in the Middle East can only strengthen the hand of those who argue against a contextually-rooted and rational reading, with its concomitant emphasis on the promotion of tolerance and dialogue.[36]

With the dawn of the modern era, and the early penetration of European influence and colonisation with respect to Islamic lands of the Middle East, there was a weakening of traditional Islamic norms of society and so a concomitant improvement in the lot of Jewish and other dhimmi communities. Although reforms were slow, eventually the Ottomans, for example, abolished the jizya tax. By comparison, reforms in Morocco were very tardy, and required high-level diplomatic pressure, especially from the British as, for instance, with the 1863 intervention of Sir Moses Montefiore and a British Jewish delegation. Stillman remarks:

> It is a great irony that during the nineteenth century, which was the very period when the legal and economic position of the Jews was improving throughout the Arab world, the physical security of Jewish persons and property was quite precarious and in many places was actually declining. This insecurity was in part because of a general deterioration of the forces of law and order in most Arab lands.[37]

For example, in Iraq, and particularly Baghdad, throughout much of the nineteenth century relations between Muslims and non-Muslims were most often quite tense. There were 'numerous anti-Jewish and anti-Christian riots, some limited and some on a large scale' often because 'Jews and Christians were especially vulnerable to

---

[34] Ibid.

[35] Ilan Pappe, 'Understanding the Enemy: A Comparative Analysis of Palestinian Islamist and Nationalist Leaflets, 1920s—1980s', in Nettler and Taji-Farouki, eds., 104.

[36] Taji-Farouki, ibid., 34.

[37] Stillman, *The Jews of Arab Lands*, 101.

accusations that they had blasphemed against Muhammad or that they had once converted to Islam and thereafter apostasized. Capital punishment was called for in either case'.[38]

By this time it would not be impossible to imagine that certain antisemitic sentiments abroad within Christian Europe were finding their way into the consciousness, and subsequently the discourse, of Muslims who were interacting with the West. One example of this is the famous—or infamous—'blood libel' incident of 1840 that occurred within the Arab world, the so-called Damascus Affair.

> This affair was touched off by the disappearance of an Italian Capuchin friar and his native servant in Damascus on February 5, 1840. The local Christians, supported by the French consul Ratti-Menton, accused the Jews of having murdered the two men in order to obtain their blood for the coming Passover. A Jewish barber was arrested and made a 'confession' under torture, implicating seven leading members of the community in the crime. All were arrested and tortured. Two died under examination, one saved himself by embracing Islam, and the others 'confessed'. ... News of the trials and confessions spread throughout the Levant and were believed by Muslims as well as Christians. The [Jewish] community in Damascus became subject to mob violence, and there were reprisals against Jews in other parts of the province.[39]

Furthermore, the late nineteenth century saw the appearance of European-type antisemitic literature within the Arab world, especially within communities under French influence. Stillman remarks that, in general, the inception of antisemitism in the Arab world could be seen

> as part of the struggle of one partially emancipated minority—the Christians—to protect itself against the economic competition of another partially emancipated but less assimilated minority—the Jews. The vast majority of Muslim Arabs did not yet perceive the Jews as an economic or political threat. This would come in the twentieth century with the confrontation of opposing Jewish and Arab nationalisms.[40]

Colonialism was certainly a mixed bag so far as Muslims were concerned. But for Jews it would seem that those in Muslim lands with British contacts fared better than Jews in Muslim lands with French connections.

Although we need to acknowledge that it is notoriously difficult to make generalisations about antisemitism in Islamic lands, nevertheless some summary comment that indicates broad patterns of experience is warranted. Wistrich remarks that there were, indeed, times when

---

[38] Ibid., 103.

[39] Ibid., 105.

[40] Ibid., 107.

tolerance towards Jews prevailed and they made real intellectual advances, enjoyed economic prosperity and occasionally even some political influence. But more often, their existence from northern Africa to Iran was punctuated by misery, humiliation and persecution.[41]

Wistrich is critical of the resurgence of Islamic attention to the idea and meaning of dhimmi status. He contends there is a 'renewed and obsessive Muslim concern with Jews and Judaism in the contemporary world and the inability of Islam to transcend obsolete stereotypes from a bygone era'.[42] While political and ideological elements play a part, the underlying paradigmatic driver is, arguably, theological or religious. For example, from a Muslim perspective 'Islam didn't supersede Christianity and Judaism, it preceded them. Islam, in fact, was the faith of Abraham, which his descendants twisted for their own purposes'.[43] First and foremost of the descendants doing the twisting is, of course, the Jews.

In the twentieth century, the decade of the 1930s saw not only the rise of German National Socialism as a force to be reckoned with in the European context, but also succour lent, by Nazism, to latent antisemitism within Palestine and the Arab world in general. Arab anti-Zionism grew stronger in tandem with German-focused antisemitism. Thus, there were many Arabs who 'clearly realised that German antisemitism was above all anti-Jewish and evidently rejoiced that a great European power was putting Jews in their place'.[44]

Arabs were portrayed by some, at least, as the 'natural allies of Germany, as could be seen by their mutual enemies: the British, the Jews, and the communists'.[45] The Grand Mufti of Jerusalem, Haj Amin al-Husseini was a significant figure who identified with Nazi political rhetoric concerning the Jews. Wistrich notes the significance of the silence of Palestinians and other Arabs in respect to the complicity of the Grand Mufti in the Holocaust. It is clear that, in terms of rhetoric and polemics, if not in underlying ideology, the 'post-war struggle for Palestine was strictly divorced from the Jewish tragedy in Europe'.[46]

It must be remembered, of course, that the 'other' in terms of Palestinian religio-political discourse was, and probably still is, identified as the Zionist, or Israeli, rather than the Jew *per se*. In consequence, as Wistrich wistfully, if not resignedly, comments:

Ethnocentrism and religious arrogance on both sides are now too strong to permit subtle distinctions between Zionists and Jews among the masses. The atavistic hatred between

---

[41] Wistrich, *Anti-Semitism*, 195.

[42] Ibid., 221.

[43] Feiler, *Abraham*, 176.

[44] Wistrich, 245.

[45] Ibid.; see also Joan Peters, *From Time Immemorial: The Origins of the Arab–Jewish Conflict over Palestine* (London, 1984).

[46] Wistrich, 246.

the sons of Isaac and of Ishmael, between the followers of Moses and Mohammed, threatens to drown out the still, small voice of reason.[47]

Since the 1960s there has been a voluminous output of Arabic antisemitic literature that is quite independent of any connection with earlier European antisemitism. In no way can the apparent paradox of Arab, or Islamic, antisemitism be apologetically defended as a 'foreign import'. As Wistrich has remarked, today 'antisemitic diatribes against Zionism in an international forum, when used by Arabs, aim to find common ground with a Western Christian audience. In a Middle Eastern context, it would be more common to vilify Jews and Israel as expressions of Western culture'.[48]

The twentieth century has seen a distinct upsurge of anti-Jewish—antisemitic—literature within the Islamic world, most disturbingly with the coming together 'of archetypes fixed in the consciousness of early Islam with the theories of a "world Jewish conspiracy" adapted from modern European antisemitism'.[49] And as Wistrich points out, Islamic antisemitic attitudes 'are actively encouraged and spread into the Muslim diaspora in Asia, Africa and Europe by government financing coming particularly from Iran, Saudi Arabia and Libya'.[50] As far as the world-conspiracy idea is concerned, Wistrich avers that it 'has long served to compensate Muslims for the unpalatable reality of repeated defeats at Israel's hands. It has sought to make Israel's existence and its goals appear sinister in the eyes of Arabs, Muslims and sympathetic outsiders in the Third World'.[51] Furthermore, Zionism is constantly linked to Western imperialism as

> a deceptively powerful, omnipotent force which would otherwise dissolve without sustenance from outside. Above all, the antisemitic conspiracy theory serves to mobilise the destructive passions in the Muslim and Arab population, in order to reinforce the will to fight for Islam. In the words of Hamas in one of the opening sentences in its official Covenant: 'Israel will exist and continue to exist until Islam will obliterate it, just as it obliterated others before it'.[52]

Wistrich makes the point that there is both a theological and metaphysical dimension to the clash between Islam and the Jews.[53] The Arab–Israeli conflict is not simply territorial and political. It is inherently religious. 'Palestinian Arab leaders repeatedly asserted that anarchism and revolution were inherent in the

---

[47] Ibid., 251.
[48] Ibid., 257.
[49] Ibid., 222.
[50] Ibid., 223.
[51] Ibid., 239.
[52] Ibid.
[53] ibid., 223.

Jewish "character",' and Palestinian anti-Zionist rhetoric earlier in the twentieth century tended to focus on the desire to protect the Islamic and Arabic character of Palestine and its people from a perceived secular threat.[54] Polemical use has been made of the scurrilous and discredited *The Protocols of the Elders of Zion*, which has found recent ominous resurgence in Egypt as the subject of a TV soap opera.

A report of some field research, undertaken not too long ago and involving an interview with a local Imam in East Jerusalem is most telling. Although, of course, hardline exclusivist perspectives can be found to a degree in all religions, not least Judaism and Christianity, as well as Islam, the point is made that, in this context at least, the viewpoint of the Imam does rather represent wider and more generally held popular Muslim perspectives. Jews and Christians are alike dismissed as inferior to Muslims in their devotion and correct worship of God. These People of the Book are given 'opportunity to submit ... and follow the rule of God. But you ignore him because you have become strong. ... You do the opposite of what God wants. ... God gives you many chances, but of course we know you are not going to follow'.[55] Furthermore, from the very heart of Israel comes an Islamic view—by no means should it be thought to be an isolated or idiosyncratic view—that sees Jews as necessarily following the wrong path and thereby attracting the punishment of God. And the reason given is 'because you abhor Islam and try to destroy the religion of the Creator. By forcing your ideas and way of thinking on the world, you show your hatred for God'.[56] The chillingly sinister opinion is offered that 'punishment is going to come from the Creator, but of course through the people. Like Hitler, for instance'.[57] Islamic antipathy to Jews appears to run very deep indeed. Of course, in the context of contemporary Israel-Palestine, such profoundly negative views come as no surprise. But that does not lessen the problematic, nor diminish the thesis, of relational paradigms I am here exploring. Contemporary attitudes have contemporary referents; but in this case they also have a paradigmatic history. Unless and until that is addressed – together, of course, with the contemporary socio-political referents of such attitudes – there is little chance of any attitudinal change being brought about, and so little prospect for an advance in Jewish–Muslim relations.

Conclusion

A brief account such as this is sufficient only to demonstrate a disturbing trend in terms of the paradigms of relationship between Islam and Judaism, or at least between Islam and Jews. The issues underlying this trend, intimated by use of the hermeneutic of paradigm development, are complex and deep. At the birth of

---

[54] Ibid., 242.

[55] Feiler, *Abraham*, 179.

[56] Ibid., 180.

[57] Ibid.

Islam, in the city of Medina, the first intimations of the nascent religious system were positive so far as relations with both Christians and Jews were concerned. But it is matter of historical record that things changed for the worse. As Esposito has remarked, the resulting confrontation

> became part of the baggage of history and would continue to influence the attitudes of some Muslims in later centuries. Recently, this legacy can be seen in official statements from Hamas and Osama bin Laden. Both not only condemn Jews for Israeli occupation and policies in Palestine but also see the current conflict as just the most recent iteration of an age-old conflict dating back to the Jews' 'rejection and betrayal' of Islam and the Prophet's community at Medina.[58]

It would seem that, at first reading, the originating paradigm is dominated by the notion of the Jew as untrustworthy; the dhimmi development is predominated by a sense of contempt, and the contemporary paradigm is clearly one of resurgent antisemitism of the worst kind. This is not a comfortable picture, but does it necessarily suggest a rather sombre, if not hopeless, conclusion?

Historically, there have been many examples of good relations between Jews and Muslims, and there is good recent work that asserts close religious and other parallels between Islam and Judaism sufficient to strike a hopeful note for the future. Indeed,

> Judaism and Islam are comparable in that they concur that God cares deeply not only about attitudes but actions, not only about what one says to God but how one conducts affairs at home and in the village. God aims at sanctifying the social order, not only private life. Both religions agree that God aims at the reconstruction of society in accord with norms of holiness and that God has ... specified precisely the character of those norms.[59]

Furthermore,

> In general, seen up close Judaism and Islam as religions of law exhibit significant divergence, but, viewed in the larger context of world religions, they stand side by side in their fundamental convictions about God and the social order.[60]

There is a legacy of shared fundamental convictions, as well as a history of divergence. Distinctions are real, and so too are the prospects for peaceful co-existence for, as it has been affirmed:

> Both history and contemporary affairs testify that Islam and Judaism know how to co-exist in a comfortable and tolerant relationship, each honoring the other for its faith in

---

[58] Esposito, *What Everyone Needs To Know About Islam*, 81.

[59] Neusner, Sonn and Brockopp, *Judaism and Islam in Practice*, vii.

[60] Neusner and Sonn, *Comparing Religions*, vii.

the shared, one and only God. Not only in such Muslim countries as Turkey and Morocco, but also in the West, both secular and Christian, the faithful of Islam and Judaism, along with Christians of every communion, work at living together in harmony.[61]

This appears hopeful, and certainly must not be underplayed. Equally, however, the realisation that signs of hope come under a constant barrage of undermining rhetoric and terrorising action cannot be ignored or dismissed as an irritant aberration.

There are deep issues to be addressed and resolved, and, I suggest, one starting place is with the underlying paradigms that each side in any relationship holds with respect to the other. On the one hand the arena of basic religious prejudice, expressing itself in variant forms of superiority or exclusivity of one over another, needs to be addressed. Both parties to any Jewish–Muslim interfaith dialogue need to recognise 'that each religion is an interpretive venture'.[62] Triumphalism must be countered if there is to be any advance. On the other hand, whilst acknowledging real difficulties in terms of advancing Jewish–Muslim relations, Rabbi David Rosen nevertheless sounds a hopeful note:

> We should indeed keep the differences ... and learn to respect them. Each religion has its *particular* approach to God. But we also have a *universal* dimension to our traditions that we share, and we must emphasize that as well.[63]

Unfortunately, it would seem, the present-day impasse in the Middle East concerning Israel and the status of Palestinians (not all of whom are Muslim, it must be said) is the touchstone to global Jewish–Muslim relations. However, simplistic and all-too-common dichotomous views that rely, for example, on a superficial assessment of the situation of Jews and Judaism, and of Palestinians and Islam, in the context of the Middle East, do not help. Assessments of the struggles besetting Israelis and Palestinians are reduced by some—in particular, religious fundamentalists—to a generalised religio-ethnic clash. Arguably for Israel, however, the issue is not simply a question of a just settlement for Palestinians *per se*: Jewish sensitivities concerning justice and human co-operation with the divine might have otherwise resolved that long ago.

At its historical inception through the Prophet Muhammad, Islam emerged in the religious lineage of, and as a rival to, both Christianity and Judaism. There is, I have suggested, a critical factor which militates against Israel and impugns Jews and Judaism, namely the negative dimensions of the predominant and contemporary Islamic paradigms of Jews and Judaism. Such paradigms of ideological leitmotifs require careful scrutiny and contextual understanding and, if

---

[61] Ibid., xi.

[62] Feiler, *Abraham*, 202.

[63] Cited in Feiler, 204.

there is to be any change, any advance in the relationship pattern to which they have been applied, they need also to be critiqued, addressed, and countered by recourse to the development of alternative paradigms. The three broad sets of Islamic attitudes toward Jewish–Muslim relations, identified here in general preliminary terms as originating, historico-legal, and contemporary paradigms and discussed above, constitute but a sketch, an interpretive overview, of a complex issue. Much more is to be discerned and debated.

Chapter 8

Islamic Identity and Ideologies
Contemporary Contours

A wide spectrum of humanity adheres to Islam. Indeed, over a billion people—representing many different races and cultures—are Muslim. Yet within this diversity there may also be found the idea of a universal Islamic culture (*adab*) which includes mores, language, behaviour, and so on, and which unites Muslims across the divides of ethnicity. As Akbar Ahmed remarks: 'It is *adab* that defines a Muslim: one can be a bad Muslim from the orthodox point of view and yet be a good one because of *adab*, and vice versa. A convert to Islam may master Arabic and be an orthodox Muslim yet be weak on *adab*'.[1] There are, of course, several major languages that predominate in different parts of the Muslim world of which Arabic is only one. But being the language of the Qur'an it holds pride of place. Key Arabic religious words and phrases are found throughout the Islamic world, or 'abode of Islam' (dar-al-Islam), whatever the local *lingua franca*. In Islam religion (*din*) and culture (adab) intimately intertwine: there is not really one without the other. Personal Islamic identity is bound up with communal identity, which is itself located and contextualised within the bounds of time and space. Today, in many lands, Muslim people are seeking to recover and assert their identity as Muslims, and Islamic communities are seeking to shape their destiny according to Islamic ideology. This is happening all across the abode of Islam, involving countries as different as Turkey, Afghanistan, Iran, Pakistan, Nigeria, Somalia and Malaysia; and none of these is ethnically or culturally Arabic.

In this chapter I shall briefly review a range of factors that contribute to what might be called the 'contours' of Islam in the modern world. I begin by looking at the construction of Muslim identity in general terms then undertake a brief exploration of the issue of Islam and modernity. A range of ideological options that express something of the diversity of Islamic identity, and which features within the Muslim world today, will then be outlined. Finally, at the risk of some oversimplification of what is in reality a very diverse and complex subject, I shall discuss the Middle East as, arguably, something of a 'hub' of Islamic identity in the contemporary world, at least in respect to the place and impact of Saudi Arabia and Egypt.

---

[1] Akbar S. Ahmed, *Living Islam* (London: BBC Books, 1993), 17.

Islamic identity: some factors

There are, I suggest, at least six key factors that cumulatively construct the essential, or grounding, Islamic identity. They are what make people 'Muslim' in a generic sense. Specific and local Islamic identity develops from there. These factors are interrelated, comprising a structure that leads into the development of a fuller, locally or regionally contextualised, identity that comprises other contributing elements as well. In simple terms, I would argue that, at heart, Islamic identity is a function of the complex interrelationship of community (Ummah), tradition and history, personal piety, daily life (belief and duty), relationships and society (especially as mediated through the regulations of Shari'a), and finally geographic location. The starting point for understanding Muslim identity is undoubtedly the idea of Ummah as such, which was discussed at some length in Part I, especially Chapter 4. The concept, and concrete reality, of the Ummah is found in the sense of belonging to a single overarching community under God that is at once both an ideal yet-to-be-realised and an everyday, diverse, localised context in which a Muslim actually exists.

As we have seen, during the course of his lifetime Muhammad instigated a new political identity within Arabia and laid down the basis for universal Islamic religious belief and communal life. The net result was a theocracy, a community believed to be shaped and guided by God: the Islamic Ummah. This, I suggest, is the foremost key to understanding Islamic identity. The outcome of the early emergence and development of community, with its central stress on unity and cohesion, was the postulation, and indeed execution, of a theocratic model that, though in practice over time has been variously modified, nevertheless remains a powerful and venerated ideal. Islamic identity is grounded within community.

The division of Islam into two broad groups, Sunni and Shi'a, signals of course the dual context for the development of tradition and history: there are, in reality, two major Muslim stories to be told—and within these two, even more. Nevertheless, this foundational two-fold distinction signals differing views on the nature of the Islamic community and related issues of Muslim identity. If the ideal of 'Ummah' is couched in terms of a single unified community, the socio-religious reality from early on was of diversification of tradition and history. Islamic identity thus contains within it a tension, even dialectic, between singularity and diversity. This dialectic flows into the element of personal piety that contributes to identity. There is but one Qur'an, the pious goal being to recite it entirely from memory in its original Arabic. But, as we have discovered, there are multiple collections of hadith: the Sunnah of the Prophet lends itself to great diversity of interpretation and application. Sufism, as we saw, is the phenomenon within Islam that gives particular evidence of both deep experiential piety and the diversity of religious expression and experience.

Muslims everywhere, of whatever race and culture, are united in the requirements of belief and duty, and this is given concrete expression and realisation on a daily basis. To that extent, Islamic identity is something overt and obvious. Furthermore, Muslim identity is reinforced and refined by the canons of Islamic Law (Shari'a). Though grounded in the idea of a singularity of Divine Law, Shari'a is nevertheless diversely expressed and interpreted within the wider world of Islam. Furthermore, diversity of identity is found in terms of geographic location. Whereas the rise of the Ummah eclipsed its Arab origins and resulted in a trans-national entity—Islam embraces many races and ethnic identities—a significant feature of the contemporary Islamic world is that, in some cases, an identification of ethnic with religious identity has occurred. Islam presents, on the one hand, as a universalising global religion; yet, on the other hand, in countries such as Turkey, Malaysia and Indonesia, ethnic identity equates with religious identity. One can be a Turkish citizen and hold a religion other than Islam, but one cannot, by definition, be an ethnic Turk and not be Muslim. Similarly, ethnic Malays and Indonesians are, by definition, Muslim.

Religious identity is also a function of values. That is, certain values find expression in religion and, conversely, the expression of the values contributes to particular religious identity. Ethical values and religious identity are often intimately intertwined. Compassion, justice, benevolence, reason, and wisdom may be reckoned as among the principle values of Islam. Of course, we might recognise such values as universal: they can be found expressed in just about any religion. More distinctive to the Islamic religion *per se* are values such as *unity*, derived from tawhid, and *submission*—that grounding of the being of all things in a particular relationship to the Creator, a relationship of 'onto-theological deference'. The being of human being exists in deference to the being of the Divine.

The third distinctive value for Islam, I would suggest, is that of the Divine Law—Shari'a—itself. By this I do not just mean mundane law codes and rules, but rather more the sense of law expressing justice and giving voice to wide-ranging principles of jurisprudence. In this sense Islam is a religion whose leitmotif is submission to living the divinely prescribed way for humanity. In consequence, leading Muslim scholars and religious leaders (mullahs, ayatollahs; scholars as a group—the ulema) are not just theologians but are also jurists: the essence of Islam is conveyed in both belief and law. There is not one without the other.

Identity and modernity

The nineteenth century saw a revival of interest in classical Islam within the Muslim world. Two chief reasons were the dominance of Sufism during the late Middle Ages, which posed something of a threat to normative Sunnism, and the rising dominance of the West as a colonising force. By the term 'the West' I mean, of course, the complex political, cultural and religious entity of Western Europe of the day. With its rival religion and culture, the West—once overshadowed by the unity and power of the world of Islam—was seemingly united against all things Islamic. The Muslim response to this marks the beginnings of contemporary Islamic reformism and revivalism and underpins Muslim reaction to, and struggle with, modernity. The discussion in this section will touch on some salient background factors then briefly address issues of unity and diversity, Islamic fundamentalism, decline, political and social responses to modernity; and offer some comment on the contemporary socio-cultural climate of Islam.

Background Factors

Prior to the modern era the most powerful Islamic empires had been the Safavid empire in Iran, the Mughal empire in India, and the Ottoman empire radiating out from Turkey. The spread of their impact was felt not only in Europe but also in North Africa and West Asia as well.[2] Indeed, no less than four races 'were responsible for moulding the political aspect of Islam down the centuries: the Arabs, the Iranians, the Turks and the Indians'.[3] But then came the aggrandisement of an economically powerful and consumer-hungry West. The advance of colonisation and the spread of European civilisation—warts and all—are not to be underestimated for their impact upon the contours of the Islamic world. Ever since Napoleon Bonaparte's incursion into Egypt in 1798 the world of Islam has been continually subject to a relentless 'onslaught' from the West.

> The grabbing game reached its climax in 1920 at the end of World War I when British troops occupied Damascus and Baghdad, once the two most powerful centres of the Umayyad and Abbasid Caliphates. Everywhere Muslims found themselves utterly defeated and thoroughly demoralised. More shameful was their sense of religious subjugation at the hands of Christians, whom they had always regarded with contempt. The loss of political power was understandable; but what irked them was the superior behaviour of the new rulers whose forbears they had always vanquished in the past.[4]

Whereas the ruling cliques acquiesced, fanatics and puritans rebelled. European influences became ever more pervasive and persuasive. 'The fundamentalists could do little but helplessly witness the disintegration of the Muslim polity and society. Christian values were presented in a way which made many Muslims doubt whether theirs was, as the Qur'an had proclaimed, "the best community".'[5] Islamic secularists go with the flow of change and modernity; Islamic fundamentalists resist and react. Muslim revivalists feared both colonial imperialism on the one hand and modern nationalism on the other. The one undermined Islamic culture, the other threatened the ideal and identity of the trans-national Ummah. And, of course, religious leadership was deeply antithetical to secular leadership: success of the

---

[2] Rafiq Zakaria, *The Struggle Within Islam: the conflict between religion and politics* (London: Penguin, 1989), 114.

[3] Ibid., 130.

[4] Ibid., 157.

[5] Ibid., 164.

secularists would undermine the authority and position of the Muslim scholar-leaders, the clerics (ulema).[6]

Turkey is perhaps an outstanding example of the Islamic conflict between religion and modernity. Once, as the seat of the Ottoman empire, it was—to the West—'the citadel of Islam'. But for the greater part of the twentieth century Turkey pursued a modern secular path.[7] Indeed, so aggressive was the embrace of secularism and Westernisation that Turkey was a pariah within the Islamic world for a long time. Turkey today, though more openly Islamic, remains on the whole averse to Islamic fundamentalisms of whatever sort. The legacy of the founder of modern-day Turkey, Kemal Mustafa Atatürk, lives on.

By contrast, Islam in the Middle East is often perceived as a hotbed of 'fundamentalism'. In this context the term 'fundamentalism' or, better, the phrase 'fundamentalist movement'

> refers to modern political movements and ideas, mostly oppositional, which seek to establish, in one sense or another, an Islamic state. The model for an Islamic state is sought by these movements in a 'sacred history' of the original political community of the faithful established by the Prophet Muhammad in Medina in the seventh century and maintained under his four successors, the *Rushidun* ...[8]

However, Golam Choudhury argues that the laws and ordinances of politics that derive from the Qur'an and the Sunnah do not themselves yield any one specific form of Islamic state, and he avers that an Islamic state is not one which is framed by or run by Islamic theologians:

> It is the people or people's elected legislature which is committed to the task of working out an interpretation of the Islamic state and not the '*ulama*' ... Muslim scholars in the contemporary period emphatically refuse to identify the 'Islamic state' with theocracy.[9]

Choudhury holds that modern Muslim countries, such as Malaysia or Pakistan—indeed any contemporary Muslim country as such—cannot simply adopt institutions or activities within the contemporary world that were suitable for Arabia in the seventh century.[10] Choudhury may, of course, be a relatively lone voice. On the other hand, he may well be expressing a more widely held moderate view than much contemporary rhetoric and news reports would have us think. If so, this is a valuable Muslim viewpoint that needs to be heard.

---

[6] Cf. ibid., 169.

[7] Ibid., 10.

[8] Sami Zubaida, *Islam: The People and the State. Political Ideas and Movements in the Middle East* (London: I. B. Taurus, 1993), 38.

[9] Golam W. Choudhury, *Islam and the Modern World*, 2nd edn (Kuala Lumpur: WHS Publications, 1994), 56.

[10] Ibid., 57.

Unity and Diversity

Ideologically, Islamic nations constitute one vast notional socio-geographic and religious entity—dar-al-Islam—to which minority Muslim communities elsewhere are associated to form an overarching single religious community. The Islamic Ummah is spread across some four dozen countries where Muslims form the majority, and throughout many other lands where Muslims are in the minority. In many of these latter cases individual Muslims are often members of minority Islamic communities within the larger, usually secular, society. Contrary to the ideology of the one worldwide Islamic Ummah, there have in fact been many Muslim 'worlds', or particular major communities, that have both existed through time—empires, kingdoms, caliphates—or which exist in the present.

The diversity of these Muslim worlds, so to speak, reflects varieties of contemporary political orientation and regional geography. Against the *notional* singularity of the Ummah, undergirded by a religious ideology of unity (tawhid), there is today a multiplicity of *national* Islamic entities and identities. Pluralist reality co-exists in tension with the ideology of a global communal unity. Thus categories of contemporary Islamic community include, for example, Islamist government (Iran, Sudan); Islamic monarchy (Saudi Arabia, Jordan); the secular state with an Islamic predominance (Morocco, Malaysia); the secular Muslim state (Egypt, Turkey); and the situation of significant Muslim minorities (North America, Great Britain). The tension between the reality of socio-political diversity and the ideals of religious unity is an inherent problematic within the world of Islam. The contemporary context has, of course, changed radically from that which pertained at its inception. This, of course, is no surprise, but awareness of its implications is often lacking. Fazlur Rahman has commented that:

> Whereas in the early centuries of development of social institutions in Islam, Islam started from a clean slate, as it were, and had to carve out *ab initio* a social fabric ... now, when Muslims have to face a situation of fundamental rethinking and reconstruction, their acute problem is precisely to determine how far to render the slate clean again and on what principles and by what methods, in order to create a new set of institutions.[11]

In this astute observation Rahman highlights two interconnected facets of Islam. First, that in its inception and early development as an historical religion, Islam, under the leadership of Muhammad, effected novel and radical social change, and a wholly new religious expression and identity. Second, the emergence of an ethic of radical, even revolutionary, change and disruption as being valid, even needful, was evident. But such change was intended to effect a return to the pristine forms of the perceived original Islamic institutional structure and religious life, not to

---

[11] Fazlur Rahman, *Islam*, 2nd edn (Chicago: University of Chicago Press, 1979), 214.

engender further novel development of the religion as such. Thus there is a deep inherent tension between conservative tendencies (the maintenance of the received tradition of religion) and radical tendencies (the return to the roots of religion). Each can engender change, yet each can resist further novelty: it all depends on context and circumstance. The conservative may call for revitalisation of institutions and the revival of religious sensibilities and in the process may be labelled a 'fundamentalist'. But this could apply equally to the radical who critiques the socio-political status quo and advocates revolutionary change in order to regain true values and the realignment of the institutional expression of Islam.

Islamic fundamentalism

The use of the term 'fundamentalism' can be very misleading when applied to Islamic contexts. It ought really to be avoided, though its widespread usage makes that difficult. Indeed, while the apparent resurgence of Islam in the late twentieth century reflects an element of religious extremism and fanaticism from some quarters, for the most part Muslims are moderates. 'Fundamentalism' is a religious term arising out of Christian religious history. It is often quite inappropriate to apply it within the Islamic context where the religious situation is quite different. Interpretation of the 'fundamentals' of Islam has never admitted a wide range of options. The parameters of belief are tightly proscribed. Religious resurgence is more a matter of 'holding the line'; of more diligent application and overt assertion of a faith and practice that, in its essentials, has not greatly changed, if at all, since its inception.

Although there is a tenor of strictness and discipline that adheres more or less naturally to Islam by virtue of the very nature of the religion, the headline-grabbing excesses are just that: an excess of fervour and zeal rather than an expression of the essence of this religion whose name—Islam—means *peaceful* submission (to the Will of Allah). However, in the modern world, the theme of submission cannot be taken to mean quiescent acceptance: Muslims are being challenged at depth to rethink and to reclaim their position in the world. In the process there is considerable intellectual activity taking place that addresses questions of modernity and the radical (back to the roots) rethinking and reconstruction that has been occasioned by modernity itself.[12]

Decline of the Ummah

The Islamic Ummah, having known a period of ascendancy and an epoch of domination, has in recent centuries fragmented and declined. As Rippin comments, once a major political force and a relatively united empire, the world of Islam

---

[12] Cf. Andrew Rippin, *Muslims: Their Religious Beliefs and Practices, Vol. 2: the contemporary period* (London: Routledge, 1993), 12. Rippin relates work on issues of modernity by the sociologist Peter Berger to the Islamic context.

'found itself subjugated politically and exploited economically'.[13] Muslim scholars are in consequence sometimes inclined to offer poignant reflections upon the fate of Islam[14] and may indulge in raising the rather haunting question of the 'failure of Islam'. In large measure this is because success within the world is a central motif for Islamic ideology. Religion and the political life are intimately intertwined: submission to Allah is in respect of all things, and the blessings of Allah are not limited to the 'spiritual' realm in distinction from the mundane.

There is a perception in many quarters of the Islamic world that the Muslim community has suffered as a consequence of its relationship with the West. Such a perception has serious repercussions, both potential and real. A number of issues touch on this, and on the wider question of Islam's reaction to modernity. The first has to do with political life itself. For example, on the one hand the Arab world is a significant part of dar-al-Islam, even though the Arab Muslim population is numerically in the minority so far as the worldwide Ummah is concerned. On the other hand, the Arab world can be seen as constituting something of a singular entity embracing one language, one religion, and one culture. However, as a consequence of the processes of modernity, even this Arab world now embraces a great diversity of socio-political identity and expression. This arose, by and large, out of the complexities of regional history and the evolution of Arabic societies, first under the Ottomans and then under Western European sway. A complex artifice of nation states was the legacy bequeathed by European withdrawal following World War II. Ahmed comments that, as a result, there are many Arabs who

> complain today that although they are ostensibly free their societies are still in bondage to Western imperialism—whether political or cultural. Their rulers, they say, depend on the West for support and, in return, give away rights to natural resources or military bases.[15]

Political responses

In recent centuries many Islamic nations found themselves in submission to a colonial power. But that submission has since been cast off. The political response to the collapse of colonialism, and a way forward for Islamic communities, has very often been to embark on one form or other of nationalism and socialism. As a programme, socialism can be perceived to embody Islamic principles and values.[16] In theory, democracy is natural to Muslims given the egalitarian principles that underlie the Ummah: all Muslims, male and female, are equal in status. Yet the

---

[13] Ibid., 15.
[14] Cf. Ahmed in *Living Islam*, for example.
[15] Ibid., 127.
[16] Cf. Rippin, *Muslims.*

practice of democracy within the world of Islam is acknowledged by some to have been problematic in many instances. Ahmed, for example, comments that:

> While Muslim countries are generally if erratically moving towards the acceptance of the notion of democracy, or some form of controlled democracy, the old structures— feudal or tribal or monarchic—continue to remain in place. True democracy cannot function with such structures constantly interfering and subverting it.[17]

He also remarks that

> In the present situation Muslim societies find themselves in a quandary. They cannot fully convert to the democratic process without jettisoning traditional structures. Too much democracy would mean a straight plunge into anarchy for some states which are still evolving and whose borders are still flexible. Internal groups demand autonomy and sometimes secession; external enemies cast covetous eyes on chunks of territory.[18]

Also, in many places, Muslims reject their own post-colonial ruling elites, the single-party establishments that have utilised Western models of government, including socialism and nationalistic totalitarianism in particular. Muslims often assert that their religious culture needs no alien influence: Muslim civilisation was once the leading light of the world during the golden dynastic age of Islamic learning and political ascendancy.

Another political dimension, of course, is the fact of the State of Israel and Islamic perceptions of Zionism. Rippin suggests that, ironically, Israel may yet serve as the grit of irritation that produces the pearl of beauty in so far as Zionism has 'led to a strengthening of Islamic identity'.[19] On the other hand he acknowledges that the existence of Israel represents, for many Muslims, an eternal reminder of the decline of Muslim civilisation. Real difficulty is posed for Islam by the existence of the State of Israel as a product of the modern era. Ahmed rather idealistically argues that Muslims can, logically, be neither anti-Judaism nor antisemitic, for that would be to deny their own religious heritage and would beg the question of the ethnic origins of Islam. But Muslims can be, and indeed are, opposed to Zionism on the grounds that it was 'politically organized in modern Europe, was basically alien, a foreign import, to the Middle East'.[20] And we have seen, in Chapter 7, the extent to which Islam is indeed susceptible to enacting ant-Jewish, or antisemitic, paradigms. However, here the point is simply to highlight the consequences for Islamic prejudice in respect to dimensions of modernity that have been, almost by definition, Western dominated.

---

[17] Ahmed, *Living Islam*, 130-131.

[18] Ibid.

[19] Rippin, *Muslims*, 16.

[20] Ahmed, 128.

Social responses

Emphasis upon the role and place of the family is another significant element in the Muslim response to modernity. Such an emphasis is by no means limited to Islam, although there is a particular dimension to this in respect of the role of women in both Islamic family life and Muslim societies more widely. Issues here are very complex and include the fact that in many parts of the Muslim world pre-Islamic customs regarding women and sexuality have persisted. As a result they have often been taken to be part of Islamic culture and so have assumed religious sanction. These can include not only dress codes but also the deeply problematic issues of genital mutilation by way of female circumcision, clitoridectomy, infibulation, and so forth.

The core issue has to do with the theme of submission, which lies at the heart of Islamic piety and identity. Ahmed casts it in rather lofty tones, yet nonetheless underscores the point:

> The reversion to primordial identity, the falling back to old ways, is one way of regaining lost dignity. A woman wearing *hijab* or a man cultivating a beard are both attempting to relocate a sense of pride. They are making a point: by asserting themselves and their sense of identity they aim to recapture some of the dignity that is so deeply required by all human beings.[21]

Noting that its source as an Islamic dress code is most certainly debated within Islam, Ahmed also points out that the

> covering of the face by a veil has never been universal in the Muslim world. ... But the Quranic injunction to modesty, however it is applied, cannot be set aside. Its interpretation has varied, and does vary, but its importance is basic. ... The *hijab* or veil presents us with some useful sociological insights into Muslim society.[22]

All is not necessarily as it seems.

Other dimensions, with social and economic consequences that are involved in the complex interaction between modernity and Islam, include oil and television. The fact that oil production rests with a significant group of Middle Eastern Muslim countries brings those particular nations, and the religion which they vigorously espouse, into the eye of global politics and media attention. This has consequences for both the religion of Islam, *vis-à-vis* its perception within the wider world in particular, and the oil-producing countries themselves. But, furthermore, the wealth so created within these Muslim countries not only makes

---

21 Ibid., 134.
22 Ibid., 148.

them significant players on the global economic scene, it provides them with power and prestige—and the gaze of envy and criticism—in respect of the wider Ummah.

So oil has been a mixed blessing. So too has television, which is the prime symbol and tool of mass communication. Of course, what is communicated is to a large extent the mass culture of the West: the amoral, consumerist, self-satisfaction-seeking image of the 'good life' that is daily portrayed around the globe. All of these things impact upon Muslims who have access to a TV and, in particular, a satellite dish. For where local censorship curtails programming options, more and more people in Muslim lands are able, with the help of a little technology, to access international broadcasts. There seems to be no shortage of this technology in the oil-rich Middle East, nor beyond, for that matter. Thus a tension of values is set up with the result that Western amorality quickly becomes anathema and is judged to be inherently immoral so far as purist Islamists are concerned. And as the seduction of culture threatens religious sensibility, so the combating of cultural hegemony gains religious sanction. One way, of course, is found in the rising sophistication of Muslim Arabic television broadcasts, at least one of which (*al-Jazeera*) has widely international, if not global, coverage.

The contemporary climate

The scene is thus set for a 'clash of civilisations', to use Samuel Huntington's celebrated phrase, in the cause of protecting cultural identity and values. And more than anything else television can represent within the Muslim world a symbol and agent of cultural invasion and value displacement. This can be so even though, at the same time, the medium of television can be an agent, in the local context, of the promotion of a trans-national Islamic identity.

Many scholars and commentators, both Muslim and non-Muslim, have acknowledged that the role of Islam in the modern world is problematic. As Rippin notes, 'Islam is the civilisational basis of the Muslim world in politics, in society, in life'.[23] Islam, the religion, provides not just the base but also the frame and structure of Islamic cultural and political life. Integral to this, of course, is the legal code of Islam, the Shari'a. However, for much of the Muslim world the Shari'a had been displaced by other legal codes introduced through colonisation. As a result there have been adverse consequences for Islamic religious and cultural life. Rippin has remarked that

> under the impact of the rapid change which the modern world has inflicted, many
> Muslims have experienced a severe weakening of the traditional conception of the
> eternal, unchanging Muslim legal code, the *shari'a*. At the same time, it is within the

---

[23] Rippin, *Muslims*, 19.

shari'a that various strategies have been employed in order to try to face the challenge of change.[24]

It has been in response to the exigencies of the modern world, and the struggle to find identity and a place within it, or in distinction from it, that contemporary Islamic ideology needs to be understood.

Ideological options

The seemingly exponential expansion of European power, both military and economic, which during the nineteenth century imposed itself upon much of the world of Islam, evoked a mixture of ideological responses that have given shape to the socio-political dimension of Islam ever since. A useful definition of an 'ideological option' is given by Rippin who speaks of the 'ideological level' as 'the system of thought which orients and interprets an individual's life within society'.[25] Such orienting systems apply, of course, not just to individuals *per se*, but to communities of individuals within societies and, indeed, to the dominant paradigms by which the life of whole societies may be ordered. Responses have varied also to the loss of identity through the colonising replacement of Shari'a by various secular Western law codes, and the concomitant dilution of Islamic religious, cultural, and also political identity.

The range of ideological responses within the Islamic world has included, at one end of the spectrum, the call of the radical Islamist for total Islamisation: the call for Shari'a to govern every part of life. At the other end Muslim modernists have advocated the abandonment of early Islamic politico-religious ideals in favour of the privatisation of religion. This is the model of Western secularism and, of course, is anathema to the dedicated Islamist. But, between modernist reform at one end, and Islamist revivalism at the other, there are many variant positions on the spectrum of ideological option that may be—and often are—taken. For example, Rippin[26] delineates three major groupings or categories of Muslim response to the modern age: Traditionalist; Revivalist (sometimes referred to as 'Fundamentalist'); and Modernist. William Shepard classifies the variant responses as Islamic secularism, modernism, Islamism, traditionalism, and neo-traditionalism.[27]

However, irrespective of the option pursued, the main issue concerns the place of religion in public life: be it social, legal, political, intellectual. Wilfred Cantwell Smith once remarked that the 'fundamental problem of modern Muslims is how to

---

[24] Ibid.

[25] Ibid., 36.

[26] Ibid., 28ff.

[27] William Shepard, 'Islam and Ideology: Towards a Typology', *International Journal of Middle East Studies*, 19 (1987), 307–36.

rehabilitate their history; to set it going again in full vigour, so that Islamic society may once again flourish as a divinely guided society should and must'.[28] The options confronting Muslims, with respect to the all-pervasive phenomenon of modernity, are to deny value to modernity as such; to view it as the root of all evil; to see modernity as a mixed blessing, bringing boon as well as bane; to hold to a critical or modified modernism; or perhaps to go outside Islam altogether by virtue of taking on an alternative and sectarian identity, or a modern secular identity; that is, becoming 'agnostic', relatively speaking, at least *vis-à-vis* the identification of religious with political life.

As already noted, in contrast to the ideal of the one worldwide Islamic community, there have been, and indeed are today, many Muslim 'worlds'. What has been the ideological implication of this for Muslim identity? How has Islam responded to the changing contexts and political vicissitudes of the modern era? My own attempts to delineate the ideological options that have predominated within the Islamic Ummah during the modern era, suggests the broad groupings of Traditionalism, Modernism, Pragmatic Secularism, and Islamism.

Traditionalism

This option refers to Muslims who follow an ideology of affirming the *received traditions* as practised, such that 'change should not and does not affect the traditions of the past. Change is to be rejected'.[29] This tends to yield an entrenched conservatism, an outlook that holds to past methods and perspectives, come what may. Westernisation is viewed, in particular, as a 'temptation ... to be resisted'.[30] Traditionalism is the conserving ideology, the perspective that seeks to maintain the religious tradition as such, which eschews change for change's sake, but which may employ coping mechanisms, not to effect change, but to uphold the tradition through changing circumstance.

Variants within this category include, on the one hand, a 'rejectionist' hard-line view and, on the other, an 'adaptationist' stance which makes some concession, at least in respect of process. Rippin notes that, as a cultural entity, Islam has 'always been able to cope with change and has built into its structures ways of dealing with change'.[31] Thus, whilst its sources (Qur'an and Sunnah) remain unchanged, novel situations could be managed by way of the institutionalised legal systems pertinent to the particular local Islamic community. The sub-category *neo-traditionalism* is a development from the adaptationist strategy, which allows for gradual change to take place whilst maintaining the essential tradition and identity in the process.

---

[28] Wilfred Cantwell Smith, *Islam in Modern History*, (Princeton, 1957), 41; cited in Choudhury, *Islam and the Modern World*, 83.

[29] Shepard, ibid., 29.

[30] Ibid.

[31] Ibid.

Modernism

The option of modernism has its genesis in the nineteenth century when the spirit of European optimism, liberality and progressivism, encapsulated in such slogans as 'The Fatherhood of God and the Brotherhood of Man', impacted pervasively upon both European and colonial life, and hence colonised Islamic countries. Indeed, it impacted upon any Islamic country that had a close relation to the West. Islamic modernists in this context emerged with an ideology that attempted a defence of contemporary civilisation in terms of traditional Islam, striving to adopt whatever was perceived to be beneficial so far as Western European culture was concerned, yet retaining the framework of the Shari'a, which for the modernists, as David Waines comments, 'provided the basis of Islam's unquestioned religio-moral superiority over Europe'.[32]

Some key representatives of Islamic modernism include *Jamal al-Din al-Afghani* (1839–97CE) *Muhammad 'Abduh* (1849–1905CE) and *Rashid Rida* (1865–1935CE) from Egypt, all of whom advocated pan-Islamism coupled with a synthesis of features of the West, such as scientific rationalism, which were deemed desirable. However the desirability of such features was premised on their being in concert with, or their capacity to be incorporated within, the essential truths of Islam. The advocated synthesis was expected to be positive and complementary. Golam Choudhury, a Muslim political scientist, identifies al-Din al-Afghani as 'the father of modern Muslim nationalism, proponent of Pan-Islam and the main aspiration for the reform movement in Islam'.[33] Afghani sought to 'open the door' to ijtihad, to end the apparent intellectual stagnation of Islam. Thus Afghani

> pinpointed the Muslim's lack of progress in science and technology. He attributed the success of European colonial powers to their achievements in science. He strongly argued that the Muslims acquire modern scientific knowledge without which the Muslims would not be able to get rid of European subjugation.[34]

'Abduh, a student of al-Afghani, 'advocated a modernizing reform of traditional religious education and put forward an interpretation of Islam by which he hoped to open the door to progress and new life'.[35] Following the death of 'Abduh, Rashid Rida became the 'mouthpiece' of this movement of modernist reform thinkers emanating from the Middle East. Rida, it is said,

---

[32] David Waines, *An Introduction to Islam* (Cambridge: Cambridge University Press, 1995), 218.

[33] Choudhury, *Islam and the Modern World*, 84.

[34] Ibid., 85.

[35] Ibid., 86.

attributed the decline in Islam to stagnation and the blind following of the medieval schools of Islamic jurisprudence. ... Rida was in favour of the reform and reconstruction of Islamic law through the process of *ijtihad* – the use of analogical reasoning in legislation.[36]

From India, representatives of Islamic modernism include *Sayyid Ahmad Khan* (1817–98CE) and *Muhammad Iqbal* (1876–1938CE). They advocated modern Western forms of knowledge and use of reason as being required to bring back vitality to Islam. They separated Islam, as religion and law, from Islamic rationalism, that is, reason and science. Khan advocated co-operation with the British, and learning the English language together with modern Western sciences. Iqbal gave expression to the idea of a separate Muslim state in India. He favoured a modernising process of reform of Islamic polity and legal structures and held a dynamic approach to interpretation that was consonant with the modern age.[37]

Modernists extract values and principles from the authority sources and traditions and argue for, and allow, modification of practice in accordance with contemporary need. Indeed they would argue that this is in fact how the different traditions have arisen through time and what keeps a religion vibrant and relevant. Islam knows this as 'reconstruction' (*islah*): change is embraced and religion is subject to change. Rippin notes the modernist principle as 'differentiating basic moral precepts from specific legal prescriptions'.[38] John Esposito comments that, whereas on the one hand 'premodern revivalist movements were primarily internally motivated', on the other hand 'Islamic modernism was a response both to continued internal weaknesses and to the external political and religiocultural threat of colonialism'.[39]

In general terms, Islamic modernists sought neither to expunge modern society of religious guidance in favour of a wholly secularist approach, nor did they look to a supposed pristine origin to provide past solutions to present problems. Rather they took the line of acceptance of the reality of change and endeavoured to reinterpret and reapply Islam in the light of the reality of the modern world. Although, again in broad terms, modernisation has come to be equated with Westernisation—a crude but widespread identification, which has had the tendency to spawn either reactionary rejection or uncritical adoption—modernists, as a group, attempt a more critical response. While their secular counterparts tended to look to the West somewhat uncritically, and traditionalists tended to obstinately shun the West, Islamic modernists have generally attempted

---

[36] Ibid.

[37] Cf. ibid., 90f.

[38] Rippin, *Muslims*, 31.

[39] John L. Esposito, *Islam: The Straight Path*, Expanded Edition (Oxford: Oxford University Press, 1994), 124.

to establish a continuity between their Islamic heritage and modern change. On the one hand, they identified with premodern revivalist movements and called for the purification of internal deficiencies and deviations. On the other, they borrowed and assimilated new ideas and values from the West.[40]

Modernists attempt to adapt Islam to changing conditions and circumstances. To that extent they are the champions of the view that religion is a living thing; change and adaptation are a natural component of living entities of whatever type. Modernists claim the right of contemporary interpretation, the contemporary exercise of ijtihad. James Piscatori notes that

> Islamic jurists long ago accepted that it was impossible to attain complete uniformity of interpretation, and in fact sanctioned the diversity that flows from the exercise of *ijtihad*. This is the idea of *ikhtilaf*, that there is a permissible diversity of doctrine in Islamic law.[41]

However, whereas it was the orthodox Sunni jurists who 'closed the door' to ijtihad in the tenth century, during the nineteenth century the intellectual response of emerging modernists

> argued that the restriction on *ijtihad* had been disastrous and that its door must be thrown wide open. The eighteenth-century reformers had laid the groundwork by calling for *ijtihad* to restore the early legal sources, but from the late nineteenth century the call was intentionally for *ijtihad* to reinterpret the sources in line with modern circumstances.[42]

The propounding of modernist ijtihad—that is, of promoting a radically different process of interpretation and investigation than has been traditionally the case—poses a considerable problem. For this leads to a questioning not only of traditional ideas, but also of traditional practices, and so runs the risk of losing appeal among more traditionalist-oriented Muslim peoples, let alone the rising tide of the more aggressive and self-assertive 'Islamism' (see below). In short, Islamic modernism, or modernist reform, identifies a reinterpreted Islam as the basis for both political and religious life. It draws on an inherent capacity within Islam for flexibility of application and interpretation. A high idealistic valuation of Islam becomes the ideological leitmotif driving political engagement. It promises much but it would seem, at least in the present day, it has difficulty in successfully engaging with the broad realities of contemporary Islamic life.

---

[40] Ibid. 140.

[41] James P. Piscatori, *Islam in a World of Nation-States* (Cambridge: Cambridge University Press, 1994), 5.

[42] Ibid., 8.

Pragmatic Secularism

This option views Islam in the modern world as a purely religious phenomenon, without a political dimension or force. Radical social reorganisation occurs without recourse to religious jurisdiction as, for example, was the case in communist Albania. As noted above, Turkey has pursued a secularising process of separating religion from politics throughout much of the twentieth century. As well as replacing the Arabic script with the Latin alphabet, Turkey's 'suppression of Islamic legal and educational institutions and the outlawing of mystical Sufi groups were other steps in the removal of religion from the apparatus of the state'.[43]

In countries that are officially secular so far as their political constitution is concerned, Islam can find itself confronted with the challenge of adjusting to, or contending with, variants of nationalism, capitalism or socialism. As a result, further pragmatic variants, identified by William Shepard, include 'religious secularism' (as in Indonesia's multi-faith system); and 'Muslim secularism' (as in Egypt's constitutional placing of religion, specifically Islam, as having a role in, but not being the basis of, political life).[44]

Islamism

This last option is the relatively recent development that refers to the position of contending for the application in a society of Quranic principles and values—Shari'a—and the dismissal of all else. Islamism, or Islamic revivalism, certainly accepts change, albeit in a controlled fashion. It pushes beyond the conservative tendencies of predominant Traditionalism. It tends to use authoritative sources of the past to legitimise changes in the present. Ibrahim Karawan states that Islamism

> refers to the movements and ideologies that claim Islam, as they interpret it, as the basis for restructuring contemporary states and societies according to an idealised image of Islam's founding period ... Hence, Islamists talk of the need to return to Islamic roots and a 'golden age'....[45]

John Esposito summarises the ideological framework of Islamic revivalism, or Islamism, as follows.[46] First, Islam is a total and comprehensive way of life. Second, the failure of Muslim societies is due to their departure from the 'straight path of Islam' and their following a Western secular path. Third, the renewal of society requires a return to Islam and the advancement of an Islamic religio-political and social reformation or revolution. Fourth, Western-inspired civil law

---

[43] Rippin, *Muslims,* 36.

[44] As cited in Rippin, ibid.

[45] Ibrahim A. Karawan, *The Islamist Impasse* International Institute for Strategic Studies, Adelphi Paper 314 (London: Oxford University Press, 1997), 7.

[46] Esposito, *Islam,* 163.

codes must be replaced by Shari'a, which is the only acceptable blueprint for Muslim society. Fifth, although Westernisation of society is condemned, modernisation as such is not, that is to say, science and technology are accepted, but they are to be subordinated to Islamic belief and values; and finally, the process of Islamisation requires organisations or associations of dedicated and trained Muslims.

Many Muslims hold that, during the historical period of Western modernity, especially during the height of colonialism, there was a steady decline in both the fortunes and the integrity of the Islamic Ummah. Thus, 'reality has diverged from what they perceive the ideal to be ... practice bears no relationship to the theory'.[47] From this perception, and the viewpoints as to the underlying causes, there have emerged the distinctive late-twentieth-century forms of Islamism for which James Piscatori identifies four underlying reasons.[48]

The first has to do with the 1967 war with Israel. The defeat of Egypt, Syria and Jordan was *al-nakba*, the disaster. It impacted on Muslim identity *per se*, not just Middle East society and sensibilities. It precipitated a general spiritual and intellectual malaise throughout the Ummah. The second reason concerns the processes of socio-economic development, particularly urbanisation and allied demographic dislocations with consequent stress and strains on the social and political fabric, 'thereby leading people to turn to traditional symbols and rites as a way of comforting and orienting themselves'.[49] The third reason is the 'universal crisis of modernity' which has lead inexorably to the breakdown of authority and other stabilising social structures. This has involved a loss of the sense of meaningful 'incorporation' or communal identity for individuals and a concomitant increased sense of 'dis-connectedness'. It has led to a wide appeal of the religious revivalist's strong communal identity and orientation. But also, and fourthly, political conditions have often led to a heightening of Islam as political ideology. Thus, 'governments have been able to use Islam with such ease because, as an ideology, it is vague in content yet highly charged: people instinctively respond to it as a general symbol but also as a guide to their loyalties'.[50]

A singular defining characteristic of Islamism is the concern to gain political power: religion is not confined to the realm of the private and personal, but is necessarily in the public domain and so carries with it an active concern for the political life of the society. Therefore obtaining the controlling interest in politics is critical for Islamists 'if they are to reshape society, politics, the economy and culture in accordance with what they deem to be God's ultimate will'.[51] Rippin notes that, for this group, 'reliance on text ... opens up possibilities of independent

---

[47] Karawan, *The Islamist Impasse*, 22.
[48] Piscatori, *Islam in a World of Nation-States*, 26ff.
[49] Ibid., 28.
[50] Ibid., 32.
[51] Ibid.

reasoning through the rejection of authority by that very process of the return to the text and the ignoring of traditional interpretations of those texts'.[52] Thus the way is cleared for the revivalist to adopt radical, even relatively novel, strategies and policies, on the basis of a closely reasoned Islamic ideology that is grounded in the primary texts.

Ironically, then, the revivalist, sometimes called 'fundamentalist', can actually be quite radical in contrast to the conservative position of the Traditionalist. But at the same time the revivalist can often incline to anti-intellectualism that eschews any intentional hermeneutics. To such a perspective, interpretation is both imposition and distortion. The revivalist position, from its own perspective, is not seen as an exercise in interpretation. Of course, this pattern is not unique to Islam: it may be found in the so-called fundamentalist movements of other religions. However, Muslim revivalist movements are often also characterised by their concern for the socio-moral decline of Muslims and, in response, they advocate an intentional return to the origins of the religion and the shedding of all accretions of legal and mystic traditions. They tend to reject the predeterministic outlook of popularist Islam and the predominant theology of the day, and in some circumstances they are inclined to effect, or at least attempt, revivalist reform through armed force if need be. The Islamic revivalist will use the authority sources of past tradition to legitimate present-day change in the sense of an active promotion of change from an unsatisfactory state of affairs to that of an ideal 'what should be'. Thus the goal of establishing an Islamic state is viewed as a necessary precursor to achieving an Islamic society, *per se.*

> Islamists commonly believe that Islam has to be implemented in society *as a whole.* Individual adherence to the faith cannot in itself lead to an Islamic society. For Islamists, Islam encompasses the three 'Ds'—*din* (religion), *dunya* (life) and *wa dawla* (state)—and has to be implemented in its entirety. ... Islamists consider it their duty to overcome challenges to Islamic teachings and norms to bring about the rule of God in place of the rule of human laws.[53]

Three proponents of Islamic revivalism within the twentieth century need to be noted, if but briefly, at this stage. They are by no means the only ones, but they are representative of the narrow and at times 'hardline' perspective that often accompanies revivalist intentions. Mahmud Faksh refers to them as three activist theorists who have provided 'theoretical paradigms that inspire contemporary Islamic fundamentalism'.[54] Previously of India, *Maulana Maududi* (1903–79CE) of Pakistan founded the *Jama'at-i Islami* political party. The perspective of Maududi and his party involved 'a return to the Qur'an and a purified *sunna* so that Islam

---

[52] Rippin, *Muslims,* 30.

[53] Karawan, *The Islamist Impasse,* 14.

[54] Mahmud A. Faksh, *The Future of Islam in the Middle East: Fundamentalism in Egypt, Algeria, and Saudi Arabia* (Westport, Connecticut: Praeger, 1997), 3.

might be revitalised' and furthermore that 'this could only truly happen if Islam became the constitution of the state'.[55] *Sayyid Qutb* (1906–66CE) of Egypt was the intellectual force behind the Muslim Brotherhood. He advocated 'a return to "pure Islam" and a move away from the materialism of the West which he perceived as contaminating Islam'.[56] For Qutb only Islam alone can provide a universal social system applicable to all humanity. And such a system 'will cure all the ills of the modern world.'

The third figure is that of *Ayatollah Khomeini* (1900–1989CE) of Iran, whose advocacy of a resurgent Islam within the Shi'a world has provided a very particular paradigm of Islamic revolutionary change. Furthermore, in the twentieth century, revivalist movements on the whole contrast with other Islamic groups in respect to organisation and discipline, among other factors: 'Their emphasis on discipline, loyalty, and training as well as social-activist programs resulted in more cohesive and effective organizations'.[57] Also to be noted is the sub-category *Radical Islamism* (see below) often referred to as 'extremism', which calls for a strict application of Shari'a under which all Muslims—indeed often all members of the society regardless of personal religious identity—should live, and also for the creation of an Islamic state in which Muslims can so live free from needing to account for the religiously 'other'. It is often the case, of course, that Islamic revivalism, at some point at least, takes on the more extreme contours of radical Islamism, which may later moderate once the revolutionary overthrow phase has passed, as was the case, for example, in Iran.

Islamist themes

In respect of the phenomenon of Islamism, Makmud Faksh identifies a set of five 'synthesised themes' from his examination of the work of Maududi, Qutb and Khomeini.[58] The first is the *fusion of religion and politics*, which is the expression of the holistic view of Islam as 'both an ideology and a system of life comprising religious, legal, and moral aspects in accordance with God's commands' and therefore the 'establishment of an Islamic order is prerequisite to the actualisation of Muslim life'.[59] The second is the notion of *Divine Sovereignty or Rule* (*hakimiyya*) which expresses a cardinal principle of Islamism wherein the political order is subservient to the rules of Shari'a: human rulers and political leaders are merely God's representatives and are to be judged according to the fidelity and integrity of their representation. The third theme is that of *Islamic authenticity* being asserted over against jahiliyya, the state or condition of spiritual ignorance.

[55] Ibid., 31.
[56] Ibid.
[57] Esposito, *Islam*, 152.
[58] Faksh, *The Future of Islam*.
[59] Ibid., 5.

A shared element in Islamic revivalist discourse is the 'restoration and reassertion of Islamic authenticity in response to Western hegemony'.[60] The new jahiliyya against which Islam is pitted is the seduction of Western culture and values viewed as inherently antithetical to Islamic culture and values. However, Faksh notes that

> for the fundamentalists, the most insidious aspect of the new *jahiliyya* is the internal dissemination of debilitating notions by Muslim reformers and rulers who are deemed to be secularists in Islamic disguise. ... To fundamentalists, the post-independence pseudo-Muslim rulers, desirous of mimicking the West, adopted nationalist-secularist policies that are inimical to Islam.[61]

Thus *Islamic universalism* (as in the idea of the Ummah), over against nationalist particularism (*qawmiyya*), constitutes the fourth theme. The contemporary jahiliyya is viewed as an expression of secularity and nation-statehood within the world of Islam. Therefore, any and all forms of nationalism, including pan-Arab nationalism, are rejected. As Faksh comments:

> Today, under political Islam, religion is the primary source of political identity and loyalty. To Muslim fundamentalist thinkers of all kinds, the underlying strength of an Islamic order is its universality – the bond of religion is the heart of community solidarity.[62]

Indeed, from the perspective of the Islamist:

> The Qur'an does not glorify the Arabs or any other group of people based on nationalism. Rather, the Prophet of Islam struggled against the chauvinist identities of the various Arab tribes in order to establish a Muslim *ummah*, wherein the only relevant bond is the religious bond, which supersedes all other affiliations. The Islamic state therefore is not nationality-based; it is an ideological Qur'anic-based state that transcends race and nationality.[63]

The fifth and final theme, one that is found throughout much revivalist and fundamentalist literature and rhetoric, is that of jihad. This is a critically important theme. The dynamic and comprehensive interpretation of this core religious motif gives a sharp edge to revivalist ideologies. Thus Sayyid Qutb

> was inspired by Maududi's advocacy of political struggle through direct action ... When the Muslim community is so debilitated by the godless *jahiliyya* culture, the obligation

---

[60] Ibid., 8.

[61] Ibid., 9.

[62] Ibid., 10.

[63] Ibid., 11.

of *jihad* devolves upon the virtuous who have renounced that culture. ... to Qutb, *jihad* in Islam is permanent, timeless, borderless.[64]

And Faksh notes somewhat trenchantly that 'Ayatollah Khomeini's conception of *jihad* is divinely sanctioned violence directed against internal and external enemies of Islam, and he takes his cue from the historical Shi'a theme of martyrdom'.[65]

Islamist orientation

Karawan identifies Islamists as falling into two broad categories, namely, militant Islamists and political Islamists. The former combine 'ideological purity and deep contempt for political compromise with a keen sense of urgency for direct Islamic action'. Thus, their 'primary obligation is to act as dedicated fighters against states which they see as embodying contemporary "ignorance"—*jahiliyya*'.[66] Militant Islamists will pursue destructive and destabilising strategies in the interests of waging a war of attrition against the state. As the current socio-political order is, by definition as it were, totally rejected by a militant perspective, such Islamists continue the struggle for as long as it takes: surrender is unthinkable, compromise anathema: anything less than the achievement of the goal is tantamount to apostasy. However, it is the nature of this phenomenon that militant groups are highly competitive, fractious and exclusivist. As a movement, militant Islamism is highly fissiparous.[67] By contrast, political Islamists are inclined to pursue more constructive and social-supportive strategies.

> Political Islamists believe that violent struggle is futile and self-defeating, and reject the assumptions of urgency advocated by militants. ... violent struggle against regimes is futile, and offers those regimes the opportunity ruthlessly to suppress *all* Islamic movements and activists. Political Islamist leaders focus instead on propagating *al-da'wa* (the 'Islamic Call') and purifying individual minds, and society as a whole, of all traces of secularism.[68]

In commenting on Islamic reform up to the 1960s, David Waines has remarked that whereas 'secularist Muslims were often guilty of an uncritical admiration of the West', conservative Muslims 'tended on the whole to dismiss the West as irrelevant to the needs and aims of Muslim society.' On the other hand, Reformist Muslims

---

[64] Ibid., 13.
[65] Ibid., 14.
[66] Karawan, *The Islamist Impasse*, 16.
[67] Karawan, *passim*.
[68] Ibid., 20.

'had tried to find a thread of continuity between the Islamic past and the modern present'.[69]

Esposito has noted that the 'dominant theme of contemporary Islam has been its resurgence. ... However, the contemporary revival has brought a noticeable increase in emphasis on religious identity and practice in individual and corporate life'.[70] Although Golam Choudhury advocates 'Islam and its ideology, if they are interpreted and applied in their true perspective (are) perfectly compatible with a modern Muslim nation's aspirations for progress towards modernisation, science and technological advancement',[71] reformist tendencies have led to the more aggressive or assertive revivalist phenomena. Choudhury has identified one powerful revivalist tendency as being 'the rejection of what is regarded as alien to Islamic values and a vigorous search for renewed strength from Islamic ideals and principles'.[72] He makes the point that disillusionment with Western culture and values has been a major factor in the resurgence of Islam in the 1970s and 1980s. The reality for many is that the resurgence of Islam is precipitated by 'the inherent strength of religion in the minds of Muslims; they attach great significance and importance to Islamic ideology in both their private and public lives'.[73]

Radical Islamist ideology

John Esposito also points out that radical Muslim Islamists will go much further, advocating violent revolution.[74] They can be viewed, ideologically, as 'crusading', that is, by giving expression to a crusader mentality in the advocating of opposition to all colonialism, and especially Zionism. They live by an imperative, namely, that an Islamic government is not simply an alternative but is in fact a divine requirement to which, in submission to Allah, there is no hesitation in obeying. This leads to the next element, that of an impositional execution of aims and objectives. The radical Islamist will not hesitate to criticise Muslim governments perceived as not following Shari'a: political leaders may thus be judged atheists or apostates and so viewed as subject to the full imposition of jihad. They also tend to be *a priori* oppositional in that opposition to Muslim governments is often extended to the religious establishment (that is, ulema, mosques, and so on) that are deemed to have been co-opted by the status-quo government. All this means that radical Islamists view their programmes for change, and the actions taken to effect their change, as divinely sanctioned, for jihad against such unbelief and unbelievers is in fact a religious duty. Finally such Islamists are radically exclusive, to the extent that

---

[69] Waines, *Introduction to Islam*, 233.

[70] Esposito, *Islam*, 156.

[71] Choudhury, *Islam and the Modern World*, 96.

[72] Ibid., 189.

[73] Ibid., 193.

[74] Esposito, 163f.

160 ·· The Challenge of Islam

Christians and Jews are generally regarded as unbelievers, rather than as 'People of the Book', because of their connections with Western (and so Christian) colonialism and also Zionism. Warrant for either perspective can be found in the Qur'an: the attitude taken is, of course, a reflection of the governing ideological stance if not also predominating paradigm (per Chapter 7, above).

The Middle East hub of Islam

The Middle East is a diverse and complex region. In terms of the worldwide Muslim population it represents only a minority. But in terms of influence on the wider world of Islam, it remains the ideological hub and rallying heart. The Middle East has given to the wider world the legacy of Islamic political life, one where religion is integral to both social policy and political praxis, among other things. By way of teasing out the significance of the Middle East context, I shall briefly comment on aspects of two key countries, namely, Saudi Arabia and Egypt.

The question of the relationship of culture and religion is rather like the question of the relation of the chicken and the egg: which comes first? Nowhere is this more acute than in reference to the Middle East and, in particular it would seem, with respect to the Arab world. As Karawan has commented:

> Numerous regimes in the Arab and Muslim worlds have used Islamic symbols and concepts to increase their political legitimacy. Examples include the Hashemite regime in Jordan; King Hassan's political identification as *Amir al-Mu'minin* (Commander of the Faithful) in Morocco; and King Fahd's status as *Khadim al-Haramyn al-Sharifayn* (Custodian of the Holy Places) in Saudi Arabia.[75]

Egypt's Anwar Sadat styled himself *'al Rais al-Mu'min* (the believing President)'. Mahmud Faksh argues that no Arab state is actually 'democratic' in the normal (that is, 'Western') sense of that term. 'In no single case is government based on the consent of the governed, with constitutional rules and procedures guaranteeing participation and access to power by all groups'.[76] But Islamic states and regimes do not always sit comfortably with Islamist ideology and goals. Indeed, often they are in deep opposition. This has provoked two models, if not modalities, of action in respect of the stance taken by Middle East Islamic regimes towards the political threat posed by dissenting Islamist groups. On the one hand there is the *inclusionary* model which aims to 'to co-opt Islamists into conditional participation in a political process which is in essence managed by the state' and, on the other

---

[75] Karawan, *The Islamist Impasse,* 13.
[76] Faksh, *The Future of Islam,* 33.

hand an *exclusionary* model which seeks 'to deny Islamists the opportunity to influence society, primarily through repression'.[77]

Most Arab rulers resist, to a greater or lesser degree, the inclusion of the general populace in decision-making processes. They also tend to distrust open and free communications. Hegemonic control is the order of the day. 'The reality of current Arab-Muslim politics is best characterized as hegemonic, closed state structures superimposed on emasculated societies'.[78] Faksh is thus trenchant in his critique of Middle East Islamic societies.

> Modern Middle Eastern states have grown increasingly supreme in the lives of their people, overwhelming civil society and inhibiting freedoms. The political area is controlled by the dominant elites presiding over increasingly centralized state authority. They are intolerant of independent tendencies outside the realm of their fiefdoms and are bent on barring the citizenry from open political participation. ... this has been the established practice from Morocco to Saudi Arabia: by and large, demands for political reform and popular involvement have either been suppressed or gone unheeded.[79]

Ironically, however, it has been the repression of political diversity and the suppression of rivals that has empowered the Islamic revivalist movements, especially in the closing decades of the twentieth century. The so-called 'Islamists' have not been slow in filling political vacuums, and taking on what to them, if not the majority Muslim populace, is perceived to be a bankrupt, even apostate, ruling elite.

So it is that the wider region of the Middle East (including countries such as Algeria and Lebanon) has spawned a number of Islamist groups that have impacted not only on the local political scene, but on the world stage at large. Such groups include the Egyptian-founded Muslim Brotherhood; the Egyptian ultra-militant organisation, the Islamic Group, which uses violence and assassination in the attempt to overthrow the Egyptian government and social structure in order to replace it with an Islamic state proper; and in Israel/Palestine the Islamic Resistance Movement, or Hamas, which, formed in 1987, is a development out of the Palestinian branch of the Muslim Brotherhood. This group embraces both political and militant Islamist principles.

In Algeria the *Groupe Islamique Armée* (GIA) is a militant organisation, which since 1992 has been dedicated to the overthrow of the secular Algerian regime by whatever means. In Lebanon the *Hizbollah*, or Party of God, is a radical Shi'a group dedicated to the creation of an Iranian style of Islamic state.

---

[77] See Karawan, *The Islamist Impasse*, 13.

[78] Faksh, *The Future of Islam*, 33

[79] Ibid.

Saudi Arabia

Founded in 1932 by the Saudi tribal patriarch Abdul Aziz ibn Saud, who became known as King Ibn Saud, the state of Saudi Arabia is the outcome of some two centuries of unity between two powerful groups: the Al-Saud tribal-warrior family and the assertively religious al-Wahhab family. Saudi Arabia is relatively unique as far as modern Islamic nation states go, for it has had no historical experience with Western colonialism or liberal secularism. Except for the Ottoman-Turkish suzerainty over the coastal areas on the Persian Gulf and the Red Sea, it has not been exposed to disruptive foreign control and influences. But, as Faksh notes,

> Saudi Arabia has not been the source of significant inspiration and leadership (ideologically and intellectually) in the region. It has long been shielded by a veil of traditional Islam. ... The Saudi system is the product of a desert culture marked by tribal division and conflict, harsh and austere living conditions, and religious piety and fanaticism. Family and religion are the sources of its legitimacy. ... It is a state propelled by Islamic ideology and consolidated by Saudi power.[80]

In 1722CE Ibn Abd al-Wahhab joined forces with Muhammad ibn Saud in the Arabian peninsula to form a religio-political alliance to their mutual benefit. The result of this development was the creation of the religious *Wahhabiyya* movement, or *Wahhabism*, which was, and is still today, an uncompromising assertion of a form of Sunni orthodoxy and orthopraxy. In particular, it is an aggressive self-interpretation of Islam consciously directed against all perceived innovations in doctrine and practice. Denis MacEoin comments that

> Wahhabism was not, in the strict sense, a new sect within Islam but a revival of orthodox Sunnism based on the teachings of the fourteenth-century scholar Ibn Taymiyya and the rulings of the Hanbali law-school, the strictest of the four recognized within the Sunni consensus. The particular targets of Wahhabi wrath were the Sufi brotherhoods ... Shi'ism, and the cult of saints common to both groups.[81]

The specific religious underpinning of Saudi Arabia has been provided by the revivalist Wahhabi doctrine, which has supplied motivation, direction and an answer to the quest for an extreme revivalist, or strict Islamist, state system.

> The spirit of Wahhabism exults in the ethos of piety, austerity, and egalitarianism as it is believed to have existed in the days of the Prophet. Its doctrine emphasizes a revivalist-fundamentalist-puritanical interpretation of Islam, calling for a return to the true religion of Islam as practised by *al-salaf* (the pious ancestors at the dawn of Islam) by insisting

---

[80] Ibid., 89.

[81] Denis MacEoin, 'Islam in the Middle East' in Peter Clarke, ed., *The World's Religions: Islam* (London: Routledge, 1990), 152.

upon a literal meaning and application of the original sources. In addition, the quintessential monotheism in Islam (*tawhid*) must be maintained against any elements of polytheism (*shirk*) or any practice even remotely suggestive of polytheism. Therefore, corrupting outside influences and innovations (*bid'a*) must be vigorously fought.[82]

Wahhabi ideology and Saudi power co-exist in a symbiotic relationship. Wahhabi Islam constitutes the basis of Saudi state identity and national unity. Islamic revivalism, or assertive fundamentalism, is state-sponsored within Saudi Arabia. Thus, 'armed with Wahhabi Islam as its official ideology, the state has always posed as the Islamic state *par excellence*. ... above all, it does not countenance religious diversity; the society wears a strait-jacket'.[83] But Wahhabism is neither a sect of Islam nor a school of Islamic jurisprudence apart from the four classical schools (Hanafi, Maliki, Shafi'i, Hanbali), which had crystallized by the middle of the tenth century. Though it follows Hanbali teaching in terms of its dogmatism and strict adherence to the primary sources—the Qur'an and Sunnah—Wahhabism does not repudiate the other schools of Islam. Wahhabism is more a movement, with a particular pietistic and political flavouring, of the Sunni Islam of Saudi Arabia, albeit a flavouring that is now being tasted elsewhere.

In many ways the hard line taken by the Saudis on religious and related matters could be seen as an idiosyncratic divergence from the wider Muslim ethos. Furthermore, although Wahhabism is formally the official viewpoint and worldview perspective of the Saudi state, expressions of dissident Wahhabism, or neo-Wahhabi fundamentalist resurgence as with an Osama bin Laden, for example, in fact stand in opposition to the Saudi monarchy. Such revivalism is dealt with harshly by the Saudi authorities. Nevertheless, the challenge of neo-Wahhabism has made significant impacts with, for example, an uprising that resulted in the takeover of the Grand Mosque of Mecca in November 1979.[84]

Of course, Saudi Arabia's petrodollar power, and the custodial prestige it enjoys on account of having two of Islam's holiest cities within its borders, including the great pilgrimage city of Mecca, mean that the Islam of the Saudis receives a high profile and is widely influential. Despite its problems—and in some ways, perhaps, because of them—Saudi Arabia is nonetheless a model, an ideological option and exercise of Islamic identity, which cannot be overlooked. It certainly stands at the hub of Islamic identity today.

Egypt

By contrast to Saudi Arabia, Egypt seems to be much more urbane. Here the life of Islam rubs shoulders with the remnants of an ancient civilisation, and the culture of

---

[82] Faksh, *The Future of Islam*, 90.

[83] Ibid., 91.

[84] Cf. ibid., 92.

contemporary Egypt is a confluence of many streams of ideological contribution, both ancient and modern. Zubaida remarks that, in Egypt,

> modern political Islam started in the second half of the nineteenth century in anticipation of a modern state on the European model which it mostly welcomed, but constructed in terms of 'original' Islam, as against the degenerate religion of the dynastic polity it opposed.[85]

This was a form of Islamic revivalism that was cast firmly in the mould of modernist reform. Indeed, nineteenth-century modernist aspirations led to a revivalist movement that advocated a synthesis of Islam and modernity. The spirit of the age, namely, liberalism and nationalism, contributed to Egypt's advance into the modern era. It continued under British rule (1882–1922CE) and also, after independence, under the monarchy (1922–52CE) that ushered in liberal constitutionalism and nationalism led by a Western-oriented elite. The emphasis was on building an integrated modern national community. Thus modernity was viewed as the medium wherein Egyptian society could advance, but within an Islamic context.[86]

The assumption of reformers in this context was that true Islam is not in conflict with modern life and can be reconciled with science and progress. They called for the restoration of ijtihad in order that Islam could assimilate Western ideas and culture without foregoing its essential principles. Such reformers tended to seek a societal awakening that was derived from religion, but not limited by a narrow interpretation, or inhibiting application, of religion. They would certainly defend the essence of Islam and its relevance to *al-nahda* (renaissance). Once Islam was purified of the accretions that had corrupted its essence and led to *al-jumud* (stagnation), it would adapt to modernity. Further, it was deemed easier to institute reforms based upon religious revival than upon European secular rationalism.[87]

The 1952 revolution led by Gamal Abdul Nasser emphasised populism and Arab radicalism and ushered in a period of nationalist socialism (1952–70CE). However, under Anwar Sadat (1970–81CE) Egypt experienced a shift toward a more politically open and economically liberal state of affairs. This produced an era of relative entrepreneurial activity and limited democratisation, which has been continued to a greater or lesser degree into the twenty-first century under President Hosni Mubarak. Throughout, the machinery of state resisted the efforts of a variety of Islamist activists to achieve their aims.[88]

---

[85] Zubaida, *Islam*, 39.

[86] See Faksh, *The Future of Islam*, 41ff.

[87] Ibid., 42.

[88] See ibid., 43.

Nevertheless, the modernist dream was severely challenged by the establishment of the Muslim Brotherhood (*Ikhwan*) in the late 1920s, and its rise during the 1930s and 1940s, both within Egypt and in neighbouring Arab countries.

Starting as a reform movement concerned mainly with religious activities and individual and social morality, the Ikhwan—or Brotherhood—grew in the 1940s into a populist Islamic movement with an activist political bent, advocating an Islamic polity based on Islamic norms and laws.[89]

This was a movement that rejected the modernist reform ideology of the intellectuals and instead aimed for, and received, much popular support for its own Islamist revivalist platform. Although it has harboured a political wing since the 1940s, its primary focus since the 1970s has been on the provision of social services, especially in the urban areas. The meeting of concrete human need, apart from being itself a virtue, is also the means of recruitment and the avenue of furthering the more abstract religio political goals.

The original aim of the Brotherhood was the reform of hearts and minds, to guide Muslims back to true religion, and away from the corrupt aspirations and conduct created by European dominance. The early politicisation of the movement placed this objective in the context of a virtuous community and an Islamic political order.[90] In the decades since its inception the Brotherhood has played a significant political role, much to the consternation of the Egyptian government and ruling elites. Zubaida remarks of the Muslim Brotherhood that:

In terms of ideology and organisation it represents a radical departure from historical forms of Islamic political agitations and actions. It is primarily urban and orthodox, distinct from the rural heterodox movements led by charismatics and often featuring messianic expectations. ... The Brotherhood is distinguished from these past patterns in being a modern political party, with a systematic organisation and recruitment, and a political programme imbued with the assumptions of the modern national political field[91] ...

In short, the Brotherhood is modern in style, but revivalist in substance. It would use modern methodologies to promote its atavistic aims. The Brotherhood was ideologically influenced by Sayyid Qutb who viewed twentieth-century Egyptian society as in a state of jahiliyya 'from which the true believers must separate themselves until sufficiently strong to conquer it for Islam'.[92]

---

[89] Ibid.
[90] Zubaida, *Islam*, 48.
[91] Ibid., 155.
[92] Ibid., 54.

Qutb's originality lies in the fact that, from the outset, he radically dissociated Islam from all other human societies of his time, not excluding self-styled 'Islamic' societies. He held that there was no longer any Islamic society, and therefore no point in seeking Islam in a world that had cast it out. There was nothing in the world but *jahiliyya* ... [93]

In Qutb's radical view, a true Muslim is one who breaks with the jahiliyya society, struggles to destroy it, then out of the ruins builds the Islamic state. Qutb gave coherent theoretical expression to the revivalist mentality of which the Brotherhood was a leading expression. But it has not been the only Islamic revivalist group to draw on the ideas of Qutb. The Indian (later Pakistan) Islamic Society, *Jama'at-i Islami,* for example, extrapolated a very rigorist view and 'declared all people outside their group to be infidels' on the one hand, whereas, on the other, the group calling themselves *Islamic Jihad* 'declared only the rulers to be infidels, while ordinary people were Muslims'.[94]

Mahmud Faksh casts the discussion of Islamic revivalism in the Middle East in the context of 'three periods of Islamic revival associated with the failure of various societies to deal with an accumulation of internal and external crises arising from sociopolitical and economic weakness and from foreign hegemony'.[95] The first is the religious reaction of the nineteenth century, which finds focus in the Arabian Wahhabi movement and in modernist reform in Egypt, among others. The second phase, spanning the early decades of the twentieth century, comes to focus in the Muslim Brotherhood of Egypt, and the Muslim Society—Jama'at-i Islami— of the Indian subcontinent.

The third phase begins in the aftermath of the 1967 Arab–Israel war 'and continued through the 1970s amid social and economic dislocation, class disparities, and authoritarian state structures'.[96] This is contemporary 'Islamism', in the sense of a highly charged political ideology where Islam is not just viewed holistically as a religio-political ideology but is asserted as such, becoming the vehicle for the activist's struggle against the ruling powers. Faksh judges such Islamism to be 'a product of the failed modernisation policies of the past fifty years, which have eventuated in unmet expectations and consequent militancy'.[97] Although much of the expression of Islamism in Egypt has been of a militant nature, Egyptian revivalism has been offset by the modernist forces of liberalism and nationalism. On the other hand, Saudi Arabia 'has had no experience with

---

[93] Gilles Kepel, *The Revenge of God: The Resurgence of Islam, Christianity and Judaism in the Modern World* (Cambridge: Polity Press, 1994), 19. See also William E. Shepard, 'Sayyid Qutb's Doctrine of Jahiliyya', *International Journal of Middle East Studies,* 35 (2003), 521–45.

[94] Zubaida, *Islam,* 54.

[95] Faksh, *The Future of Islam,* xi.

[96] Ibid., xii.

[97] Ibid., xiii; cf. Olivier Roy, *The Failure of Political Islam* (Cambridge, MA: Harvard University Press), 1994.

Western colonialism or liberal secularism. The country has long been kept behind a veil of tradition Wahhabi Islam, the nexus of the Saudi state since its inception in 1932'.[98] Nevertheless, despite its extreme Islamic identity and ideology, even the Saudi state is not immune to internal challenge and attempts to undermine the ruling powers.

Conclusion

Islamism is a multifaceted phenomenon. It involves piety, but increased devotion does not just focus on religious observance. It also looks to the application of social, economic, and political values. The critical factor is that it is *Islam*, and not a secular ideology, which shapes attitudes and directs actions. Islamism involves a high-level conscientisation process and a deeply held intentionality. Further, there are many disquieting elements associated with it that act as catalysts for revival, together with a wide range and number of attempts to make Islam politically relevant. Religion is cast in the role of the critic of government. But Piscatori also observes that there is no real or overall co-ordination to the phenomenon of Islamic revivalism. Rather it is marked by a high level of idiosyncretism and local flavour: 'the form that revival takes and the effect that it produces vary according to circumstance and place'.[99] And of course, as he notes, that revivalism within Islam attracts a perception of militancy is a function of the way in which it has 'has captured most attention in the West and generated negative, undifferentiated images'.[100]

John Esposito, in commenting upon the ideological worldview of Islamism, or Islamic revivalism as he prefers to term it, states:

> At the heart of the revivalist worldview is the belief that the Muslim world is in a state of decline. Its cause is departure from the straight path of Islam; its cure a return to Islam in personal and public life which will ensure the restoration of Islamic identity, values, and power ... radical movements assume that Islam is not simply an ideological alternative for Muslim societies but a theological and political imperative.[101]

Esposito identifies four options for an Islamic response to Western colonialism.[102] The first is the way of *rejection*: following the model of jihad as a sacred struggle to fight against, and overcome, the forces of antipathy and threat. The second is the way of *withdrawal*: following the model of hijra that is, leaving the territory no

---

[98] Faksh, ibid., xiv.

[99] Piscatori, *Islam in a World of Nation-States*, 38.

[100] Ibid.

[101] John L. Esposito, *The Islamic Threat: Myth or Reality?* 2nd edn (New York: Oxford University Press, 1995), 19.

[102] Ibid., 53ff.

longer under Muslim rule. Directly opposite is the third way, which involves the embrace of *secularism* and *Westernisation* viewed as movements of positive modernist reform. Here the values of Islam are coupled with taking up the practical advantages of the colonising culture and power. But Esposito notes that:

> A major result of modernization was the emergence of new elites and a growing bifurcation of Muslim society, epitomized in its legal and educational systems. The coexistence of traditional religious and modern secular schools, each with its own curriculum, teachers, and constituencies, produced two classes with divergent worldviews: a modern Westernized elite minority and a more traditional, Islamically oriented majority.[103]

The fourth way, Islamic *modernism*, attempts to bridge the gap between Islamic traditionalists and secular reformers. As Esposito notes, 'Islamic modernists incorporated the internal community concerns of eighteenth-century revivalism with the need to respond to the threat of European colonialism and the demands of modernity'.[104] Such modernist reformers

> preached the need and acceptability of a selective synthesis of Islam and modern Western thought; condemned unquestioned veneration and imitation of the past; reasserted their right to reinterpret (*ijtihad*) Islam in light of modern conditions; and sought to provide an Islamically based rationale for educational, legal, and social reform to revitalize a dormant and impotent Muslim community.[105]

It must, of course, be stressed that the vast majority of Muslim people are moderate in their outlook, in that reform would be seen as something that occurs through the gradual transformation of Muslim society rather than being effected through violent revolution. Indeed, the Islamic advocacy of violent overthrow and revolutionary aggression is, in reality, a minority perspective even though it is the one that hits the headlines. In an ever-changing modern world the issues of identity and ideology will continue to be crucial within and to Islamic life and religio-political discourse. They will be equally critical with respect to the matter of dialogue with Islam. It is to this challenge I now turn.

---

[103] Ibid., 54.

[104] Ibid., 55; cf. Albert Hourani, *Arabic Thought in the Liberal Age* (Oxford: Oxford University Press), 1970.

[105] Esposito, *The Islamic Threat*, 55.

PART III
ENGAGEMENT WITH ISLAM
PROSPECTS FOR DIALOGUE

Chapter 9

Barriers to Dialogue
Perceptions of Islam

The issue of Western perceptions of Islam, and Western perspectives on Muslims and things Islamic, constitutes a topic of ongoing concern both for Muslims and non-Muslims alike. It has come to the fore in a dramatic and global sense ever since the terrorist attacks that damaged the Pentagon and destroyed the World Trade Centre in Manhattan, New York, on 11 September 2001. The twenty-first century seems hardly to be underway and already the hopeful signs for improved relations with Islam and the Muslim world, at least from a Christian perspective as intimated in Chapter 6, seem highly problematic. The matter of how Islam and Muslims are perceived by Westerners and the Western media will require sustained work if there is to be any significant change for the better. But the issue nevertheless needs to be addressed, especially in the context of interfaith dialogical encounter. And this encounter takes place at many levels, from everyday mundane and serendipitous interactions to intentional acts of interactive discourse. Furthermore, in this latter context questions of mutuality of perception necessarily arise. How does each dialogical partner view the other? How is each viewed by the other? These will be answered, inevitably, within the process of any actual discursive dialogue itself. But often the issue needs some preliminary consideration before dialogue can proceed, especially if there is to be any real hope of achieving open and honest interaction.

Identifying, and thereby in some measure overcoming, barriers to dialogue that arise from distorted perception and uninformed presumption is a necessary prolegomenon. Each party to dialogue must do that for themselves in the first place, of course. Each of the parties to dialogue ought to be prepared to encounter the other in dialogue by identifying their own barrier in respect of that other. Such owning of barriers and seeking to overcome them is an exercise in humility, a self-declaration of vulnerability, an openness to correction and growth in self-awareness which, if undertaken well, can lead to a climate of greater openness toward, and empathetic awareness of, the other with whom we are engaged in dialogue.

In this chapter I wish to address the issue of barriers to dialogue by undertaking a critical review of some key dimensions of Western perspectives on Islam. This task will be guided by a dual hermeneutical approach that makes use of the terms and concepts *image* and *imagination*. In this regard I shall review and discuss some of the perceptions—or images—of Islam that are prevalent in the West, then undertake a critical analysis and review of these. That is to say, I shall bring to bear critical analysis, and an intelligent use of imagination, both to examine the nature of these perceptions and explore and suggest, albeit in a limited and provisional way, how they might appropriately be addressed and perhaps countered.

Ignorance and media image

It goes without saying that the Western perception of Islam is dominated by misrepresentation and distorted image, which derive largely from past misunderstanding and ignorance. I contend that 'ignorance' may be manifest in at least three modalities, namely innocent, blind and culpable. On the one hand there is *innocent* ignorance, or ignorance *simpliciter*. This is the situation of a naïve 'not-knowing', yielding the direct and unequivocal 'don't know' response when a question of knowledge or perception is posed. However, this form of ignorance provides opportunity for correction through the provision of information and the processes of education. It implies no intentional prejudice on the part of the one who is innocently ignorant. It is the default position of cognitive deficiency that provides the impetus to learn.

On the other hand, *blind* ignorance is something else again. It is ignorance born of an intellectual incapability, or cognitive barrier, that effectively prevents any 'seeing' or 'knowing' other than what has been dictated by the worldview perspectives held. It yields a 'can't know; its beyond our ken' response: knowledge and image, of the other are so utterly proscribed by the worldview of the knower that no alternative perspective or image is admissible. Here the notion of applying a corrective simply through information is inadequate. Any educational process, if attempted, will require sustained and careful execution to effect any real change. But it can happen, nonetheless. Change is not precluded *a priori*. Even if change is unwelcome or resisted, the premise of this mode of ignorance is basically cognitive inertia, which in principle can be overcome. Indeed it is this modality of ignorance that yields to the great shifts in social ordering and cultural life as happened, for instance, in the momentous changes brought about in the USA by the civil rights movement in the twentieth century.

However, there is yet another kind of ignorance that goes beyond even that occasioned by the blinding effect of a limited perspective and an intransigently closed mind. This third kind is *culpable* ignorance, that is, an active ignoring: the deliberate refusal to know, the avoidance of the challenge to cognitive change, the reinforcement of a prejudicial perspective by deliberately ignoring the issue at hand. This is ignorance born of an active dismissal of alternative possibilities, the out-of-hand rejection of options presented for alternate ways of thinking, understanding and interpreting. This modality goes hand-in-glove with the attitude and mindset that harbours most forms of fundamentalism. It produces an intentional 'won't know' or 'not wanting to know' response. It is resistant to any information contrary to its own; it is inimical to educational process; it treats cognitive change as effectively, if not actually, treasonable.

It is worth noting that all three forms of ignorance surfaced in the context of acts of global terrorism perpetrated by the extremism of Osama bin Laden's al-Qaeda network, and the subsequent battle over Afghanistan to neutralise the network and crush the extremist Taliban regime there. As a result, many people became aware of their innocent ignorance of things Islamic and sought knowledge. Others found to their discomfort that their secure understanding of the world and the reality of Islam was challenged: their 'blindness', born of their cognitive *sitz-im-leben*, was shaken. They may have joined with the innocently ignorant to redress their ignorance, but would likely find it a more disturbing process, possibly precipitating some into the 'culpably ignorant' camp: those for whom 'Islamic' terrorism requires no educational rethink, but confirms a prejudicial perspective of all things Islamic, and their own worldview in respect to that.

But, of course, as with all conflicts the first casualty, it is said, is truth. How much of the media portrayal and the deluge of analytical articles, for and against either side in the so-called 'war on terrorism'—with the unspoken, but generally universally assumed, understanding that it is Islamic terrorism that is in the frame— is the product of propaganda, the machination of so-called political 'spin-doctors'? How much is simply the uncritical reflection of stereotypical image and biased (mis)perception? The former Prime Minister of Malaysia, Mahathir Mohamad, was one Muslim political leader who spoke out vociferously about Islam and terrorism. He lambasted the Western stereotyping of terrorism as 'a Muslim monopoly' while presenting all others as 'just terrorists unconnected with their ethnic group or culture or religion'.[1] A politician's rhetoric may overstate the case, but a salient point is made nonetheless. Image distortion derived from ignorance, of whatever kind, continues to impact upon the world in ways that now make even more urgent the issues I am seeking to address.

What, then, could be identified as predominant Western perceptions of Islam? Or perhaps, better, what is the predominant perception, at least so far as that can be detected, in the 'Western' mind, be it Christian or secular? Of course, the way the question is put, and the way it is usually answered, is a gross oversimplification of a complex issue. But, for the sake of discussion and argument, the simple approach is not without foundation and validity. For the answer, arguably and sad to say, is a negative one. It is best summed up by the word 'threat'. We may see this negative reaction both through media image and report, and, more particularly, how people in the West may be observed reacting to such image and reportage. Western newspaper articles are likely to feature headlines and items that speak, for example, of Egypt's 'largest Islamic extremist group'; Algerian 'Muslim fundamentalists'; Afghanistan's 'Taliban terrorists' and so on. Indeed the word 'Taliban', Arabic for 'student', is now likely to be absorbed into most languages as a synonym for 'terrorist'. But, in reality, such negative and arresting headlines utilising Islamic terms of reference are commonplace, and have been so for years. Indeed it can

---

[1] Mahathir Mohamad, *Terrorism and the Real Issues* (Malaysia: Pelanduk Publications, 2003), 14.

seem that nearly all news concerning Islam that is reported in our papers or covered on television concerns aggressive Muslim action of one sort or another.

The media image of Islam that is portrayed is all too often a threatening one, and in the uncritical Western imagination the particular and dramatic activities of some specific Muslims is generalised: thus the religion, Islam, is perceived as itself a threat. And, in recent years, it would appear that, apart from Bosnia, Kosovo, and perhaps Kuwait and Kashmir, Muslim countries or regions as a group have been tarnished with the brush of aggression, with Muslims in them branded as 'bad guys', every one. Or so it seems. Of course, as already acknowledged, this is a gross oversimplification. Or is it? Even as we recognise its limitation, the picture I am portraying is perhaps not so far from the reality of what passes for the predominant Western *perception* of Islam and Muslims, particularly at the level of the masses and the popular press.

Although there is genuine interest from within some western communities to find out more about Islam, often such interest is derived from an assumption that Islam, and Islamic countries, pose a potential, if not real, politico-military and/or religio-ideological threat. Of course we are to remember that there are several competing ideological options for Muslims (see Chapter 8 above) of which it is 'Islamism', largely because of its apparent ascendancy within much of the Islamic world, that is really being referred to in the context of this discussion. The respected American scholar of Islam, John Esposito, is one who has written on the theme of Islam perceived in this sense. In one article he noted that the 'many faces of contemporary Islam have tended to be subsumed under the monolith of "Islamic fundamentalism", which has become equated with violence and terrorism'.[2] Thus the incidents that hit the headlines have reinforced images of Islam as a militant, expansionist religion, rabidly anti-American, vigorously anti-Christian, relentlessly anti-Jewish, and intent upon war with the West. This became blatantly evident in connection with the emergence of the Taliban movement in Afghanistan, and its associations in Pakistan and elsewhere in the Muslim world, as an expression of resurgent Islamic extremism. The result of situations such as this is that, as Esposito concludes, 'Islam's relationship with the West has often been marked less by understanding than by mutual ignorance and stereotyping, confrontation and conflict'.[3]

Esposito himself has identified the Western perception of Islam as a threat in three interconnected arenas, namely political, demographic, and religio-social. Leaving aside the rather more obvious political and religio-social arenas, what might be meant by 'demographic'? Esposito views this as the identification of a perceived threat in reference to population shifts. That is to say, it is now a commonplace, for example, to see the presence of significant Muslim minority populations within North America and Europe, as well, indeed, in most other

---

[2] John Esposito, 'The Threat of Islam: Myth or Reality?' *Concilium* (Vol. 3, 1994), 39–47.

[3] Ibid., see also John Esposito, *The Islamic Threat: Myth or Reality?* 2nd edn (London: Oxford University Press, 1995).

countries within the so-called 'Western World'. Until recently such countries, for the most part, saw themselves as either secular or Christian, even if nominally so. But although ethnic rivalry and prejudice, irrespective of religion, must not be underrated, more recently it would seem that the growing overt self-identification of migrant communities as intentionally Islamic has fuelled a burgeoning xenophobia so far as the perception of Muslim communities and people is concerned.

In England, a report entitled *Islamophobia: A challenge for us all,*[4] showed how, during the 1980s and 1990s, there emerged within segments of British society a 'culture of contempt for Islam and British Muslims'.[5] The report contrasts open and closed views of Islam and Muslims. An open view sees Islam, rather like Christianity, as a diverse, multifaceted, and dynamic complex phenomenon, in ongoing dialogue with the wider society in which it is set. The closed view, however, 'presents Islam as monolithic and static, an aggressive and ideological enemy to be combated'.[6] The *Church Times* article reported on how the authors of the Report—a Commission comprising Christian, Jewish and Muslim members— were 'shocked by the dread and dislike of Islam across all sections of English society.' It drew attention to the report's findings on the image of Islam in the media.

> In the press, contemptuous stereotypes and cartoons were not confined to the tabloids but included the broadsheets across the political spectrum. If some of the political cartoons had featured a Jewish rather than a Muslim character, they undoubtedly would have been judged anti-Semitic. ... The danger in this is that a 'conceptual Muslim' will be fixed in the public mind, as the 'conceptual Jew' was in the history of anti-Semitism.[7]

The substance of a report such as this, and the issues it identifies, is not unique to Britain. It represents a Western mindset forged by misleading image and fuelled by distorted imagination. Interestingly, the article and report indicate that it is the secular Western imagination that often has far greater trouble coming to terms with Islam and Muslims than the Christian one.

Germany provides an interesting example of the interaction of Islam with a Western Christian society. Germany is a modern secular democracy with a particular dominant Christian religious identity. The Basic Law (*Grundgesetz*), in existence since 1949, guarantees freedom of conscience to individuals and

---

[4] Published by Runnymede Trust, London, 1997.

[5] See review article 'Facing down the bogeyman of Islam' in *Church Times*, 24 October 1997.

[6] Church Times, ibid.

[7] Ibid.

protection to social institutions, including Churches.[8] The predominant Christian category of religious identity is subdivided between Catholic and Protestant. This division, reflecting antecedents of modern religious history and the historical geography of Germany—with the North substantially Protestant and the South dominantly Catholic—is embedded within German cultural identity as well as in the structures of education, particularly at the tertiary level. German religious identity, by and large framed as Christian, is irrespective of active Church membership or allegiance. But of particular significance—especially in what is now a post-modern pluralist era—is the question of shifting relativities of religious identity. The Christian 'Catholic versus Protestant' delineation is fast becoming an anachronism in the face of both the relentless rise of a secular mentality on the one hand, and the ascendancy of Europe's new major religion, Islam, on the other. What is happening to German religious identity as the parameters set by the past come increasingly under question in consequence of inevitable changes to religious demographics? How well does Germany's Basic Law apply to and protect the freedoms and sensibilities of Muslims in that country? Similar questions can be asked of other European countries, of course, and indeed of just about any major Western nation today.

Islam emerged as a significant element of German life through the post-World War II use of foreign workers and immigrants. Turkish immigrants largely define the character of contemporary German Islam or, more accurately perhaps, Islam in Germany. Bosnian Muslims, who fled the civil war in the former Yugoslavia during the 1990s, constitute the second-largest immigrant group, albeit one that maintains close ties with the Turkish community. Thus Islam is presented as substantially a Turkish 'other' in terms of German religious demographics and cultural identities. Yet a 1999 figure of 2.6 million Muslims in Germany, being equivalent to roughly 5 per cent of the combined Protestant and Catholic Christian population, is identified as comprising 'Muslims from 41 nations'[9]. Islam is identified as 'not-German', but how many Muslims might actually be German citizens, even German-born? And how many ethnically European Germans now belong to this religion? Figures are opaque, but clearly Islam in Germany, as elsewhere, is on the rise, and it is not all due to immigration. One authoritative statistical report cites a figure of 3.2 million Muslims in Germany in 2001.[10] However, it notes that of that figure only 10 per cent hold German passports, and only 11 000 are stated as actually being Muslims of Germanic origin (*deutschstämmige Muslime*).

Islam is reckoned as the second religion of Europe.[11] What does this mean for Germany? Formal and informal Muslim organisations are crucial in achieving both

---

[8] See *Tatsachen über Deutschland* (Fankfurt/Main: Societäts-Verlag, 1999), 409–12.

[9] Ibid.

[10] *Religionswissenschaftlicher Medien- und Informationsdienst e. V.*, web-site: http://www.uni-leipzig.de/~religion/remid_info_zahlen.htm

[11] See Francis Clark, 'Religion and State in Europe' in Jørgen S. Nielsen, ed., *Religion and Citizenship in Europe and the Arab World* (London: Grey Seal Books, 1992), 53.

collective and individual recognition within the European cultural mainstream. In Germany, for instance, Islamic networks and affiliations often serve as intermediary structures representing the unique educational and doctrinal interests of many diverse Muslim communities. And this extends to the extremisms of an al-Qaeda network as evidenced by the investigations into the so-called suicide pilots of 11 September 2001, some of whom had been current students at a university in Hamburg.

Clearly there are growing social and political implications—not to mention theological ones—in respect to the incursion of Islam within contemporary German life. And of course the media can, and do, play a major role in respect of the integration or otherwise of different religious communities into the larger matrix of German identity. Media presentation, and the image thereby created—with its resultant stirring of the popular imagination—is all important. In respect to Islam, stereotypes still strengthen fears of radical Islam despite the fact that only a small minority among the over 2000 registered mosque associations in Germany identify with militant theologies.[12] Such perceptions persist even in the face of a newly emerging Islamic consciousness characterised in part by the adoption of Western dress and music within normatively Muslim urban Turkish communities. Yet, as I have been led to understand, an attempt of the government of Gerhard Schroeder to establish dual citizenship in respect of the majority of Turkish Muslims in Germany was thwarted by the widespread belief, promoted in part by the German right and the popular media, that the planned reform to the existing citizenship law would afford such immigrants special status. Under the guise of not wanting to offer an elite advantage that might upset the appearance of egalitarianism, a situation of religiously demarcated disadvantagement was retained.

Ironically it is the participation of various Islamic organisations in democratic processes—as opposed to the anti-democratic stance of most extremist groups— which Esposito identifies as posing a further, even formidable, threat so far as the West is concerned. In some respects this is because the West does not see that Islam and democracy are really compatible: but this is surely to beg the question of the nature of democracy. However, Esposito has identified the essential religio-social conundrum: in contrast to the image of Islam as a monolith, and therein a threatening entity, within the world of Islam there are differing forms of government and the ordering of the instruments of government, ranging from the monarchical and autocratic to various forms of socialist and democratic states.

Western media and commentators often overlook the fact that from within Islam there have come democratic movements that have critiqued their own autocratic rulers and have sought change through the ballot box rather than by the bullet. Tragically, there have been recent examples of the exercise of the popular democratic vote being quashed or thwarted by ruling forces and the power of the status quo as happened, for instance, in Algeria late in the twentieth century. There

---

[12] See 'Islam in France and Germany': http://www.csis.org/europe/frm990412.html

is a history of vigorous internal critique and dissent within the world of Islam. Democratic influences have been—and in many situations in today's world still—strongly held and advanced. The outcomes may not be as the proponents would wish, or readily identifiable from a Western perspective. In this respect Esposito, rightly in my view, identifies the challenge of resolving tensions between Western and Islamic forms of democracy as a contributing factor to redressing the Western misperception of Islam.

The problem of tolerance of minorities within Islamic countries—or in nations with a dominant Muslim constituency—is an ongoing challenge within the Islamic Ummah which also impacts on the Western perception of Islam. In particular, the status of 'non-believers' is again an issue.

> A modern, liberal, secular pluralistic approach is contested in many quarters today by those who argue that the state's Islamic ideology requires a commitment to Islam. This would preclude non-Muslims from holding key posts in government ... Without a reinterpretation of classical Islamic legal doctrines regarding non-Muslim citizens as 'protected people' (*dhimmi*), an Islamic ideologically-oriented state would at best be a limited democratic state with a weak pluralistic profile.[13]

However, Esposito ends on a positive note: Islam is to be perceived more as a challenge than a threat:

> It challenges the West to avoid reducing the richness and diversity of Islam and the Muslim experience to a monolithic threat. Followers of Judaism and Christianity are challenged to become aware of the faith of Islam, to acknowledge their Muslim brothers and sisters as children of Abraham, and to distinguish between Islam and its exploitation by extremists much as it demands that others do so when confronted by the violence and fanaticism of Christian and Jewish extremist groups.[14]

Furthermore, political Islam 'challenges the conventional Western secular world-view': just as 'Muslim governments are challenged to be more responsive to popular demands for political liberalization and greater popular participation' so Western powers 'are challenged to stand by the democratic values they embody ...'.[15] In other words, there is a multifaceted dimension to the challenge posed within the secular and political arena by religious sensibilities and values simply because such values impinge on real life, on the lives of communities and the individuals within them. When communal existence proceeds in a relatively stable fashion, religion can appear to be relegated to the margins of social life. But in

---

[13] Esposito, in *Concilium,* 45.
[14] Ibid.
[15] Ibid., 46.

times of stress, crisis, or social dysfunction of one sort or another, religious perspectives and identities tend to come to the fore.

However, to attribute either the cause of, or the solution to, the particular societal malaise simply to religion alone is to misunderstand the nature of the religion and misplace responsibility and accountability. For example, Jürgen Moltmann and Hans Küng, in their editorial to the issue of the journal *Concilium* which contained Esposito's article, made reference to the thesis that, on the whole, wars of the twentieth century have been wars of civilisations rather than religious wars *per se*, which was often the dominant situation previously. Thus they stated that the idea that Islam 'could emerge as an aggressor in such a "clash of civilizations" is the fear of many people in the West and perhaps the hope of some Muslim fundamentalists and radicals'. They added 'we have to grant that certainly in our days there is no lack of tensions and aggressions, not only on the part of Islam but also on the part of some "Christian" countries (one need only look at Bosnia-Herzegovina)'.[16] Indeed. And many more places since.

Image and perception

I wonder, though, whether in fact the perception of Islam as a threat is obtained by superimposing an image of particular religious identity, and therefore of root cause, onto a situation that may be better understood in terms of socio-economic imbalances of one sort or another. These may relate to, but are not materially caused by, religion or religious factors. Thus it is not Muslims struggling for justice, even taking up arms, *simply* because of their Islamic faith, but rather Muslim people, as people, *striving* for a better political deal, a more just context for their existence. It so happens that their political rhetoric and will-to-succeed is informed and strengthened by their Islamic ideology and language. But in principle this is no different to the situation of, for example, Christian people, as people, struggling for justice wherever they are, and finding succour and inspiration from their particular faith. Of course, the history of Christian warfare has given *that* faith such a bad press that the secular assumption of the West is that *all* religion should be kept out of the political arena so as not to confuse religious sensibilities with political realities. This viewpoint is transferred to Islam, and it is there underscored as being a problematic perception simply because it is of the inherent nature of Islam *not* to divorce religious ideology from political reality.

Differences in politico-institutional arrangements both within and between religions reflect differences in religio-political ideology and underlying religious philosophy. Mutual misunderstanding is the outcome of not grasping the significance of this and, as a corollary, of adjudging the overt arrangements of one through the ideological lens of the other. Typically, from the Western side, this

---

[16] *Concilium*, vii.

means perceptions of Islamic social and political life (which life is necessarily grounded directly upon religious sensibility and outlook) are skewed because of the uncritical application of secular assumptions. Thus religious sensibilities are set to one side when it comes to matters of social and political arrangements and, because of this, there is a negative judgement placed on societies that allow for, or even look to, the informing and formational effect of religion: this, to the secularised West, is anathema. The Christian Church may, ideally, wish it were otherwise, but the reality of plural religious identity within Christianity means that Christian churches accept the secular context as at least allowing the freedom to co-exist without interference from state authorities, and rely then upon moral suasion and the enunciation of principle to influence change in the political arena, albeit indirectly. This is a vastly different climate of religio-political interaction to that which pertains within intentionally Islamic states.

To take the discussion further, I identify the following as among the critical issues pertinent to addressing the overall question of Western perspectives on Islam: a *structural parallelism*; the impact of what might be termed a '*dhimmi-parallel effect*'; the phenomenon of *religious identity displacement*; the use of the term *fundamentalism*; and the use of *negative descriptive terms*.

The first issue concerns the application of a *structural parallelism* of the contemporary sacred-versus-secular, or church-versus-state, outlook which, when taken into the Islamic arena, obscures, for Westerners who apply it, the reality and scope of the Islamic outlook for Muslims themselves. That is to say, the drawing of any sort of structural and/or institutional parallel between Christianity and Islam, for example, is very fraught and likely to be highly misleading. At the same time, to make the observation that this difficulty indicates an inherent problematic within Islam *vis-à-vis* relations with Christianity, or the West, is likewise highly problematic. Whether applied positively or negatively, the problem of assuming structural parallelism leads the side that makes the application to indulge in unwarranted judgements and conclusions about the other. The church–state structures that apply in the West—and which are by no means uniform in any case—do not apply to Islamic countries. This may lead to pragmatic problems, as for example the difficulty often in getting a balance of 'representation' at Christian–Muslim dialogue events when one side has institutional organisations (Churches) used to mandating representatives, but there is no parallel structure on the Muslim side to do likewise. However such institutional differences ought not to gainsay a negative judgement about the nature of Islam from a western perspective. To the extent it does, then this is yet another barrier to be dismantled in the cause of interfaith dialogue.

The second issue concerns the impact of what might be called a *dhimmi-parallel effect*. By this I refer to a parallelism—in regard to both experience of, and perception about—that holds in respect to 'outpost' or diaspora communities of one religion residing within the geographic and socio-political boundaries of another religion. That is to say, there is a parallel of sorts between the minority communities of religions X and Y residing, respectively, within majority societies of Y and X. In this case, the perception in the West would be—and often is—that minority Western-type or Christian communities that live within Islamic countries can be, or indeed are, treated at best as only second-class citizens; at worst they may be actively discriminated against, even persecuted, as has been the case for many other dhimmi communities down through the ages. This perception, or image, applies in particular to such countries that, to varying degrees are, or are attempting to be, intentional Islamic states. Despite the rhetoric of dhimma that Muslim apologists might offer to reassure the minority community involved, the persistent negative image of an inherent ascription of inferiority and consequential discriminatory practice predominates. And where today, as in Pakistan for example, there are calls by some Islamic activists to subsume all citizens under Islamic Shari'a, this only serves to fuel a deepening disquiet in the West and underscores the tendency to jump to the worst conclusions and assume an uncritical deprecatory outlook toward all things Islamic. The negative impact of Islamic ideals upon the Western image of Islam only deepens.

However, Muslims themselves, both as individuals and in communities, can and do encounter a parallel experience when living as a minority group within Western societies, whether self-proclaimed Christian countries, or secular states of Christian origin. Muslims in these contexts may be subject to prejudice and negative, even hostile, reaction. This may occur independently of, as well as being directly fuelled by, the Western image such as outlined above. The British report mentioned above drew attention to the fact that negative English reaction in one city to proposals by Muslims to build a mosque there was prompted, at least in part, by an awareness that British service personnel in the Gulf War had to hold church services in secret. 'We Christians were repressed: why should we grant favour to Muslims?' was the essential retort.

More generally, there was evidence of a general perception that Muslim countries repress and even persecute other religions as a matter of course. Again the responsive retort was to conclude that favour should not be granted. So, Muslims constituting a minority in a Christian country, having nothing to do with the policies of Middle East Muslim countries, and who are themselves, indeed, citizens or residents of that country, find themselves treated as inferior persons. Minority Muslim communities find themselves compromised in terms of religious sensibility and the demands of local laws or the imposition of local mores. Hence the phenomenon of a 'parallel effect' with respect to the experiences of minorities, ostensibly protected (dhimma) with regard to the stated policies of rights, duties and obligations on the part of the host societies. Such experience applies both to Muslims within many Western or 'Christian' societies on the one hand and, of course, a number of Western communities within Islamic countries on the other.

A third critical issue arises from the above: the impact of contemporary demography and what I would call *religious identity displacement*. It is a *sine qua non* of life today that the earth has become a global village, or to use a more contemporary phrase, a single 'global marketplace'. This can be seen not only through the agency of modern communications, but more particularly as an outcome of the trans-nationalisation of trade and commerce, the manifest economic interdependency which excludes virtually no country. All this means that people in the contemporary world no longer need—whether by choice or necessity—to remain bounded by their ethno-geographic origins.

As never before people are on the move. Individuals, families, even whole communities, relocate spatially. And most usually this means a linguistic and cultural relocation. This in turn can be a spur to religious response: the religious identity that adhered to the original location is carried, and conserved, yet at the same time challenged, and, like as not, changed. Even where there is a high intent to preserve the originating faith, the history of religions shows that the displacement effects of demographic relocation disrupt religious identity. The long-term result is to render the relationship of the 'diaspora' identity with that of the 'homeland' problematic, whatever the religion.

Thus the fact that many Muslims themselves experience the effects of geographical displacement, to varying degrees, needs to be taken into account with respect to the issue of Western perceptions of Islam. There needs to be a more openly acknowledged recognition of the principle that within a given society all communities who value and seek to preserve the essence of their particular cultural or religious identity must, as it were, 'present' themselves—both to themselves as well as to the wider society in which they are situated—as 'other'. That is to say, they must identify themselves as being 'other than' the society in which they are set: their identity is a matter of difference. And this is necessarily so even where there is, at the same time, a manifest desire to be 'good citizens' of the society in which they find themselves, that is, to be to that extent the 'same' as their fellow citizens.

Good citizenship of the wider society requires law-abidingness, which may involve a measure of compromise so far as strict adherence to religious codes pertinent to particular communal identity is concerned. But the essence of religious piety and the observances of practices may be maintained nonetheless, perhaps even more intently. This is so as to provide a counterpoint to necessary cultural adaptation and compromise in the inevitable dialectical tension between holding 'difference' and promoting 'sameness' as the relocated community seeks both to retain originating identity and adjust to its new environment. It behoves Western communities, who are the hosts to other ethnic and religious groups and communities, to take greater cognisance of this principle and the effects of religious identity displacement, especially in respect of Muslim communities and the issue of the image of Islam.

It is all too easy for an unthinking attitude, articulated from within a host community, of expectation that a newcomer ought to deny original identity and get on with the business of assimilation: to become as quickly as possible 'one of us'. This attitude holds that the newcomer, if desirous of full acceptance and integration, ought to adopt a new identity—namely, 'our' identity—by virtue of taking on 'our' language, cultural practices, even religion. Although this attitude still abounds among many people in the West, history has shown that the outcome may not be as clear-cut as it first appears, as assimilated Jews in Nazi Germany, for example, found to their cost. And as the 'melting-pot' model of intercultural relationships within Western societies gives way to the larger recognition and acceptance of the model of pluralist co-existence—the basis of religious pluralism as such—so the reality of the presence of the religio-cultural 'other', now situated within an otherwise 'homogeneous' community, is becoming a more widespread experience. But this reality, while manifest, has yet in many places to issue in the fullness of acceptance of diversity and affirmation of plurality of religious identity as culturally enriching. Until that occurs, the likelihood of the expression of threat to identity, both in regard to the newcomer as well as in regard to the host community, will remain, with attendant deleterious outcomes.

The fourth critical issue concerns the use of the term *fundamentalism* to label all things intentionally Islamic, that is, where Islamic motives, goals, and programmatic ideals are clear and overtly promoted by the Muslim community concerned. The loose and uncritical application of this term has led to all sorts of confusion and has been a prime source of media mischief-making. The term 'fundamentalism' itself is of uniquely Christian origin and is loaded with a particular and theologically nuanced meaning. Arguably, in its 'soft' application, referring to a declared belief in the fundamental propositions of a faith-perspective, then all good Muslims are fundamentalists, and to that extent are happy to be so identified. But that is not how the term is applied or intended in the West's use of it with respect to Islam. Here a particular, politically nuanced, meaning is loaded onto the word. In this application, fundamentalism means political extremism: forms of radical fanaticism which find direct expression and engagement in the world of everyday affairs; the resurgent Islam that disrupts the status quo. But to label Islamic resurgence as fundamentalism in a theological sense, and imply by that a relatively new phenomenon, is to misrepresent the reality of Islam as religion and to completely overlook the reality of Islamic history. The course of Islam has been replete with pietistic revivals and socially disruptive resurgences in the name of reform and re-assertion of pristine perspectives of one sort or another. Such an ebb and flow is of course not unknown to the history of Christianity in the West.

Ironically, it should be a source of reassurance to the West that by far the most common focus of Islamic resurgence has been internal and is likely to remain so: the overthrow of the Islamic ruler or government adjudged apostate; the jihad of a faith community seeking to be true to its own principles within its own specific spatio-temporal sphere. Even da'wah, the Islamic outreach or call to faith, has been, and is primarily, addressed with urgency to those within dar-al-Islam. That those without may also hear and respond is coincidental, a matter of *alhamdullah*— thanks to God, a gracious or serendipitous bonus—but in no sense the discharge of a divine missionising injunction as, for example, has traditionally motivated the Christian evangelical enterprise.

The fifth and final of my critical issues follows on from the discussion of fundamentalism: this has to do with a list of decidedly *negative descriptive terms* used regularly by the West in its reference to Muslims. Along with 'fundamentalist' and its variants we find media and other reports on Muslims and things Islamic containing terms such as 'extremist', 'fanatic', 'terrorist', 'martyr', 'suicidal' and so on. The impression given is of a people who live at the edges of value, who stand on the boundaries of life and death, who seem not to hold to the apparently agreed common human values (from the West's perspective at least) of honouring and preserving life in the context of upholding such governing ideals as mercy and compassion. And this even though the first reference ascribed by Muslims in virtually any context is to the name of Allah: the most constantly enunciated Islamic principles are, in fact, compassion and mercy as articulated, for example, in the frequent enunciation of the *bismillah*.[17]

That there are minority groups and news-making individuals who warrant negative descriptive appellations goes without saying. But that fact is true of other religions and societies as well, even though it takes an American bomber in Oklahoma and a Jewish assassin in Tel Aviv to make the point. There has been, without doubt, a terminological prejudice applied to Islam in modern times such that when bombings and assassinations occur the first response is to assume the involvement of Islam, or at least Islamic activists of one sort or another. Perhaps nowadays, though, Islam and the Muslim community in general will be seen by the West to have no monopoly on such negative terms of reference as inherently apt descriptors. Perhaps a consciousness that the use of such terms has been rather oversubscribed when discussing things Islamic may now moderate their future use. Time will tell, but the point of the requirement for terminological alertness is, in my view, one of the key issues in addressing the question of the West's perception of Islam, and so the issue of barriers to dialogue.

Media image analysis

A review of issues such as I have undertaken may aid us in addressing the question of the perception of Islam held in the West. But we are still not quite there. These contribute to the image, or better, the *process* of imaging Islam, and thereby to the construct of the Islam of imagination. Perhaps a more significant task at this juncture is to reflect upon the question of what constitutes the imaging process as such: what are the factors that shape and influence the Western perceptions of Islam? This is the issue of image analysis—where does the Western image derive from? What critical factors are at play? By way of a first foray into the subject the following outline of a programme of analysis seems to me to be appropriate. I contend that to all intents and purposes the Western perception of Islam is *media-shaped; politically dominated; contextually loose; religiously skewed; ideologically oppositional,* and *sociologically misrepresented.* I will define and comment briefly on each of these in turn. To the extent I have correctly identified key factors in the

---

[17] *Bismillah al-Rahman al-Rahim*: 'In the name of God, the merciful, the compassionate'.

imaging process then the fact that the image is predominantly negative can be appropriately addressed and, hopefully, corrective steps undertaken.

Perceptions media-shaped

The picture of Islam portrayed in the West is first and foremost an imaginative construct shaped by media images. It goes without saying that the primary, and for many the only, exposure to Islam is via television news coverage, newspaper reportage, and cinematic presentation. All too often, however, these media project images of Islam that are little more than stereotypes. However, it is the stereotypical image that powerfully influences the formation of imagination, both for the individual and also in respect of the collective or common communal perception. Of course, the predominance of visual image, in a video age, hardly needs to be stressed. But as well, the impact of the printed word, whether in newspaper, news-journal, popular book or tract, contributes significantly to the image-making effect of the media.

Yet, all this really doesn't tell us much. What gives form and content to the image-shaping so conveyed? What constitutes the image held in the imagination? Given the incontrovertible pervasiveness of the media in the process of image-formation—and even allowing for the recognition that there is more than a grain of truth in the adage that 'the medium is the message'—what gives the image its substance? This brings me to the second item of this critical analysis.

Perception and political domination

This is the two-edged sword of the predominance of political material as the source and focus of much media coverage, and the filtering effect of editorial choice and decision-making by those who control the media. Whether intentional or not, the selection of material, the way it is presented—the casting of the news—will reflect at least prior assumptions and agendas of a broadly political nature.

Arguably all editing—all redaction—is a political act in the sense of not being undertaken in a cognitive vacuum but rather being guided, at least, by consideration of desired effects or the dictates of subtext message, propaganda, and the like. Despite the profession of objective neutrality of a reporter, and the supposed neutral objectivity of the camera—which 'never lies'—the outcome, in terms of presented image, necessarily yields to the language of the report and the angle of the camera-shot (the more graphic, stark, or dramatic, the more likely it will be aired or printed). This undoubtedly implies, even in a broad sense of the term, that there is a dimension of political domination in the image product, which is then projected through the media. But what does this all mean? We can begin to construct an answer by turning to the third critical item.

Media image of Islam contextually loose

For the most part the image of Islam projected via the media lacks an authentic framework for interpretation: it is lacking in context, or is 'loose' in the sense of only a simplistic—often assumed and thus likely false or misleading—contextual reference being given. So, that which feeds the collective imagination, which in turn holds, embellishes, and draws upon the image for a variety of purposes, lacks appropriate contextual reference points. Certainly, for the most part at least, it would be true to say that both the projection and reception of the image of Islam is conducted with a bare minimum, if any, of attention paid to proper contextual factors. Of course good investigative journalists and reputable news reporters will defend their locating of reportage in context.

I am not saying that good contextualising of the image does not happen at all. Only that the predominant image of Islam in the West does not, in fact, come with an appropriate or authentic hermeneutical guide. Thus, for example, Islam is too frequently and falsely perceived as a monolithic entity; as an avaricious self-aggrandising religious culture; as neither self-critical nor reflective; as archaic, time-locked, and Middle Eastern. So the *image* of Islam, for the most part at least, is in reality contextually loose—it is not rooted in sound contextual appreciation and understanding—so far as the Western *imagination* is concerned.

Religiously skewed image of Islam

Here I refer simply to the fact that Islam is not perceived as religion (*din*[18]) as such. It is not, as it should be, presented as being a spiritual path, inherently holistic in its outlook and application. Rather the idea of religion that is attached to the term 'Islam' is itself skewed or conceptually twisted. It is off-centre, unbalanced such as to reinforce negative, even false, representations of Islam. For instance, the politico-juristic elements of Islam are overstressed in comparison with the theological and pietistic dimensions; the pragmatics of Islamic programmes predominates over an awareness of Muslim ethical sensibilities and reflections. And the underlying and deeper *raison d'être* for any given Islamic action is thereby lost to view. The religious depth is trivialised: the picture remaining is two-dimensional. And so we are brought to the fifth component of my critical analysis.

Islam as ideologically oppositional 'other'

Islam is consequently portrayed as the *de facto* oppositional religion to Christianity, and vice versa. Furthermore, and in the context of a general or wider Western perspective, Islam is the presumed ideological rival, the necessary ideological opposition to the West. Inherent in the image is the product of the process I have

---

[18] Pronounced, and written sometimes, as *deen*.

analysed so far. Islam is no friendly rival as in a competing sports team. Rather this rival is so completely 'other' that the prospect of confrontation is couched in dramatic terms and fearful expectation.

Thus Islam is portrayed as the Great Threat, the opponent *par excellence* in a climatic and apocalyptic clash of civilisations, the historical antithesis to the West's thesis. Religious extremists of variant Christian types will transmute the antithesis to an anti-Christ image. Islam is then portrayed, ideologically, as the great contemporary satanic opponent. And, ironically, the vice versa holds: to many in the Islamic world it is the West that is the demonic opposition, with America itself identified as the Great Satan. But such ideological oppositions are little more than mirror images of extremely fundamentalist and exclusivist religious postures.

A sociologically misrepresented image

The cumulative effect of the foregoing is that Islam is deemed by many to be, in a variety of ways, sociologically 'out of control'. It will produce a Saddam Hussein, who for a long time no one seemed able to curb; an Osama bin Laden, with his network of terrorists evoking massive retaliatory and expurgatory action, and whom no one seems able to pin down. It will produce a plethora of countries where political volatility and/or communal violence seem commonplace. On the one hand, there is much Islamic rhetoric concerning peaceful co-existence and membership in the world community yet, on the other, virulent policies of opposition to the West and to Zionism and, in some cases, to Christianity or at least to Christian churches and related organisations are frequently enunciated. Such active opposition may be directed against Israel and may even produce a negative response to Judaism, Quranic injunctions to the contrary notwithstanding. This misrepresentation will reflect on Islam as having an aura of inner conflict and lack of concerted direction for its own good, politically speaking.

To be sure there *is* great social and political, and even ideological, variety throughout the world of Islam, and much diversity in localised political expression and difference in the way specific issues and agendas occupy the energies of Muslims. This diversity does not mean Islam as such is a threat by virtue of being, in some vague sense, out of control as a sociological entity. Indeed the countervailing impetus to unity within the Ummah, which acts as an internal check and corrective upon some of the more volatile elements, is not to be misread as suggesting the possibility that Islam may yet become the monolith it is feared to be already. Rather, it suggests that the dialectic implied in the tension between the ideal of an overarching unity of the Islamic community, and the variegated reality of the Islamic Ummah only reflects the fact of Islam being an authentic and complex religio-political entity.

Conclusion

So we are led to a concluding comment and reflection: what may be done to counter the effects and outcomes of the issues and image-making processes adumbrated above? How might we apply ourselves in addressing the issue of the predominantly distorted image of Islam in the West?

Three things spring to mind: education, apologia, and dialogue. *Education* is an ongoing task for both the Islamic community itself to engage in as well as for the West to take up more urgently. A greater understanding of each other, the laying to rest of prejudices, the dispelling of misinformation, and the general allaying of fears and concerns constitutes an educational task that ought to be a priority. The educative task is the first response to the challenge that is posed by Islam.

Together with education, in which both Muslim and non-Muslim can be equally engaged, there is a more specific task that rightly belongs primarily to the Ummah, the Muslim community as such, both as a whole and in its local expression and context. This is the task of *apologia*, of rendering one's position, one's outlook, one's beliefs and teachings, in language and form that make them intelligible to another. Apologia is the discourse of outward-directed engagement, a discourse that is quite different from the internal discourse of, for example, da'wah. However, while the task of apologia belongs properly to the Muslim community, there is no reason why it cannot be assisted by appropriate scholars—both theologians as well as scholars of religion more broadly—from the West, acting as a kind of 'bridge' for the sake of communication and interaction. Indeed, I would hope that what I have attempted here—especially in Part I of this book—is just such a contribution.

Finally, it is the very possibility of an educative apologia that brings us to the third item, namely the ever-pressing task of *dialogue*. This is the proper arena for interreligious discussion, the fulcrum point of inter-communal engagement and relationships. The purpose of this book is to address the first and third of these three tasks: a foray into the field of an introductory education about Islam, and a dip into the waters of interfaith dialogical encounter with Islam.

Chapter 10

Dialogue and *Da'wah*
Elements of Encounter

This chapter consists of two sections. In the first I shall discuss some general elements that seem to me to be important in approaching the matter of the interfaith dialogue with Islam. In the second I shall extend the discussion with special reference to a consideration of Islamic da'wah, and this will itself lead to a consideration of a number of critical issues.

Dialogue elements

All too often it seems that religions, especially—but not only—Christianity and Islam, are caught in an apparent hypocrisy. For even as religions actively promote peace, they nevertheless can be found endorsing and blessing the battle-tanks of military might. On the one hand religions tend universally to espouse justice and liberation, yet they can also be found, on the other hand, giving sanction—whether directly or indirectly—to structures of injustice and oppression. And in so doing they fuel the secularist's cry that religion must go if true peace and justice is to be found.

The world looks on aghast at the terror and havoc that are once again wrought in the name of religion or a religious ideology. Religion is viewed as the enemy of peaceful human co-existence, even though—or perhaps because—it is more stridently asserted and embraced in many parts of the world today. It would seem that if there is ever to be a lasting peaceful cohabitation of human communities, not to mention the prospect for a just and ecologically sustainable future for all, then religion is going to have to back off. Religion, on the evidence of history, endangers peaceful co-existence. For the sake of peace and justice in a pluralist world, the future of religion could seem rather precarious: humanity can't really afford it. But, history also shows that humanity can't live without its sacred paths. So, as Theodore Ludwig has noted, 'the real question is not whether there will be religion in the future. It is whether the sacred paths can help shape the future of humankind in a creative, beneficial, hopeful way'.[1] The dialogue between religions is a dialogue among different 'sacred paths' in the interests of a future for all.

---

[1] Theodore Ludwig, *The Sacred Paths* (New Jersey: Prentice-Hall, 1989), 510.

Overcoming the competitive clash that has so often coloured the interactions between the sacred paths of religion is one of the aims of dialogue. Although much has been written, and even more discussed, by both proponents of, and participants in, interreligious dialogue, yet relative to the history of interreligious encounters it could be said that the truly deep and searching dialogical task has hardly begun. And this is acutely the case with respect to the relationship between Islam and Christianity.

The Muslim perspective on Christianity begins with the Quranic call to the religiously other—the 'People of the Book'—to join with Muslims in a united affirmation of the One God.[2] While a shared point of affirmation is always possible, in reality Jews and Christians *per se* could not embrace Islam, even though some communities, and many individuals, did just that during the early years of Islamic expansion.

Islam holds an ambiguous view of Christianity. Christian doctrines concerning the Trinity and the divinity of Christ are traditionally viewed by Islam 'as compromising the unity and transcendence of God'.[3] Yet there is an acknowledged salvific efficacy in Christianity: 'they shall have their reward'.[4] Toleration is affirmed with the injunction that 'different religious communities should exist in complete freedom'.[5] Indeed, as the Qur'an affirms: 'There shall be no compulsion in religious matters'.[6] Charles Kimball remarks:

> With few exceptions, most Islamic literature on Christianity has been framed in the language of polemics. Recurring themes include charges of altering or forging parts of the divine revelation, seriously errant doctrine (e.g., original sin, incarnation, atonement, the Trinity) and grievous mistakes in religious practice (e.g., celibacy, veneration of saints, 'idol' worship).[7]

Perspectives on both sides have been based, for the most part, on limited information and an inadequate understanding about the wider tradition of the other. The interplay of ignorance about each other, and the pervasive impact of the world-view presumptions of each, was at work. Also, and in particular, Western scholars on the subject

> began with the assumption that Islam was, by definition, false. The finality of God's redemptive action in Jesus Christ was the definitive event for human history. A new

---

[2] Cf. Sura 3:64.

[3] Charles Kimball, *Striving Together: A Way Forward in Christian–Muslim Relations* (Maryknoll: Orbis Books, 1991), 46.

[4] Sura 2:62 and 5:69.

[5] Kimball, ibid.

[6] Sura 2:256.

[7] Kimball, ibid., 47.

religion arising after Christianity, the reasoning goes, must be false or a heretical deviation from the faith.[8]

It was but a short step to link Muhammad to the Devil or the Antichrist. On the other hand, Muslims

> began with the assumption that Jesus was one of the greatest among the special messengers from God. They assumed that the revelation he brought was true and accurate. The frustration and fear vis-à-vis Christendom was never vented through fraudulent or derogatory assaults on Jesus. Rather, it is the distortions and even blasphemous teachings and practices of the Christian community that Muslims feel need to be addressed.[9]

For dialogue to proceed in the hope, if not expectation, of a productive outcome, then the misapprehensions of the past, together with the prejudices of the present, must be addressed in a climate of mutual and reciprocal correction. So, when Christian and Muslim meet in dialogical encounter, each first needs to know that they faithfully represent and thereby empathetically understand the position of the other. In the process, of course, each must be open to correction by the other, and be prepared to engage in an honest self-reflective critique in the light of the dialogue process. A shorthand way of tackling this process is to think in terms of discerning identity: partners in dialogue need to know their own and their partner's identity. Only so can genuine dialogue proceed. So, with this in mind, and in order to grasp something of the nature of Islamic identity as a necessary corollary to dialogical engagement, I shall revisit in a succinct manner some of the topics raised in Chapter 8, and so review the range of factors that contribute to that identity as I understand it.

The primary factors that contribute to the construction of Islamic identity can be readily sketched, and I make no claim to an exhaustive or definitive list. But it would surely include the elements of ummah, of tradition and history, of personal piety, of the beliefs and duties expressed in daily life, of matters of geographic location and relationships to society. Let me elaborate. Muhammad initiated and effectively developed a new socio-political identity within Arabia and laid down the basis for the belief and communal life of Islam. The Islamic Ummah was conceived as a theocracy: a community under God. The development of the Ummah was premised on unity and cohesion. It was a theocratic model that, although it has been subject to change and development throughout the history of Islam, it continues to provide a powerful ideal and ideological template. Islamic corporate identity, as well as individual belonging, is sustained by ideal of the one community existing in perfect submission to God.

---

[8] Ibid.
[9] Ibid., 47-48.

Any religious identity is, in part, constructed by the experience of everyday life, of the living out of duties and obligations, of the concrete expression of belief. This is eminently so with Islam. The Islamic religious life is given visible and daily expression in terms of the obligations to fulfil the requirements of piety. This active life of faith is summed up in the 'five pillars', the divinely required ordinances of duty (arkan). But alongside this universal element of Islamic identity sits the particularity of geographic location. If Islam espouses trans-national identity—the transcendent solidarity of the Ummah, given graphic expression in the hajj—the realities of geographic location or origin, thus ethnicity, also play a significant part.

In its relatively rapid development the Ummah quickly extended beyond its Arabic origins to embrace a diversity of races and ethnic identities. The legacy of Muhammad was that Islamic identity transcended race, language and ethnicity. However, as previously pointed out, a significant feature to be found in some places within the contemporary Muslim world is an identification of ethnic with religious identity. So, paradoxically, Islam to be understood as a universal and global religion without racial boundaries yet, at the same time, in several Islamic countries—Turkey, Malaysia, Indonesia, for example—ethnic identity is equated to religious identity. Turkish, Malaysian and Indonesian ethnicity are identified as inherently Islamic. This equation of ethnicity with religion creates problems with respect to trans-national mobility and also to matters of freedom of religion. But I shall not go into those issues here. Rather, I come to the matter of relationships with society as the final of this set of factors contributing to Islamic identity.

Belief is not a matter of simple intellectual assent: it also has to do with living by certain principles, with the application of a perceived divine intention in respect to the business of mundane life. Much of the beliefs of Islam have to do with ways in which human beings are to live in accordance to the Will of Allah. The primary goal of human existence is submission in the service of Allah, and this gives the guiding leitmotif to matters of relationship to the wider society. In terms of Islamic identity it is spelled out in the Shari'a law codes. The dialectic of living out a religious identity in the light of such a legal code, but in the context of a non-Muslim, or constitutionally secular, society, gives rise to a complex set of tensions. In some situations it leads to calls for full Islamisation as the ultimate resolution. In others, it means a measure of adaptation and compromise of detail whilst endeavouring to maintain principles and values intact.

Religious identity is also a function of values. That is, certain values find expression in religion and, conversely, the expression of the values contributes to particular religious identity. Distinctive to the Islamic religion *per se* are values such as *unity*, derived from tawhid; and of course *submission*, that grounding of the being of all things in the particular relationship to the Creator: submission to the Divine Will. The third distinctive value for Islam, I would suggest, is that of Law, or Shari'a, itself, in the sense of law expressing justice and giving voice to wide-ranging principles of jurisprudence.

Together with such key or lead values that play a part in the construction of Islamic identity, we need add the consideration of Islamic identity as a function of ideology in terms also of the discussion in Chapter 8 above. The interplay of the ideologies of Traditionalism, Modernism, Pragmatic Secularism, and Islamism constitutes, in terms of concrete socio-political realities, the various expressions of Islamic identity with which, in the context of any dialogical engagement, we have to contend. But there is yet another dimension of Islamic life and practice—da'wah—to take account of. Islam is not just a religion of action in terms of the five pillars of religious duty and a holistic approach to life. There is much more besides.

Islamic Da'wah as dialogue issue

Muslims are enjoined to the task of issuing a call, an invitation, to any who would listen, to attend to the truth of God as presented through the lens of Islam. This is the missionising task of da'wah. Much effort and energy is spent within the Muslim world on promoting da'wah to the many Muslims who are in effect 'nominal'—that is, they may be born Muslims, but they are not as diligent or intentional in their Islamic identity and life as those whose religion has been internalised and has become part and parcel of their individual identity. This is an Islamic variant of the phenomenon of the intentional believer encouraging the casual believer to deeper and more meaningful commitment, understanding, acceptance and practice.

A few years ago I was asked to speak—indeed to deliver the opening keynote address—at a Da'wah Training Conference.[10] I was asked to do this as a Christian scholar interested in Islam and the dialogical relationship between Christianity and Islam, and I was charged with speaking to Muslims about a particular dimension of concern for da'wah, namely the matter of presenting Islam to a Christian audience. In discharging this somewhat challenging dialogical task my intention was to raise some questions, share some ideas, pass on some thoughts, and generally stimulate the thinking of those present, so that, as I put it, 'we might all be encouraged in the primary task that faces both Muslim and Christian: to present the claim and good news of the One God to our fellow human beings'. It was my contention that dialogue and da'wah are not just things to be talked *about*: they are things to *do*. Indeed, as a Christian scholar, giving this address was itself an example of 'doing dialogue', for I set out to engage dialogically not by talking *at*, but by endeavouring to talk *with* the audience. In the process I raised two preliminary questions: what is da'wah? What do we mean by 'dialogue'? I then went on to a series of key issues: first, what are the kinds of problems that Christians have with Islam? What might be done about these problems? Second, what are the kinds of problems Muslims have with Christians? What might be done about these problems? And finally, how

---

10 What here follows consists of the substance of an address I gave, namely, 'Da'wah and Dialogue: Some Practical Considerations on Presenting Islam to a Christian Audience', to a 1998 Auckland Youth Training Conference, jointly organised by a regional committee of the World Association of Muslim Youth and the Federation of Islamic Associations of New Zealand.

might da'wah be carried out in a dialogical context? In what follows I effectively reproduce the substance of my address as it was given.

What is da'wah?

The Islamist scholar, John Esposito, defines da'wah as the 'call to Islam', meaning the 'propagation of the faith; more broadly social welfare and missionary activities'.[11] Another source defines da'wah as 'call, propaganda, invitation, invocation, missionary movement, missionary call'.[12] The Muslim scholar Ataullah Siddiqui states how da'wah is to Islam as mission is to Christianity. He notes that 'mission is the very *raison d'être* of the Christian community' and he reminds us how the Holy Qur'an commands Muslims:

> Invite [all] to the Way of thy Lord with wisdom and beautiful preaching. And argue with them in the ways that are best and more gracious. For thy Lord knoweth best, who have strayed from his path (al-Nahl 16:125). [13]

So, concludes Siddiqui, da'wah is 'the central part of the existence of the Muslim *Ummah*' and he cites Kurram Murad who says: '*Da'wah* is integral to Islam. To be Muslim means to continually strive to become Muslim, that means to do *Da'wah*.'[14]

We could put it this way. Being a Muslim means becoming 'muslim', and *becoming* 'muslim' means *doing* da'wah. Or we could say: to be a good person of the Islamic faith (*being* a Muslim) means to continually strive in one's submission to Allah (*becoming* 'muslim'), and that means engaging in the missionary calling of Islam (*doing da'wah*). On this basis da'wah has a twofold application: outward and inward. The inward application is the continual call from Muslims to their fellow Muslims in the interest of strengthening the Islamic life. The outward application has to do with the presentation of Islam to the non-Muslim world. And this is more than simply the selling of one religion in competition with other religions, as travelling salespeople, for example, compete in the marketing of their vacuum cleaner, encyclopaedia, or whatever. No, what we are talking about is not the promotion of a religion whose brand name happens to be Islam, but the call and way of God which invites the response of submission to the divine Will (becoming *muslim* in the sense of a relationship of self-surrender to God). That, from the perspective of Islam as a specific religion, then results in membership of the

---

[11] John L. Esposito, *Islam: The Straight Path* (Oxford: Oxford University Press, 1994), 219.
[12] Ian Richard Netton, *A Popular Dictionary of Islam* (London: Curzon Press, 1992), 67.
[13] Ataullah Siddiqui, *Christian–Muslim Dialogue in the Twentieth Century* (London: Macmillan, 1997), 70.
[14] Ibid.

Islamic Ummah, and so the individual is identified, religiously and even culturally, as a Muslim person.

Now, while the inward application of da'wah is important for Muslims, and interesting for me as someone engaged in the study of Islam and dialogue with Muslims, what is of importance to us both is the outward application: how is Islam presented to the non-Islamic world and, in particular, how does da'wah fit in with the relationship of Islam and Christianity and the quest to transcend the variety of negative encounters and clashes of the past with positive dialogical engagements in the present and for the future? This brings me to the second preliminary question.

What do we mean by dialogue?

To the question of the meaning of dialogue, Charles Kimball answers as follows:

> Dialogue, by definition, is a conversation, a process of communication through speech. It is a reciprocal relationship in which two or more parties endeavor both to express accurately what they mean and to listen to and respect what the other person says, however different her or his perspective may be. But dialogue is more than an exchange of views. In a fundamental sense, it is a perspective, a stance, an openness. Dialogue represents a way of relating ... Ideally, mutuality in dialogue is present in communication, trust, understanding, challenge, growth, and even spiritual development.[15]

I do not really think I can improve on this definition. In essence it is saying that when we engage in dialogue as an activity, or even if we engage in an activity, such as da'wah, but seek to do so in a dialogical manner, then we engage in a two-way relationship, equally speaking out our point of view and genuinely listening to the point of view of the other, trying to understand how they see things.

The goal is not to convince the other that they are wrong and we are right but, through the process of dialogical engagement, to achieve that growth in spiritual development whereby each side better understands the other, better understands themselves, and has been led into a fuller awareness of the Truth of God. Put another way, Muslims arguably honour the path of being *muslim* that is, of submitting in discipleship to the Way of Allah, through the exercise of dialogical engagement. Perhaps this is the better way to follow rather than the way of dogmatic assertion that promotes discord and disharmony. For is it not recorded in the Holy Qur'an: 'There is no compulsion in religion?' Now we have some idea of what da'wah means, and what makes up dialogue, let us now look at some critical questions and problems, first those that Christians might have in respect of Muslims and Islam, then those that Muslims might have with Christians and Christianity.

---

[15] Kimball, *Striving Together*, 86.

Christian questions and problems with Islam

What are the kinds of problems that Christians have with Islam? What might be done about these problems? What are the sorts of things about Islam that turn a Christian audience off? What makes it difficult for a Christian to really listen to and hear the Muslim point of view? This is, of course, a large and vexed area of enquiry. We can but touch upon it in a limited way for the purposes of simply identifying some of the features we ought to be aware of. I have identified three items, and I have some suggestions to make about them. The first has to do with historical timing: the religion of Islam, as an historic phenomenon, comes after the inception of Christianity. The second returns to a theme examined above, namely the association of Islam with aggression of one sort or another. Third, I shall touch on the theological question of the object of worship and devotion: do Muslims and Christians worship the same or a different God? Behind and within each one lie a complex web of issues and assumptions, of course. All that can be undertaken here is simply to sketch out what each is, and indicate some possible responses for further consideration.

Historical timing: Islam follows Christianity

This issue of temporal or historical sequencing has to do with the classical Christian assumption that revelation is fixed and that the scripture that conveys revelation, namely the Bible, is closed. It is, of course, a problem common to all revealed religions: the context of early beginnings means that at some point the message sent by God is believed to have been received, therefore there is no need for God to send yet another message or messenger. And the record of this message was deemed to be fixed at the point when the written version was formatted into a canon, that is, the Holy Bible. So Christians have typically viewed Divine revelation to have been effectively concluded with Jesus, and the record to have been completed once the canon of the Bible had been finalised. Therefore the notion that, since these closures, there could be any revelation, let alone any substantial and significant revelation, given by God which resulted in yet another scripture seems impossible, or at least highly improbable.

Significantly, allied to the timing issue is the issue of 'supersession'. For many centuries Christians believed their revelation and religion superseded that of Jews and Judaism. The claim of Islam to be a revealed religion may be viewed as a threat to Christianity because of the implication of yet another supersession which, of course, from a traditional Christian point of view, is impossible. In other words, the timing of Islam is problematic because it does not 'fit' into the classical Christian understanding of revelation, and if it does not 'fit' then it must be either irrelevant or false.

What comment can I make about this by way of a practical consideration? Simply this: the problem of timing, as I have outlined it, is eased to the extent that the focus is placed not on the historical moment or period of revelation but on the reality of the One True God, or Allah, who is the Revealer. Revelation is the prerogative of God. Allah is the author of the message. Jesus and Muhammad are different personalities, who lived in different times and different situations, and who were—and are still—differently understood; yet they are equally bearers of revelation, equally messengers of God. The respective scriptures that followed upon the completion of their work bear the stamp of human endeavour as much as they contain within them the divine revelation that was conveyed. That is why in both Islam and Christianity there has always been a great tradition of commentary and exposition.

So, I suggest, we need not argue the point *that* God 'spoke'; we can accept that there is a record appropriate to God's speaking in each case. Rather we can, and do—both within and between our respective religions—debate and discuss what God meant and how the meaning of the message is to be understood and applied in our day and time. God, and the message of God, is eternal. The issue of timing is a matter of variations in the delivery of that eternal message to specific people in particular historical contexts. Differences in historical timing do not necessarily mean one is true and the other false, or that one is better than the other, or that the earlier is superseded by the latter. Timing is determined by God. It is our duty to hear the message that transcends all time.

Aggression: Islam and militarism

Both in its inception at the time of Muhammad, and in its subsequent historical development down to the present day, Islam is perceived by many to be a religion dominated by aggressive military and political action. It often gets its way by force. It imposes its viewpoint. It is rigid in its beliefs and inflexible in its social life. At least, this seems to be the received perception, the prejudicial tradition of assumption and closed judgement.

In some ways this can be dealt with more simply, although it is also not an easy issue. All religions, Christianity and Islam included, have their concrete expression within the realities of human communities and historical processes. Religion as such may be distinguishable from politics, but in the real world political activity and ideals are intertwined with religious sensibilities and principles. So aggression has figured to a greater or lesser degree in all of the world's religions. Furthermore, the nature of Christianity and Islam has meant that each has had a history of close engagement with political authority and power. These are the broad historical facts. To quote the old saying: the pot cannot call the kettle black. The perception that Islam is somehow differently aggressive and has a particularly militaristic flavour is just that: a perception. It is neither true nor false, but it is limited and, if not countered, leads inexorably to a false assumption or conclusion about Islam as such.

We counter this kind of perception by reference to the wider historical reality that sees aggression as not being unique to Islam. We counter misleading perception by noting that in any case aggression is more often the result of political factors rather than purely religious ones. This applies to both Christianity and Islam. And we counter negative perception by a reminder that the two keywords of Islam and Christianity are peace and love. Islam, in a word, is a religion of peace: that is its aim and goal. Likewise we can say Christianity, in a word, is a religion of love. 'God is Love' and 'God so loved the world ...' are favourite sayings of Christianity. But equally, these two words—peace and love—apply to each religion. And equally human reality doesn't always live up to the high ideal. But that does not detract from the value of the ideals, or the integrity of the religions that espouse them.

Difference: do Muslims worship a different God?

Christians talk about God as Trinity; Muslims proclaim the One True God—Allah. The Christian idea of Trinity is a way of understanding the One True God, but it is a radically different monotheism from that of Islam (see Chapter 11 below for further on the theme of Trinity and unity). So Christians view Islam as very different from Christianity in terms of a foundational belief in God. Thus the third problem is that many Christians assume that, in fact, Muslims worship a different God, one who is called 'Allah'.

Once again, this is a complex issue that can, for the purposes of dialogue, be responded to at a more simple or straightforward level. For anyone who believes there is no God but God—and this would be as true for a Christian as it is for a Muslim—then it is logically impossible to believe that someone else who believes in God in a way which appears different from me must therefore believe in a completely different God. There is only one God. The real issue is a matter of difference in conception—our understanding and idea of God—and a difference of experience—our encounter with God, including the fact of revelation that I have already mentioned.

Muslims and Christians have different experiences of, different history of ideas about, different points of reference for, the concept of God. But these differences do not necessarily suggest either we are talking about a different God, or that one side is completely wrong. Instead, it could be argued that they point more to the greatness, the majesty, the mysteriousness of this God whom both Christian and Muslim respond to in discipleship and worship. After all, God is beyond final or complete human grasp; human thought can never encompass the being of Allah. So, human difference need not be divisive: it can rather be complementary and mutually enriching. That is the clue for both engagement in interfaith dialogue on the one hand, and the particular Islamic engagement in da'wah on the other. But now let us turn to a complementary set of questions, namely, what are the kinds of problems Muslims have with Christians? What might be done about these problems?

Muslim questions and problems with Christianity

I have identified three general areas of problems that I suggest would reasonably
reflect the kinds of issues Muslims are likely to have with Christians, namely
righteous arrogance, evangelical missionising, and prejudicial ignorance. I suspect
these are real enough problems that require some sort of considered response. Once
again, behind and within each one of these there lies a complex web of issues and
assumptions. I will simply sketch each as I see it, and indicate some possible
responses for further consideration.

Righteous arrogance

It would be my expectation that, to a greater or lesser extent, many difficulties that
Muslims are likely to encounter with Christians have to do with an attitude of what
might be called 'righteous arrogance'. By this I mean the set of attitudes and
assumptions wherein Christians, at least of some persuasions, view themselves as
being in a particular, unique, and privileged relationship to God. It is based on
various ideas of what Christians understand by 'salvation' or 'being saved'. Its root
is, of course, the particularity of what was accomplished by Jesus as distinct from
what he taught. Put otherwise, within Christianity there is a double view of Jesus:
on the one hand, as with any other prophet he was a messenger, a teacher, a *bearer*
of divine revelation by way of what he said and did. To that extent there is no
essential difference between Jesus and Muhammad in terms of their function as
messenger. But with Christianity there is yet another dimension: Jesus effected a
change in the state of the relationship between humanity and God. What he did in
this regard is called 'salvation'; and what it meant for those who followed him was
that they considered that, because of what he did, they would now be 'saved'. There
are many subtle variants of understanding as to what this means exactly, but all
have to do, in the end, with the nature of the relationship between the individual
and God. At the very least, because of what Jesus did, those who are his followers
have access to a new kind of relationship with God. Indeed, for the most part the
Christian Church has believed that what he did was of significance for the whole
world and for all time. Thus Christian salvation, in this sense, is understood to be
available to all.

Now, this idea can very easily be the basis for a confident self-understanding
and self-appreciation that can slide over to a righteous arrogance: Christians can
easily feel that they are completely right, not just intellectually but also spiritually.
In their eyes, they have, as a matter of fact, the right relationship to God. For the
root meaning of 'righteousness' in Christian theological terms means just that. And
they can be supremely self-confident with it, to the point of arrogance. It finds
expression in the exclusive claim made for the Christian position by quoting from
the Gospel the saying attributed to Jesus: 'No one comes to the Father but by me'.
This is not easy to deal with. But, arguably, it rests on a massive misunderstanding
of the nature of God. While we may grant the unique perspective of Christianity

resting on the promotion of a personal relationship to God, the notion of the reality of God being identified with the term 'Father', together with the notion that the only viable way of being spiritually connected to God is via the intermediary role of a 'Son' is to place severe limits upon theological understanding and spiritual experience. The bubble of righteous arrogance is deflated as we are reminded that the reality of God cannot be limited by any conceptual notion, even if those notions are conveying a valid insight nonetheless.

Evangelical missionising

The next, and related, problem I identify is what may be called 'evangelical missionising'. Like Islam, Christianity is a missionary religion: the message of God is meant for all, the followers of this message are enjoined to spread it. Typically, through the ages, the attitude of righteous arrogance has gone hand in glove with the activities of mission and evangelism within the Christian religion. It doesn't have to be this way. But to the extent it is—and this is what has been the experience of many Muslims when confronted by Christians—then it is a problem that needs to be carefully considered.

The evangelical missionary motivation has been, and still is, a very powerful force within Christianity. It is based on a genuine and well-meaning concern for people. But again, the root problem, as I see it, is a too narrow appreciation of the greatness of God and a too narrow understanding of what it is God wants of us, His creatures. Both Islam and Christianity clearly wish for all people to be in a right relationship with the God who created us all. The issue is whether the Christian can allow for the possibility that there may be more than one way wherein that relationship may be achieved and expressed. Many do indeed believe that is the case: there is more than one legitimate avenue of access to, and proper relationship with, the Divine. But the problem Muslims tend to face is with the evangelical and missionary Christian who is convinced that only their Christian perspective on what makes a right relationship with God is valid and true. There is, unfortunately, little one can do in the face of a hard-line or fanatical perspective. Nonetheless, in terms of dialogue and da'wah, I suggest Muslims must claim the integrity of the way of Islam but not emulate the hard-line Christian evangelical missionary position by then saying the Muslim way is the only valid way to God. God's ways are greater than any of the ways we know or are familiar with. No one, Christian or Muslim, has a monopoly on God.

Prejudicial ignorance

The third problem area I wish to consider relates to the previous two, of course. It is simply the problem of 'ignorance' (see also the discussion on this in Chapter 9 above). Christians who know little or nothing of Islam are ignorant: they simply lack knowledge. That kind of 'not-knowing' is blameless in itself. We can't be held accountable for something we know nothing about. On the other hand, to know something, even a little, and refuse to learn more by actively ignoring what little is known, is a different matter. And that is at the heart of many problems that Muslims have with Christians, I suspect. For the sad reality is that it is only a minuscule proportion of Christians anywhere who are prepared to breach their ignorance of Islam. Instead they pursue the path of 'active ignorance' upon which may be found a multitude of misperceptions and prejudicial viewpoints.

When the cause of Christian–Muslim interfaith engagement—let alone Muslim da'wah—runs into such prejudicial ignorance, then the need for dialogue becomes even more urgent. For the only way to combat this ignorance, and thereby also overcome prejudice, is by fostering a good mutual dialogical relationship. First, the prejudice and the fact of active ignorance need to be identified and named for what they are. But then, instead of levelling blame and indulging in counter ignorance and prejudice, Islamic da'wah has the potential to become dialogical where a Christian audience can be invited to engage with Muslims, in an appropriate and non-threatening relationship, so that mutual learning and understanding can take place. Then ignorance can be overcome and prejudice laid to rest. And the grounding reason for doing this is, of course, that Christian and Muslim, whatever else they may think of each other's beliefs, must at least agree that all are children of God; that God would want all to live together in peace and loving harmony, not in war, dissension and destruction.

Da'wah and dialogue

So we are brought to the final question: how might da'wah be carried out in a dialogical context? How might da'wah be undertaken dialogically? In discussing prejudicial ignorance above I have already given one idea. But let me suggest one more, and relate it to what Good Friday, the day of crucifixion, means for Christians, and what it might mean in the context of Christian–Muslim engagement. However, before we do this we need to be clear about the essential underlying idea, namely that whatever the issue we are faced with in terms of our religion, and especially when considering how Islam may be presented to a Christian audience, there are three things, or three elements of a process, we need to identify.

First, there is the raw data of our religion that confronts us—the issues, beliefs, stories, narratives, or whatever is the content of what we are confronted with. This is given within the Qur'an; the Gospel; the shahada; the creeds and so on. Then comes our understanding of these data, the interpretation that is placed on them, the framework of world-view perspective by which we appreciate them for what they are. This requires us to go beyond the mere presentation of an item of data as such. It requires us to seek deeper the dynamic, the divine dynamic if you like, that lies within any given datum. Third, when we have firmly grasped something of the whole of both data and dynamic, we can then speak with one another, sharing our perspectives, learning from each other and coming to a fuller appreciation of our religious identity and commitments. And this is dialogue. So we have what I would call the three 'Ds' of da'wah: *Data, Dynamic, Dialogue*.

Now, this can be explored—in an all-too-brief and tantalizing fashion, I admit—with reference to the example of the event of Easter, specifically Good Friday. There are three questions to be raised that demonstrate the three 'Ds' of da'wah in action. They are: what happened (the datum) to Jesus? What is the meaning (the dynamic) of Jesus? What do the Islamic and Christian views of Jesus teach us (dialogue)?

Christianity says Jesus died on the cross; but that was not the end of Jesus. Islam says Jesus did not die on the cross, for that could not be the end of Jesus. That is our basic data, and it is different data. But what is the dynamic that lies embedded in the data? The account of the cross, in both cases, relates to the given understanding of the nature of Jesus and the role he was playing in terms of the Will of God. In other words, given a preconception about the nature of Jesus as a religious figure (prophet; saviour) there is a concomitant account of how that figure fulfils the divinely-given task laid upon him. The details differ, but in each case Jesus is presented as fully submitting to God, as congruently manifesting both the divine purpose and his essential relationship to the divine. So, we might say, in the end the dynamic is similar, even parallel: both accounts portray fidelity to the Will of God as the primary consideration. As we take that realisation into a discussion of what Islam and Christianity have taught about Jesus, and rethink those items from the perspective of distinguishing datum and dynamic, then I suggest we have a basis for fruitful dialogue. The real dialogical issue, I suggest, is not so much which set of data is factually correct, but how it is that through such data we may yet see the dynamic of God's Will at work, and so learn from that something of what it means, as Muslim and Christian, to respond and submit to that Will.

It is to a further exploration of this arena of theological dialogue that I now turn in the next chapter.

Chapter 11

Theological Dialogue
Christian–Muslim Engagement

Although for both Christianity and Islam the cues to dogmatic belief lie in their scriptures, articulation into definitive doctrine has emerged, broadly speaking, out of the respective decrees on their faith. Each of these religions, during their early formative years, took the witness of scripture and the witness of faith-experience—for Christians the tradition of the Fathers; for Muslims the Sunnah of the Prophet—and moulded their respective orthodoxies. Doctrine and dogma cemented orthodox identity. Yet, for both religions, the task of conceptual re-interpretation and formulaic articulation, including development and change in particular beliefs and articulating understandings of them, have continued through the processes of their own scholarly debates and discussions. The definitional and delimiting decrees of orthodoxy notwithstanding, these processes continue. Furthermore, with respect to any engagement between these two faith traditions, the scholar Charles Kimball notes: 'the history of the interaction has been characterized by mistrust, misunderstanding and mutual antipathy'.[1] Not only have internal theological debates and discussions been hotbeds of high emotion and deep dissent, but such engagement between the religions, if and when it has happened, has been equally, if not more so, contentious and fraught. Religious discourse has ever the capacity to generate more heat than light.

Within a century or so of its historical inception, Islam presented to Christianity not simply a rival world religion, but a rival world view and world power. Islam was first treated by Christians as a heresy, implying that it spoke the same religious language, but that it derived alternate religious conclusions. Yet many Christians went over to this new faith. As Kimball remarks in this regard:

> With the notable exception of the Coptic Orthodox Church in Egypt, the once thriving Christian communities across North Africa virtually disappeared after the seventh century. Since forced conversion was not the primary reason for the phenomenon, the power of Islamic theology and ideology cannot be ignored.[2]

---

[1] Charles Kimball, *Striving Together: A Way Forward in Christian–Muslim Relations* (Maryknoll: Orbis Books, 1991), 37.

[2] Ibid., 39.

To be sure, the challenge of Islam to Christianity has been impossible to ignore, even though, at times, it has been downplayed. Equally, Christianity has posed an ongoing challenge to Islam: these People of the Book simply will not submit to Allah in keeping with the tenets of the Prophet Muhammad. If, at times, there has been a promotion of an active ignoring, or ignore-ance, (Islam is something to do with other people in other places: out of sight, out of mind); and if this has been aided and abetted by ignorance *simpliciter* (we know not, therefore we care not: see the discussion on 'ignorance' in Chapter 9 above); then the changes in religious demography throughout the Western world that are now manifestly obvious, as well as the impact of globalisation—modern telecommunications and global economic interdependency—mean that Christianity and the West cannot possibly ignore Islam. And so Islam is the challenge that will not go away; and in it not going away, Islam is, *ipso facto*, a challenge.

The 'challenge of Islam' now becomes the challenge of confronting the reality of Islam itself, for which I have identified the task of understanding as the first step, and to which, in the context of this book, the first part (Chapters 2 to 5) constitutes a direct response. Beyond that there are many steps that comprise the journey of dialogical exploration and discovery. However, before proceeding with the substance of this chapter, three things need to be said. The first is that we ought not to identify Christianity, as a religion, with 'the West' any more than we would identify Islam, as a religion, with the Middle East, or the Arab world *per se*. Although religion and culture intertwine they are nonetheless distinct conceptual entities. The second thing to note comes from a comment attributed to Malaysia's long-serving Prime Minister, Dr Mahathir Mohammad, as once reported on a television news item. Although it was uttered in a quite different context it contains, nevertheless, a thought that is germane to the present topic: 'We cannot allow the past to undermine our future.' If this is an appropriate sentiment in the realm of international commerce and social relationships, how much more so is it applicable to the wider religio-cultural context? For, as the third thing to be said, which is another quotation, this time from William Montgomery Watt, 'Once a misrepresentation or distorted image has become firmly rooted in the general outlook of a whole cultural community, it is difficult to change it'.[3] If there is to be a better future not only for the relationship between the Islamic world and the West, but also between the world of Islamic faith and the world of Christian faith, then we must work together so that the past will not, indeed, be allowed to undermine our future.

One of the critical areas of dialogical interaction is that of theological encounter. This arena is crucial, but it is also exceedingly difficult. Much good interaction and dialogue can take place between Christian and Muslim in respect of other areas of concern—moral, socio-political, economic, ecological—to name but a few. Nevertheless, fundamental beliefs, and critical expressions of faith, which

---

[3] William Montgomery Watt, *Muslim–Christian Encounters: Perceptions and Mis-perception,* (London: Routledge, 1991), 111.

are those things that signal the bedrock of our respective world views, need to be seriously and sensitively addressed, if only because much of how Islam and Christianity pronounce and act upon issues and problems, with respect to both worldly and spiritual matters, comes down to an extension of fundamental principles and the application of basic beliefs. And most often the succinct belief-expressions are treated as badges of identity that are not easily shared.

However, I suggest there are some Islamic statements, or articulations of Islamic piety, that a Christian or a Jew, for instance, may indeed utter in good faith and without giving offence to either their own position or that of the Muslim. For example, there are some Islamic statements which are most often uttered in their Arabic form but which, in another language, such as English, could just as easily be read, or 'heard', as a Christian or Jewish statement. Phrases such as: 'There is only One God'; 'in the name of God'; 'Thanks be to God'; 'God willing' and so on, come to mind in this regard.

Furthermore, there is also the widespread use of expressions of honour and respect. In particular, phrases such as *peace be upon him* (*pbuh*)—when acknowledging Muhammad or Jesus, for example—and *peace be upon you*—in respect to interpersonal interactions would fall into this category. Although in many contexts such locutions may not normally be part of the language of Christian piety or daily Christian expression, it would not be inappropriate for a Christian to utter such a phrase. This may be done as an expression of politeness or as an acknowledgment of the context of discourse, especially when conversing within an Islamic environment or speaking to a Muslim audience. Then there are statements that, at least in their English equivalent, would appear not to be problematic, at least in principle, so far as Christianity is concerned. For example, 'Muhammad (*pbuh*) is a Prophet of God', or 'Muhammad (*pbuh*) is the Seal of the Prophets' might fall in this category.

With these introductory remarks in mind I now turn to the substance of this chapter, which falls into four sections. The first addresses the mutuality of ideological challenge and involves reviewing a number of specific challenges that confront Islam and Christianity alike; the second introduces some particular issues of the theological dimension of the dialogical challenge; while the third and fourth involve an initial foray into theological dialogue more directly by exploring some specific issues and problems. The challenge of theological dialogue is demonstrably one of the critical and challenging arenas of Christian–Muslim engagement.

Mutual Ideological Challenges

A major dimension of interreligious dialogue is that of addressing the *mutual challenges* that Islam and Christianity, as co-partners to dialogue, face together. The underlying challenge that each poses to the other involves, it seems to me, the prospect of facing together those particular challenges which, in theory and in fact, confront each separately, yet nonetheless equally so. Put otherwise, on the one hand there are challenges that each religion faces, and which may be the same or similar sorts of challenge, but which each must face alone, as it were. These are the domestic challenges specific to each community, even if we may detect parallel instances of similar phenomena in the other religion. The resolution of these sorts of challenge is entirely and appropriately an internal affair. On the other hand, there are challenges such that their very nature—perhaps by virtue of inherent reciprocity or symbiotic interactivity, or else their being co-equal or parallel in focus and field of concern—is suggestive of a particular form of mutuality so far as Christianity and Islam are concerned. In this field there is a type of mutuality, on the one hand, with respect to direct interactive challenge—Islam to Christianity; Christianity to Islam—that occurs by virtue of these being two religions with related and overlapping beliefs, ideologies, values and so on.[4] On the other hand there is also the instance of a challenge that each may currently face, but which is, in fact, a shared or parallel challenge. Such challenges may provide an agenda for dialogue at depth, or prove to be an arena of common concern for dialogical focus.

As a particular example I have in mind the notion that, just as Islam has misgivings about, and a range of conceptual or theoretical problems with, 'the West' as an ideological 'other' (rather than more obviously a religious 'other'), so too, in similar fashion, does Christianity (both in Roman Catholic and the myriad forms of western Protestantism, if not also in Eastern Orthodox variants) find in the cultural construct we name 'The West' an ideological problematic. Responses, interactions, and value-perceptions vary, of course, but nonetheless we might identify four specific and major ideological challenges that the phenomenon of the West poses equally to both Christianity *per se* as well as to Islam. The first of these specific challenges is secularism. In many respects it is the governing challenge in respect of which the three others I shall address—pluralism, individualism and politicisation—are particular (though not necessary) subsequent developments.

The challenge of secularism

Secularism, in terms of its positive origins, is an ideology of peaceful co-existence, of freedom of choice in matters of belief and association, and freedom of expression in matters of speech, art, publication and worship. It arose out of a particular set of Western European historical religio-cultural antecedents. The secular mentality, as a context for the unshackling of the human spirit from dogmatic constraints and allowing for the free-flowing and flowering of inquiry, has been the cornerstone of recent Western secular culture and social history. However, for all its positive contribution, there has now emerged a negative consequence, or rather set of consequences.

---

[4] See for example Hugh Goddard, *Christians and Muslims: From Double Standards to Mutual Understanding* (Richmond, Surrey: Curzon Press, 1995), 169ff.

In essence I contend that the liberating and value-enhancing ideology that distinguished between, on the one hand, the religious life of individuals and their faith-communities, and, on the other, the life of the whole society in which the individuals and their faith-communities are set, has developed from being a tool of tolerance to what we might now describe as the mindset of *laissez-faire* hedonism. Communal valuations have given way to self-gratification, and very often it is of the 'instant' variety. Even the noted comedian and educationist Bill Cosby commented some years ago to the effect that it is time the West got away from the world of 'me' and back to a world of 'us'. The positive guarantee of certain rights and freedoms is one thing; a negative perspective on communal value and individual co-dependency and co-responsibility in favour of self-serving gratification is quite something else.

By virtue of being a pragmatic response, which enabled the co-existence of plurality of perspective within the context of a broadly held Judeo/Christian-based value system, Western secularism has necessarily been vulnerable to two developments—each with their own unforeseen *sequae*—which constitute the second and third of this set of mutual challenges to face Christianity and Islam, pluralism and individualism.

The challenge of pluralism

There is today a much wider range of religious and value pluralities now occurring than was ever the case at the beginning of the modern era when secularism was ushered in as a defining mark. Pluralism is a contemporary intellectual response to the fact of plurality. The fact—plurality as such—has always been around, to a greater of lesser degree, but responses to the fact have tended to be in terms of exclusivism—denying or in some way setting aside the facts concerning plurality as of no real import—or inclusivism, where the implicit challenge posed by plurality is vitiated by including it, in effect, within the singular world-view framework of a religion or cultural heritage. The differences signalled by plurality are either way neutralised; plurality is no real threat: we carry on regardless.

However, today, it would seem plurality in respect to expressions of religious identity between, as well as sub-groupings within, the major religious traditions—including of course both Christianity and Islam—is quantitatively increasing, Espousals of unity are countered by the realities of plurality which seems less amenable to earlier strategies of denial or absorption. Plurality appears increasingly problematic. However, the paradigm of pluralism, which places a positive value upon variety and difference, has emerged to account for plurality.[5] But it poses a serious challenge to both Islam and Christianity, which hitherto have been at great pains to construct their understanding of reality so as to encompass everything within it. For, like Judaism, these are religions of revealed divine truth, with the

---

[5] See, for example, Douglas Pratt, 'Contextual Paradigms for Interfaith Relations' *Current Dialogue*, 42, December 2003, 3-9.

underlying assumption that this truth is a coherent encompassing unity. Pluralism, as an acute intellectual challenge for both Christianity and Islam, raises questions concerning our views of divine reality and traditional ascriptions of absolutes. It comprises one of the mix of challenges with which we are here concerned.

The challenge of individualism

Arguably Western secularism has become subject to a creeping nihilism *vis-à-vis* value systems, whether religious or otherwise, whereby the individual is now abandoned to his or her own fate. Individuals, in terms of the prevailing western secular mentality, are wholly and uniquely responsible for their own existence. Socio-economically, this is given expression in the tide of 'user-pay' and 'free-market' programmes and sub-ideologies that have swept across the secularised and western-oriented world. The political counter of state-provided social-welfare programmes, by virtue of the ever-decreasing support actually supplied, and by their commercial mode of implementation, only serve to reinforce the nihilistic abandonment of social value of the individual. Legislation to outlaw consequential maladies, such as drug abuse, are but fingers in the dyke: the prevailing secular ideology professes to value the individual, but, in fact, values only the economic or contributive worth that an individual represents. It has effectively undercut the intrinsic value of the individual as a member of the community *per se*, and thereby devalued the ideal of communal existence as well. Very often the clue to this is the critique, or lament, of the loss of 'family' within the context of responding to a rising tide of social maladies that today beset modern Western societies.

Both Christianity and Islam profess an ideology of the individual-in-community which stands opposed to the ubiquitous ideology of the autonomy of the individual as promoted by secularism. Islamic law, for example, is arguably not simply a punitive imposed system of petty rules and regulations (which is often the uncritical perception in the West), but rather an encompassing prescription (albeit with its concomitant sanctions) wherein the life of an individual Muslim may be situated *vis-à-vis* the community (the Ummah). And the 'good news' (gospel/*injil*) of Christianity is, again arguably, not merely a matter of 'pie in the sky when you die'—a proclamation of deferred reward in return for right belief—but the implementation of a value system whereby the individual receives affirmation and guidance for life here and now, as an individual-in-community, sustained by virtue of participation within the life of a particular religious community (*ecclesia*). For both the Muslim and Christian religious communities there is a profound challenge to be addressed arising out of the contemporary secular mentality.

The political challenge

The fourth ideological challenge is the phenomenon of *politicisation,* which seems to have been consequent, to a large degree, upon the emergence of secularism. Here I refer to the transfer of religious identity, and hence allegiance, from the global or universal ideal to the temporal geo-political realm. In many ways, of course, this process long pre-dates the emergence of modern secularism. But certainly the modern era has seen an acceleration of the process and a breakdown of the dialectic, or inherent self-reflective tension, which hitherto acted as somewhat of a brake on the process. Essentially, for both Islam and Christianity, the issue is one of the regionalisation of specific religious identity over against the affirmation of, or identification with, the universal dimension of the religious identity. Thus, for example, with the eventual break up of the Islamic empire into kingdoms and caliphates there came an overlay of political, or regional, identity into Muslim religious self-identification as such.

The ideal of the Ummah was ever present, but the temporal realities of political entities, together with the emergence of theological (kalam) and jurisprudential (fiqh) differentials, demarcated and determined local or specific religious identity and allegiance. A similar process occurred within Christianity. Individual Christians sooner or later were members of, and identified as, one particular church (denomination) over against another. Indeed the emergence of terms such as 'catholic' and 'orthodox' sprang from a context of claiming a universal rightness of one particular expression of identity and institutional arrangement over against all possible others. In Islam, of course, the first broad localisation of religious identity was with the division into Sunni and Shi'a camps.

For both Islam and Christianity the modern era and the emergence of the modern national state have exacerbated the process. Now Christians are likely to belong to a community that identifies as much with a geo-political entity as it does with the sense of universal faith: so 'Church of England'; 'Uniting Church of Australia'; 'Presbyterian Church of New Zealand'; the 'Church of South India' and so on. And Muslims are Malay, Pakistani, Egyptian; Arab or Asian; African or East European, and so on. Muslim identity is as much a matter of temporal geo-political formation as it is a matter of affirming the oneness of, and personal identity with, the Islamic Ummah. The corollary and consequence is that issues of faith, belief, and the religious life become subsumed to political factors and forces, both within the world of each religion and, painfully, between them. This is an area of study and dialogical engagement requiring much ongoing research and reflection.

The theological dimension of dialogue

Theological dialogue, and in particular the ideological element or dimension inherent in that, constitutes a major arena of dialogical challenge. Here, by way of an example, we may note the manner whereby Islam and Christianity each interrelates historical founder-figure motif and ideological-religious function. If we take, for the sake of illustration, the two respective historical 'founder figures'—for Christianity, Jesus; for Islam, Muhammad—we may like to consider how each religion perceives their particular figure in terms of function. This is important because, typically (although arguably falsely), they are contrasted and compared simply on the basis that they appear, as historical figures, to function as equivalents. But in point of fact the ideological function is different in each case.

For Christianity, Jesus functions as *saviour*: the motif of *prophet* is secondary to, and indeed subsumed by, that. The ascription, 'Messiah' (Greek: *Christos*), is derived from the Judaic understanding of the particular figure, namely someone who will be sent by God to effect salvation. But, even if the function of 'saviour' is pre-eminent, it is not the *sole* function ascribed to this figure. Jesus functions also as teacher (so the title *Rabbi*) and as an exemplar of the ways of God (thus the title *Son of God*), and so, through all this, together with the activities and events that befall him according to the passion narratives of the gospels (betrayal, trial, crucifixion, resurrection) he functions as the active agent of Divine Will (thus the title or ascription *Word* or *Logos* of God). So, in the subsequent Christian perspective the function of the figure is suggestive of divine being inherent to him; hence the lengthy and complex development of Christian doctrine concerning Jesus. An Islamic reading of the Christian account might conclude that, in the Christian record, there is evidence of unique and particular submission to the Will of God: the gospel records as among Jesus' last words the petition 'Not my will be done, but Thine'. Indeed an Islamic reading of the Christian record (as opposed to an Islamic reading of the Quranic record of Jesus) may form a worthwhile dimension of cross-hermeneutical engagement within the context of theological dialogue.

By contrast, of course, the Islamic perspective on Muhammad as the founder figure is unequivocally straightforward: he was a man through whom God gave to the world the message contained in the utterances which he, Muhammad, was commanded to recite. Muhammad was a prophet, first and last. And in the Islamic view he fulfilled that role as none before him had done. But clearly he did more than just that. A close reading of the Islamic account of Muhammad reveals the motif of *exemplar par excellence*: the motif of teacher; the motif of enacting a divine—that is, divinely willed and sanctioned—mission which resulted in the establishment of a theocratic community wherein is proclaimed and promoted the way of a saving faith.

So, in other words, when considering the ideology of function in respect of a comparison of figure, we can detect aspects of a dynamic parallelism operating at one level, yet we can recognise the impact of ideological differentiation that also applies at other levels. By carefully working through the ideological dimension it may be possible to deconstruct the accretions of dogma and hagiography sufficient to find a bedrock of unique function that allows each religion to co-equally affirm and honour the other's central historical figure in a way that has hitherto been impossible to achieve.

The discussion of ideological dimensions to theological dialogue leads to the matter of the conceptual or interpretive element to theological dialogue. My underlying concern is to identify the place and function of theological reflection in the dialogical encounter process. Here the analogy of light and prism comes to mind. Both Islam and Christianity proclaim the oneness of God and the oneness of the Truth of God. Yet, to a greater or lesser degree, vast complexes of concept and doctrine—not to mention lifetimes of intellectual ratiocination—have been produced by thinkers seeking to fathom and express the truth of divine revelation on either side. As a consequence the heritage of theological encounter is largely one of competing claim, counterclaim, and, in the end, mutual dismissal of the other's viewpoint. The assumption has been that each religion is, in effect, talking about the incoming light on the basis that only it has the right prism of conceptual construct or interpretive framework in order to refract the light and thus perceive it in its full true glory.

The analogy is based on the view that there is only one light of Truth, only one Ultimate or Divine Reality; arguably different religions are, in effect, different prisms held up to that light, and the diverse theologies, explications, practices and perspectives are the product of the different prisms and the way they are held, as it were. Religions often argue on the basis of their different refractions of the Truth, assuming that their particular refraction equates to the original light itself. To recognise, in the process of theological dialogue, that what we offer to each other is a refracted perspective—unique, distinctive, and valuable as such; potentially open to complementarity from the perspective of another's refraction—may constitute no bad starting point for dialogue. Arguably, for instance, the doctrine of the Trinity is a refraction of the truth of the oneness of God through the particular prism of a historically bounded language and set of concerns and conceptual tools for dealing with those concerns.

The point of the analogy is both to help set the context for dialogue and to help unlock the process whereby dialogue tends to end where it begins—the agreement to disagree—because, among other reasons for such an outcome, there has been no recognition of the 'prism effect' in respect of religious epistemology and conceptual constructs. Without such a recognition of what is really the interrelationship of the absolute and relative dimensions to all religious discourse there is no prospect of a perspectival shift such that might allow for, in the context of dialogical encounter, the upholding of novel interpretation on the grounds that it is just that: interpretation; a new, possibly combined, refraction of a truth which in and of itself changes not nor can it be changed.

The conceptual and interpretive element is critical to interfaith dialogue: it functions as the gatekeeper—to change the metaphor—which determines what, or who, shall be admitted, and what is to be turned away. Inherent within a critical scrutiny of this element are, of course, issues such as the meaning and implication of the concepts absolute and relative, and universality and particularity, for example. The extent that issues such as these are addressed, or not addressed, will determine whether theological dialogue will be a matter of deep engagement or superficial encounter. One offers the possibility of moving beyond the parameters of past expectation; the other at best continues friendly communication at a comfortable level and superficial depth, but little more than that.

In exploring aspects of theological dialogue I shall now turn, albeit briefly, to two other elements, namely, the linguistic and conceptual (or interpretive) elements pertaining to the challenge of theological dialogue. These concern, among other things, the issue of the mode of the utterance of religious terminology, whether as vocal event or as silently read. Among the many modes that could be identified, three stand out as relevant to our present considerations. The utterance of religious terms may be *definitive*, *stative*, or *evocative*.

In some cases we need to recognise that statements belong to one, but not to another, mode. On the other hand, and this is more likely the case, statements can be verbally identical, but, as utterance *per se*, may range across all three modes. Thus, for example, the Christian utterance 'God is Love' may be made *definitively*: that is, the purpose of the utterance is to declare the predicate 'love' as the defining attribute of 'God'. Alternatively the same utterance may be made *statively*, as, for example, when quoting the scriptural passage that contains it, thus stating or asserting an item of Christian belief or understanding. But also the utterance 'God is Love' may be made *evocatively*, as in the context of prayer or worship, as well as debate and discussion, wherein the effect of the utterance is primarily to evoke a matrix of religious understanding, where it is a shorthand formula used to stimulate or excite the sense of the divine in the context of a particular (in this case, for example, Christian) apprehension of Deity as such.

The definitive sense is most typically philosophical; the stative most typically theological; and the evocative most typically liturgical. This can be further demonstrated when considering Christian Trinitarian language. The phrase 'In the name of the Father, Son, and Holy Spirit' is an *evocative* utterance typically associated with Christian liturgical—that is, worship—activity as well as other forms of language-performative events such as funerals, weddings, blessings, and so on. A statement such as 'The Son is begotten by the Father, and the Spirit proceeds from the Father and the Son' is a *stative* utterance: it simply asserts, or states, an item of Christian belief despite its superficial appearance as an explanation, which is another form of utterance.

It is worth noting that creedal utterances, which are constructed and construed as theological statements, thus as statives, are actually used liturgically for the most part. That is, their usage and setting is evocative. Hence Christians may find themselves apparently saying things they don't really believe, or using language that has no contemporary meaning, if they are not tuned in to the appropriate mode of their utterance. On the other hand they can be accused of hypocrisy or double standards if, for example, a creedal formula spoken in good faith as an evocative utterance, is presumed by an outside 'listener' to be a stative or even definitive utterance.

As a final example, the sentence 'God exists as one substance in three persons' is a *definitive* utterance that derives directly from philosophical consideration upon the meaning of theological statements, which then frame the language of the faithful at worship. In this case there are three modes of utterance around the one subject matter. Thus they are interlinked, but it is a matter of considerable confusion when the modalities are transposed, which they sometimes are in an uncritical environment. If the evocative utterance 'In the name of ...' is taken as a stative, for example, then it is likely to be received, and will certainly appear so in the act of utterance, as a statement about three different entities, one called Father, a second called Son, and a third called Spirit. If the utterance is made with definitive effect, it may well indeed infer a (albeit unintended) tri-theistic conceptuality.

If we consider for a moment the two keywords for Deity in the Christian and Islamic traditions—'God' and 'Allah'—it is worth noting that, in the evocative context of Christian usage, the term 'God' is most usually prefaced with a preposition of address. Thus, '*Oh* God', '*Dear* God', '*Father* God', '*Almighty* God' and so on, the import of which is to evoke the degree of familiarity or distance appropriate to the context of address. By way of comparison, the term 'Allah' in its very locution seems adequately evocative as it stands. Yet the oft-used *al-Rahman, al-Rahim* (the Merciful, the Compassionate) as standard corollaries of address in the Islamic context wherein the name of Allah is invoked, would seem to function to extend the evocative utterance. They are terms of primary identification and reference for the divine, at least in the evocative mood. Further, depending on context, they may be perceived as stative or as definitive utterances. More work on examining and teasing out the range of linguistic modalities, and in particular examining how they are applied or misapplied, might prove very useful in furthering the cause of theological dialogue between Christianity and Islam.

Some theological issues in Christian–Muslim dialogue

Two key issues and themes have emerged through the history of Christian–Muslim encounter, namely scriptural revelation and the concept of God. They deserve our attention at this juncture. The place of Holy Scripture—Bible and Qur'an—as the locus of revelation is a primary theme in Muslim–Christian encounter. From the Muslim perspective, 'the Qur'an repeatedly claims continuity with Jewish–Christian tradition and is seen by Muslims as the last Scripture in a long line of Scriptures given to the Prophets'.[6] Other scriptures and other religions are mentioned within the Qur'an. Indeed, both Jews and Christians are challenged from within the Qur'an to live by the will of God as revealed in their books. But it is clear, for example, that the principle of abrogation and the doctrine of tahrif—in respect to the notion of the corruption of meaning and the assertion of the corruption of the religious text of the religious 'other'—are critically determinative decreed perspectives, even though 'most Quranic scholars claim that the Qur'an does not assert general corruption of the Judeo–Christian Scriptures, but rather that texts have been misused and certain passages concealed'.[7] A typical Christian response to Muslim polemics in respect of the Bible asks 'if it is held that the

---

[6] Michael Nazir-Ali, *Frontiers in Muslim–Christian Encounter* (Oxford: Regnum Books, 1991), 45; cf. Sura 2:136.

[7] Ibid., 46.

revelation to the Jews and the Christians was time-, people- and place-specific, why should the Qur'an not also be regarded in the same way?'[8]

The answer is that there is a fundamental difference in the way the two religions understand the meaning and phenomenon of scripture: suffice to comment here that there is a major difference in literary type. The Qur'an, as we know, is the record of direct utterance, hence the primacy of Arabic as the language of that utterance. The Christian scripture, inclusive of the Hebrew Bible as the 'Old Testament', is manifestly a collection of many forms of document and styles of communication, from narrative history, to poetic reflection, to the address of direct epistle, to the theologically crafted gospel. In both the Qur'an and the Bible there may be discerned the address of God, the word that bears message and revelation. But the difference in style, format, and origin has to be carefully weighed: it is inadequate for one to dismiss the other on the grounds of this difference. Charles Kimball states that, with but a few exceptions,

> most Islamic literature on Christianity has been framed in the language of polemics. Recurring themes include charges of altering or forging parts of the divine revelation, seriously errant doctrine (e.g., original sin, incarnation, atonement, the Trinity) and grievous mistakes in religious practice (e.g., celibacy, veneration of saints, 'idol' worship).[9]

As with Christian understandings of Islam, Muslim positions in respect of the understanding of Christianity often developed on limited and partial knowledge, on inadequate and superficial comprehension, and even on erroneous information about the wider Christian tradition. In other words, similar dynamics of ignorance and world-view presumptions were at work on both sides. Christian responses to Islam have often—and from early times—begun from the assumption of the false or heretical nature of this faith simply because it follows the final and unique redemptive act of God in Jesus Christ. And there was, as I have also previously noted, the popular acceptance abroad that in some way Muhammad was linked to the devil or Antichrist. Again we are reminded that the first task of dialogue is the work of mutual correction and education.

In general terms, in Islamic understanding of the relationship between God and humanity, Allah is the Master (*rabb*) and the role or place of the human being is that of servant (*'abd*). Thus all of life, both in morals and in religious duty, is a matter of service (*'ibadat*), or worship given to Allah. The primary goal of human existence is submission to, and the service of, Allah, the One God. Within this context the particular stress of the Islamic understanding of God is in terms of the unity—or ontological oneness—of Allah: the concept of God brooks no internal or inherent divisions or distinctions, and certainly no associations with any other being or entity.

---

[8] Ibid., 47.

[9] Kimball, *Striving Together*, 47.

The Islamic doctrine of tawhid is the assertion that God is One. It is expressed in the first part of the fundamental creed of Islam, the Shahada: 'There is no God but Allah'. God is unique, wholly different from all else: a perspective certainly echoed by both Judaism and Christianity although both, in different ways, admit of some measure of identity of God with the world. Islam opposes any such thoughts. Nothing may resemble Allah, no thing or person can be associated with Allah, or is equal, or in any way alike, to Allah. Any such suggestion amounts to *shirk*, the Islamic high blasphemy. Allah is utterly different from the realm of creation.

A very important dimension of Islamic belief in the One God has to do with the notion of the 'Will of Allah', a stress on a concept of a 'controlling God', a God in control of all things and who works within and upon creation through the act of Divine Will. Allah is omnipotent and omniscient: all things exist by the Will of Allah; Allah can do anything and knows all. Indeed, as one scholar has commented:

> The omnipotence of Allah was so strongly stressed in the Qur'an that not only did Allah guide the faithful to the truth, but in some sense also he led the wicked astray. ... a matter of letting people lose their way. ... it was ultimately the will of Allah which controlled (human) destiny.[10]

Islam views God as immediately present to humankind, full of mercy toward humanity. Just, sure, and merciful on the one hand, yet, on the other, there is in the Islamic understanding of deity a strong intimation of predestination. Allah, the all-merciful, expresses the Islamic notion of divine immanence as the counter to the stress of the utter transcendence of God. The all-powerful and all-knowing majesty of God is not the sole mark of Allah: the wholly otherness of deity is in Islam matched by relational motifs such as divine mercy, beneficence and compassion.

The Holy Qur'an of course contains much direct and indirect material with which to construct, intellectually, a concept of Allah. On the one hand there are the manifold descriptive names and attributes, on the other hand various ascriptions of perfection: omniscient, omnipotent, and so on. Allah is self-sufficient, and the focus on judgement provides impetus to the pre-emptive response: submission. Creation follows the biblical six days, but there is no seventh day of rest, for that would suggest 'divine weariness'. Rather the Islamic notion is that once creation is effected God continues as the direct and active ruler or regulator of all that occurs.

By contrast, Christian theism has a double origin: the Bible and Greek philosophy. Divine properties, or attributes, are implied within the Bible but articulated through the mode of Greek conceptual language. For Christianity the philosophical presentation of theology—or classical theism—was begun by the Apologists in the second century of the Common Era, developed by the Fathers and reached its height with St Augustine (354–430CE: the apex of the Platonic mode) and St Thomas Aquinas (c.1225–74CE: chief exponent of the Aristotelian mode).

---

[10] Ninian Smart, *The Religious Experience of Mankind* (London: Fontana, 1969), 488.

When we examine the theistic definition that has dominated the Judeo–Christian perspective, we may note a number of interesting features. First, there is a stress on the *unity of God*. Hebraic development on this point, by the time of Second Isaiah (sixth century BCE), had become axiomatic in Jewish theology and was held as a primary item of early Christian apologetics. This unity was discerned through biblical revelation: Hebrew religion believed God self-revealed as One God. It was also discerned by experience, which yielded the argument of inference: if the Divine Being, or Deity as such, is to be the object of absolute devotion it must possess absolute being. But one among many gods cannot possess such being, for this God would then share the divine nature with other gods; therefore the Divine must be One. The unity of God has also been argued for on the grounds of pure reason by, for example, Thomas Aquinas. The New Testament does not, of course, contain developed creeds, but rather patterns, slogans, and so on; that is, verbal conventions which signify faith and intimate patterns of belief that would, at a later date, be shaped into rigorous dogma.

In respect to the figure of Christ, the Muslim perspective sees Jesus affirmed and exalted in the Qur'an. However, where there is difference in interpretation and conception, any such points of conflict, 'according to the Qur'an, arise in relation to the erroneous teachings propagated by Christians' and this is because Islam 'began with the assumption that Jesus was one of the greatest among the special messengers from God'.[11] This revelation was assumed to be true and accurate. From the Muslim point of view it is the Christians who have both distorted the message and wrongly attributed divinity to the messenger, thus committing the blasphemy of *shirk*. Likewise the doctrine of the Trinity has proved a persistently stubborn stumbling block so far as dialogue is concerned. Let's take a closer look at the issue of Christ and the Trinity in respect to interfaith dialogue with Islam.

Two key dialogical issues: Jesus, the Christ; God, the Trinity

Two key issues, or theological 'problematics', which lay behind creedal development within Christianity and have continued to this day to be the source of much debate and scholarly activity, need to be addressed in the context of Christian–Muslim dialogue. The first is the problematic of the nature of Christ. The second is the Trinitarian concept of God. Both have to do with, or perhaps express particular aspects of, the issue of the unity of the Divine Being. What for Muslims is no issue at all—the priority of tawhid (absolute oneness) is paramount—for Christians has always been a mystery of the Divine Being: in the context of affirming divine Oneness Christian faith asserts, nonetheless, two forms of plurality. It is in the context of Christian–Muslim theological dialogue, however, that the resolution of the issue takes on a new urgency. In theory Christianity ought to be able to concur with the Muslim affirmation of *tawhid*. How might this be so?

---

[11] Kimball, *Striving Together*, 45.

In effect it is the figure of Christ that leads, in the first instance, to the problematic of unity. So long as there is belief in one God, but also a belief in the divinity of Christ—and then, added to that, the divinity of the Holy Spirit—there is a genuine problem of accounting for divine unity to be resolved. The early affirmation of the divinity of Christ as the Son of God led to the issue of the unity of God. The Trinitarian issue emerged alongside the Christological. Although dogmatic formulations were the official outcome, and these have shaped and flavoured the nature of Christianity as a belief system ever since, arguably neither unity problematic is yet fully resolved.

One judgement upon the great Christian Councils in the early centuries, such as Nicea in 325CE, is to say that they produced purely political formulae with the intent, by and large, of imposing a badge of union upon a divided church or a quaking empire. Such a hypothesis may help to explain the historical facts, but the underlying theological debate was—and still is—real enough. The priority of divine unity—or tawhid, to use the Islamic term—remains an issue for Christian theology and, of course, is a significant issue for any Christian–Muslim theological dialogue. For our purposes I shall discuss the Christology and unity issue first, then focus on the Trinitarian problematic.

Jesus, the Christ

The nub of the first problematic has to do with the Christian understanding of salvation: it is believed, among other things, that Christ undertook a divine act whereby human beings may be saved. Classically this has referred to the belief in the judgement at the end of time, in essence an item of belief shared with Islam. Now, the particular Christian belief about Christ in the context of salvation was that he effected a form of divine intervention that 'saves' the believer from the day of judgement and offers, therefore, the assurance of Paradise. This is very much an act of gracious intervention of divine justice that could only be accomplished and sanctioned by God.

By comparison, it is certainly the case that a natural concern for many Muslims is how to ameliorate, if not avoid, the Day of Judgement, called also the 'Day of Doom'. In keeping with the theme of 'submission' there is little one can do except await the Divine outcome in accordance with the requirements of the Divine Will but, hopefully, tempered by Divine Mercy. However, if one were to die the death of a martyr, that is, be killed in the act of defending the faith, then the Day of Doom is bypassed and immediate entry into Paradise is guaranteed. Hence within Islamic eschatology there is found a powerful element that has coloured and influenced the conduct of Islamic politics through the centuries. However, this is not exactly the same as 'salvation', nor is it the soteriological goal of Islam. That is arguably better understood as a matter of attaining harmony with the Divine Will in this life, with the hope, certainly, of a just reward in the next. Thus the soteriological process, or the 'way of salvation' it might be said, is a matter of submission to the Divine Will.

To follow the path of Islam involves studying and learning, teaching and reciting, praying and thinking. 'It is a life-long path, which continues from birth to death'.[12]

Certainly, for both Islam and Christianity, no mere mortal could grant or effect salvation for humankind. In the classical Christian view, therefore, Christ could not be merely human, but must also, in some proper sense, be God. But how could this be so? One early perspective, in the end officially rejected by the Church at the time as heretical, advocated that, whereas ordinary humans were comprised of mind and body, Christ was composed of a human body together with the divine *Logos* (Word, reason) in place of the human mind. After much debate around various views, in the end there emerged the theory that Jesus, as the Christ, has two natures in one person. Each nature was deemed to be a distinct subject, to which predicates could be assigned. For example, it was the human nature that wept, but the Divine that forgave.

A new heresy arose by logical extrapolation from this *two-natures* theory, however. This was the view that being born was something that happened to Christ's human nature only: therefore the divine is not 'born' as such. This had implications for the growing veneration of the mother of Jesus to whom many had given the title 'bearer of God' (*Theokotos*), and it also fuelled other forms of heresy such as *adoptionism*, whereby it was argued that Jesus, at the point of his baptism, was 'adopted' by God and, in some mystical way, thereby infused with the attribute of divinity. But the key concern was that, if it is only the humanity that suffered and died on the cross, it would appear that salvation is owed to a human being, not to God. Eventually there emerged an insistence on Christ's oneness in every respect: one person, one nature, one particular individual. However, it was reasoned, gradually, that there must be a legitimate way of speaking of the duality of being both human and divine so far as the person of Christ was concerned. This led to the theory of the union of the two natures in one individual. Thus 'being born' may be legitimately predicated of both the human and the divine, and the work of salvation, as a divine initiative, may be brought about through this human agent.

A number of subtle variations on the understanding of the two natures united in the one person of Christ have emerged, but in essence the dominant view has been that each nature is complete nonetheless: Christ is thus both true man and true God. This now famous Definition of Chalcedon—promulgated by the ecumenical council that met at the town of Chalcedon in the year 451CE—was the formal outcome that expressed the resolution. It stands as the normative Christian statement about Christ and holds that Christ has two natures, human and divine, co-existing in one person, and that the essential oneness of the person makes it appropriate to apply the predicates of either nature to the other. So it was that Christianity, some 400 years after Jesus, crystallised this fundamental belief about him. This resolution has formed one of the bedrock items of Christian belief ever since. Arguably, however, it leaves more questions unanswered and more issues unresolved than is appropriate for a foundational belief in any religious system. In

---

[12] Theodore Ludwig, *The Sacred Paths* (New York: Macmillan, 1989), 226.

fact, by no means was this the end of debate within Christianity. Indeed, in recent times Christian theologians have been much engaged in this and related questions. One could say that the essential problematic has never been resolved, only identified. By contrast, how did the problematic of the Trinity fare?

God, the Trinity

The theologian Keith Ward has stated, somewhat succinctly, that:

> The Christian concept of God has been definitively formulated as the concept of the Trinity, three persons in one substance, co-equal and co-eternal, not confused with one another, and yet not three Gods but one God. The Son is begotten by the Father, and the Spirit proceeds from the Father and the Son (except for the Orthodox Churches), and yet no person is before, after, greater or less than another.[13]

The doctrine of the Trinity admits of a variety of interpretations and has had a chequered career throughout the history of Christian theological thinking. It developed from the initial distinction between God the Father and God the Son, a distinction concerning the inherent 'paradoxical nature of God': God perceived as both 'absolutely above and beyond, and yet at the same time near and immanent'.[14] The doctrine of the Trinity endeavours to comprehend both the inner being of God, and how it is that God engages in relational activity while yet retaining the appropriate sense of transcendent otherness. The doctrine of the Trinity gives substance to the concept of the Christian God, yet not without invoking some particular problems.

It was St Augustine's particular view that came eventually to dominate the West. He began with the unity of God. For him it was divine oneness that was the prior conceptual truth, the plurality of divine 'persons' was subordinate to that. Thus he argued that the three Trinitarian names refer to three 'somethings' so-named because of the essential relation denoted: 'they are three subjects of one divine activity who are only relationally distinct'.[15] Orthodoxy—meaning here 'normative Christian belief'—finally found an answer to the perplexing question of the definition of 'person' in the dictum that a person (or 'hypostasis' to use the more precise technical term) within the Trinity, is 'an individual substance of rational nature'.[16] This definition became widely influential and accepted, at least until the modern period.

As I have already indicated, it was the particular issue of the person of Christ that sparked the whole question of divine unity, hence the development of the

---

[13] Keith Ward, *The Concept of God* (Oxford: Basil Blackwell, 1974), 212.

[14] C. C. Richardson, *The Doctrine of the Trinity* (Nashville: Abingdon 1958), 21.

[15] E. J. Fortman, *The Triune God* (London: Hutchinson, 1972), 152.

[16] Ibid., 163.

doctrine of the Trinity, or 'Tri-Unity', in the first place. The underlying issue in the early days was the problem of subordinationism. That is to say, as something other than God 'the Father', and as proceeding from 'the Father' the Son is thereby *less than* (or subordinate to) the Father (here synonymous with 'God'). The implication of this reasoning was that either Christ was some form of demi-god, or else super-human, and that consequently the Christian image of God, as portrayed through scripture in terms of divine 'Fatherhood', was in error. Neither of these implications could be reasonably entertained, therefore there had to be an intellectual resolution, albeit a complex dogmatic one. In essence it was that the Trinitarian persons are to be distinguished by virtue of their mutual relations within the Godhead (the so-called 'inner-trinitarian' relations, relations that pertain to the internal being of God) and not by external actions or relationships as such.

Unity is the foundational notion. The person Jesus of Nazareth was a man through whom God spoke and acted in a particular way; the title of 'Christ', which has dominated as the proper name[17] and thus contributed to the whole context for raising the question of the nature of Jesus as, putatively, both human and divine, first and foremost speaks of the divine function or action which was effected through this human individual. Christological definitions, which are ontological statements, arose as a result of theological reflection and debate. They are just that: definitions. They are constructs of ontological thinking; products of intellectual endeavour; the results of Christian *ijtihad* we might say. Likewise, the Trinity is an onto-theological explanatory concept. To talk in terms of inner-trinitarian relations constituting the essential life of God, or as fundamentally descriptive of the Divine Being, is arguably to ontologise a symbolic construct which has itself been derived from the diversity of the human experience of God within the Christian context.

Distinctiveness of relationship in regard to any one of the three 'persons' is distinctiveness of particularity in divine relational activity as such: there is no need to presume any other relational identity is responsible for the particular relational type, even a relational identity 'within' God. The Trinitarian names (Father, Son, Holy Spirit) can thus be seen as denoting three spheres or dimensions of divine relational activity. Analogously, Islam's 99 Most Beautiful Names of Allah are also indicative of various types and sorts of relationships that it is of the nature of Deity to be engaged in. Arguably it would be a category mistake to contrast Trinity with tawhid because the latter is the prior or fundamental concept; the former is but one construct expressing the human understanding of the revelatory experience of God-in-relationship. Clearly there is much to be thought about and carefully considered. It would be—indeed, often is—simply easier to ignore these theological issues on the grounds that there are more important ethical and practical matters to engage with dialogically. But this is to overlook the pivotal part played in the religious world view—so the life of values and actions—of such foundational beliefs and ideas. Theological dialogue needs to probe beyond the presented data of our traditions to the dynamics that both underlie and inhere to them.

---

[17] So: 'Jesus, the Christ' thence 'Jesus Christ' and 'Christ' as the alternate names for Jesus.

Conclusion

Not all modes of encounter and interaction between Christianity and Islam are 'dialogical', strictly speaking, and not all dialogue is obviously theological in nature or content. Nevertheless, theological dialogue can be—and, I suggest, needs to be—entered into creatively and with integrity in order to engage in a genuinely radical[18] rethinking of the intellectual constructs whereby we express our faith and belief. Only so can this dimension of dialogue lead into genuine advances in interfaith encounters. And in today's world such dialogical encounter between Muslims and Christians is of vital concern to both, and this for two interrelated reasons: to ameliorate trajectories of antipathy and hostility for the sake of peaceful co-existence that actually honours the deepest and best values and aspirations of these two religions; and to do that by addressing and seeking to resolve conceptually the underlying ideological, philosophical, and theological distinctions and conflicts. By this last I don't mean some intellectual reduction to a lowest common denominator, nor some idealist and quixotic reconciliation or new synthesis.

Nonetheless, given the fact that all religious ideas and conceptual formulations rest in language and the contexts of world views, and given that Islam and Christianity share certain bedrock affirmations and ideas, yet at the same time display some very profound differences in the development and outworking of these ideas, then the task of addressing the broad theological dimension of dialogue is an urgent and profoundly important one. For religious ideas underpin much rhetoric and conceptual construct that issues in socio-political policy and action. Hence both content and context of these ideas is of vital concern. Kate Zebiri points out that 'The majority of Muslims, like the majority of Christians, hold an exclusivist view of truth, in that they believe that their religion is true to a degree that others are not'.[19] The socio-political consequences of hard-line exclusivism are all too clear. But exclusivism is a mindset based on religious belief and ideology. Exclusivists may be inimical to dialogue, but the beliefs and ideologies espoused can nevertheless form the agenda of critically useful and important interfaith encounter.

On the other hand, as Hugh Goddard notes, in both Christianity and Islam one can find a wide spectrum of opinions about beliefs and ideologies such that 'the bewildering variety of opinion within each community has given rise to the suggestion that perhaps we should no longer speak of Islam and Christianity but rather of Islams and Christianities'.[20] Goddard's point is not just structural and sociological, reflecting the manifest fact of internal socio-identity diversity that applies to each religion; it applies also to the variegated range of theological and

---

[18] 'Going to the roots'.

[19] Kate Zebiri, *Muslims and Christians: Face to Face* (Oxford: Oneworld Publications, 1997), 175.

[20] Goddard, *Christians and Muslims,* 169.

ideological positions that is found in each religion and potentially across or between them. This suggests that, in the context of dialogue, it may be discovered that on some key issues and affirmations there is indeed a degree of conceptual overlap which may be greater than first thought—at least once the accretions of traditional rhetoric and prejudicial posturing are stripped away, and the issues are subject to appropriate critical scrutiny that engages equally both parties to the dialogue. In his own concluding remarks Michael Ipgrave has put it rather succinctly:

> There is a need to deepen and to broaden the base of mutual understanding between Muslims and Christians. The academic community has a particular role to play in helping to counteract stereotypes, myths and facile generalizations. ... Theological dialogue should not be avoided or made secondary to more apparently pressing social concerns, and it should have sufficient maturity to be able to address points of difference as well as areas of convergence.[21]

Finally, as John Macquarrie notes, 'Muhammad's conception of God has affinities with both the Jewish and Christian conceptions of God, and historically they all have a Middle Eastern origin. But they have certainly drifted apart.'[22] The nature and detail of the drift may be of historical interest; the fact and extent of it is of contemporary concern because it has led to profoundly variant understandings of the nature of divine and human reality, the modalities of relationships that pertain to that and to inter-human engagement—profound differences of understanding of the reality of religion and the ordering of human society. Arguably, so many of the clashes, confusions, and violent hotspots that exist today—where, for example, 'Western Judeo–Christian' interfaces with 'Islamic' cultures and societies (and here we only need to think of Iraq, or Afghanistan, or the Balkans)—are born from the legacy of unexamined conflicting religious ideologies and unresolved mutual misunderstandings and confused thinking. This is where the theological dimension of interreligious dialogue, particularly between Christian and Muslim, but also in respect to Jewish–Muslim engagement, must not be set aside. It needs instead urgent advance.

---

[21] Michael Ipgrave, ed., *The Road Ahead: a Christian–Muslim Dialogue* (London: Church House Publishing, 2002), 119–20.

[22] John Macquarrie, *The Mediators* (London: SCM Press, 1995), 125.

Chapter 12

Conclusion

In the Introduction I suggested that Islam poses something of a challenge in respect to religion, ideology and culture. The challenge of Islam is that it is there to be known, understood, and dialogically responded to. So, in this book, I have made an attempt, in the first Part, at addressing the challenge of presenting and exploring this religion through a series of introductory chapters: responding to the challenge of educational engagement has been my first task. The objective has been to offer my own contribution to the understanding of Islam. I trust the reader has adequately encountered the origins of Islam; its grounding scripture and the traditions it holds dear; its sense of community and the diverse and complex divisions that demarcate it; the beliefs, practices and the adherence to law—Shari'a—which mark out Muslim identity. I have done this, of course, as a non-Muslim scholar seeking to address other non-Muslims. A critical, yet sympathetic, understanding of Islam is needed today, perhaps as never before, within the wider Western world, whether the context of that world is secular, Christian, Jewish, or otherwise. Although the religion that stands as a primary protagonist to Islam is Christianity, it is not just Christians who are perplexed, challenged, and even fearful of Islam.

While I have endeavoured to be reasonably comprehensive, there is much that has been glossed, skimmed, or even omitted in the interests of succinctness and manageability of the material. As ever, when dealing with a potentially vast subject, an author must be selective. Hopefully, though, the major points and matters of pertinent interest have been adequately covered. As with any religion, and especially a global one, there are many variations—nuances of expression and varieties of interpretation—that make the task of presenting the religion in a coherent and encompassing fashion both daunting and fraught. Nevertheless, the challenge to do so, especially with respect to Islam, must be made and remade. For it is only in so doing that fear, prejudice, and general anxiety about this religion can be replaced with informed understanding and critical insight.

If Part I of this book is the first, or one of but a few, introductions to Islam encountered by the reader, then something of value should have been imparted by way of grounding knowledge and useful insight. Hopefully, too, some points of interpretation and informed understanding have been grasped. Of course, there is always more to learn, and greater depths to plumb. But there is also the danger, especially in this so-called 'information age', of being overwhelmed by data and propaganda—for and against—in just about any field of contention and debate, and perhaps none more so than in the case of Islam. It is the task of the sympathetic, but also critically alert, non-Muslim scholar of Islam to take up the challenge of explicating this religion to a non-Muslim readership in a manner that genuinely informs and enlightens. As much as I have enjoyed the task—and it certainly has been a profoundly challenging one—I am all too aware of my limitations. But hopefully I have executed a useful contribution to what is, really, the never-ending task of seeking to understand another religion, both critically and empathetically.

Responding to the task of educational engagement—of seeking to understand Islam both in terms of religious principles and presenting behaviours—led into a second task, namely that of exploring dialogical engagement. That the world needs more, rather than less, dialogical activity in respect to Islam and Muslim peoples goes without saying. Nevertheless, undertaking dialogical engagement, at whatever level from mundane daily interaction to the intentional and intellectually demanding, comes neither easily nor naturally. For the most part we are absorbed enough in the business of our everyday lives, and the sustenance of our own families and communities, to be taking the necessary time, and expending the required energy, to engage in some sort of meaningful dialogical relationship with someone from a totally different community. This is a commonplace of human experience and behaviour. But in respect of interactions between Islam, or Muslim communities, and other religions and their communities—not to mention interaction between Islam and secularised Western cultures—then this commonplace needs itself to be challenged. In many contexts the slogan 'dialogue or die' is all too real.[1]

Dialogue with Islam is, in a number of situations, a life-and-death necessity, not a luxury. Dialogue with Islam needs everywhere to be urgently explored and engaged in. So, in Part II, I attempted to lay some groundwork for this activity by way of a discussion of aspects of Christian–Muslim and Jewish–Muslim relations and an exploration of contemporary contours of Islamic identity and ideological issues. The review of Christian–Muslim encounters across the history of interaction between these two religions is not only meant to serve a useful informative purpose, but also to set the scene for a realistic appreciation of where the two religions and their communities have come from and what has informed the groundswell of prejudicial understanding and expectations each has of the other. In so doing, I hope some sense has been grasped, on the one hand, of what it is that the deeper discursive dialogue has to contend with; and, on the other, what might lie behind, and so possibly inhibit, various forms of dialogical activity.

Similarly, the foray into Jewish–Muslim relations, with its attempt to delineate some basic issues of Islamic paradigms that have applied—and in large measure continue to apply—to these relations, is no exhaustive coverage but rather a thought-provoking, and hopefully useful, exploration of a critical dimension of

---

[1] See, for example, Leonard Swidler et al., *Death or Dialogue? From the Age of Monologue to the Age of Dialogue* (London: SCM Press and Philadelphia: Trinity Press International, 1990).

interfaith encounter, one which is arguably of profound significance for the world as a whole. This is by no means a final word, rather the opening salvo signalling issues that need to be taken account of if there is to be any deep and lasting healing of the relational divide that presently holds between Judaism and Islam, or at least between the present-day communities of those two faiths.

Dialogical engagement does not occur in a contextual vacuum. Interfaith encounter, while it can have a theoretical and dispassionate dimension, is essentially a grounded relationship within the real world of religio-cultural identity and the vagaries of socio-political dynamics. Hence in Chapter 8 the focus was not simply on understanding something of contemporary Islam for its own sake— important though that is—but in order to more accurately know and understand Islam and Muslims as a dialogical partner in today's world. While Graham Fuller's broad identification of Islamism—which, curiously, he regards as not in itself an ideology—with political Islam tends to oversimplification, he is certainly correct in his assertion that, generally speaking, a contemporary Islamist is 'one who believes that Islam as a body of faith has something important to say about how politics and society should be ordered in the contemporary Muslim World and who seeks to implement this idea in some fashion' and furthermore that 'political Islam is not an exotic and distant phenomenon, but one intimately linked to contemporary political, social, economic and moral issues of near universal concern'.[2] Islamic engagement is certainly premised on a holistic world view, but the ideological options thrown up by contemporary Islam are nothing if not nuanced and diverse, as Salwa Ismail indicates when she speaks of Islamism 'as not just the expression of a political project; it also covers the invocation of frames with an Islamic referent in social and cultural spheres'.[3]

The chapters of Part III teased out the exploration of dialogical challenge by way of a series of reflections, discussions, and analyses. Chapter 11 closed this section on dialogical exploration by foreshadowing where dialogical activity needs to go with respect to Christian–Muslim interfaith encounter, namely, into the challenge of theological encounter. A number of themes and issues were addressed in order both to stimulate reflection and thought, and to indicate where I, at least, believe further work is called for.

So, in respect to comprehending something of the prospects for dialogue with Islam, I trust the reader has been both informed and challenged with regard to Christian–Muslim and Jewish–Muslim relations, and also with regard to the vibrant and contending ideological options in the Muslim world of today that vie for predominance. Having done that, hopefully the reader is in a better position to take up the challenge of real-life encounter and engagement with his or her Muslim neighbour. Perhaps the chapters of Part III may help in this task, if only to point

---

[2] Graham E. Fuller, *The Future of Political Islam* (New York: Palgrave Macmillan, 2003), xi–xii.

[3] Salwa Ismail, *Rethinking Islamist Politics: Culture, the State and Islamism* (London: I. B. Tauris, 2003), 2.

the way to some of the issues that require, in the end, to be resolved dialogically for the sake of good interfaith encounter.

I am acutely aware that differences between religions or, perhaps better, between religious world-view systems, are very real and cannot be glossed or easily reconciled, if at all. To be sure, the pursuit of interreligious engagements, on the basis of common values within religions and common concerns held by religious peoples, is both admirable and the basis for much good dialogical interaction. However, I am aware that such common values and concerns can be all too easily undermined. Too often, it seems, those things which bring peoples of different religions together are easily swept aside if there has been no sustained work undertaken to address the deep philosophical, metaphysical and theological issues that, in fact, signal deep divisions and polarised perceptions lurking within our religious communities. We don't have to look too far into recent world history to see evidence for this. Of course, such work has been undertaken across the ages by various scholars: but it is largely ignored or unknown. I suspect a lot more such work is required. What I have touched on has been but a foretaste of work yet to be undertaken. This is the next challenge, one that can be foreshadowed by considering the following.

First, one Muslim scholar has examined the cliché that 'Islam has no church and thus does not separate the sacred and the secular' and notes that

> no religion can exist without some sort of a church, and this includes Islam. No religion and certainly no great religion of salvation can do without a body of specialists who continuously define and redefine its boundaries, determine orthodoxy, excluding heresy, seeking to enforce its norms on the body of believers.[4]

The point here is not to suggest that Muslims are lacking in an institutional sense, or that they require some institutional structure comparable to that of Christianity. Rather it is to highlight that while Christians have 'Church', as both concept and institution, Muslims by contrast have the Ummah as their guiding concept of community, and the community of scholars—the ulema—as a *de facto* institution: indeed, in many contexts the corporate identity of the ulema is, institutionally speaking, *de jure*. This is more obvious in some Islamic countries, for example Iran, than others. Actual institutional arrangements within Muslim societies are quite varied across dar-al-Islam. Nonetheless, whereas, generally speaking, in Christianity its scholars have either served the Church as 'institute', or stood over against it as critics and reformers, there is no equivalent institute in Islam to which religious scholars may relate. Still, scholars in Islam do form, albeit loosely and varingly, an institutional equivalent of sorts that, at times, defines and critiques the temporal expressions of the Ummah. Yet despite structural differences, each of the two religions—Islam and Christianity (and, for that matter, we could easily include

---

[4] Tarif Khalidi, 'Religion and Citizenship in Islam', in Jørgen S. Nielsen, ed., *Religion and Citizenship in Europe and the Arab World* (London: Grey Seal Books, 1992), 26.

Judaism in this)—has a heritage, and an ongoing inbuilt imperative, of critiquing the social and political realities of the day. Themes of common critique may be a fruitful platform for interfaith encounter; indeed some of this possibility was canvassed in Part III above.

Second, although there are obvious structural differences between Islam and Christianity, there are also dynamic parallels of varying sorts. One is found in the tension between Church and state, which has contributed to the rise of secularism in the Christian world; and the tension in places between the ulema—the community of Islamic scholars—and the Islamic political state in which the scholars live. Historically, the ulema have often clashed with the Caliphs (in a way not dissimilar to the biblical evidence of tense clashes between prophets and kings; or the evidence throughout history of an oft-found tension between Church leaders and politicians, especially in the West). The tension between the two institutions within the Islamic world—between religious scholars and political leadership, broadly speaking—has often, in modern times, contributed to a further tension. This is the tension between secular tendencies (which allow for plurality of perspective, and tolerance of variation and difference) on the one hand, and the tendency to 'Islamic fundamentalism' (or the tendency to disavow the possibility of plurality and eschew allowance for variation and difference) on the other. In short, such polar tensions exist within Islam, as much as within Christianity.

In many ways the key challenge that faces the contemporary world is pluralism. The challenge of pluralism, in recent decades, has confronted the Western world and especially its predominant religion, Christianity. For example, immigration has fostered ethnic diversity so giving rise to a plurality of outlooks, cultures and religions, in many parts of the Western world. This has implications for relations between the state and its religious communities, as some European countries have begun to address already.

> No longer is the Christian religion the only religion with which the European nation states have to deal. ... A wider concept of citizenship and civic loyalty is being evolved that takes account of the new cultural and religious pluriformity. Islam has become the second religion of Europe, and its relationship to the secular non-Islamic state is becoming a matter of increasing importance.[5]

Francis Clark goes on to note:

> It is especially in the spheres of education and of personal law that the new religious pluralism raises problems of national identity and citizen's rights. In many of the countries of western Europe public policy for the education of children gives primacy to the Christian religion, as the religion of the majority of the population. Should that policy be reformed in order to meet the claims for more equitable treatment by believers

---

[5] Francis Clark, 'Religion and State in Europe', in Neilsen, ibid., 52–3.

of other faiths? So too in the sphere of personal law: should the state allow to such believers, Muslims for example, legal rights to lead their personal, family and community lives in accordance with customary laws of their own religion, even if that entails exempting them from some of the provisions of the general law or from existing administrative regulations?[6]

But Europe and, indeed, other countries within the orbit of Western civilisation, are not the only places confronting the impact of pluralism. The Islamic world is also confronted by its own challenge of pluralism, and this is on many fronts. One has to do with the issue of Muslim minorities in Western secular (or nominally Christian) societies. Another has to do with the multifaceted problem of minorities in the Arab world, for example. Here Muslims must contend with some who are both non-Muslim and non-Arab (for example, Armenians); some who are non-Arab Muslim (Kurds, for instance); some who are Arab Muslim dissenters from majority Sunni Islam (for example, Druzes); and then Arab Christians, for whom God (whose Son is Jesus) is called 'Allah'.

Dialogical exploration is a challenge of immense proportions for it requires us to take serious account of the 'other'. It requires us to be open to the 'other', to view the 'other' as neighbour and friend. It necessarily implies some measure of pluralism as a grounding context.[7] Whether within the borders of our own community and world view—where the religious 'other' represents various alternative, heterodox, or radical perspectives that challenge from the inside, so to speak—or whether from without, where the 'other' represents a wholly alien religion and culture, the essential challenge is the same. It is the challenge of dialogical engagement that encompasses radically different alternatives—the fact of plurality—as legitimate and potentially compatible co-partners in life. To reach the point of acceptance of the legitimacy of the 'other' and their perspective—which is at the root of the issue of pluralism—and to rethink our world-view constructs as a consequence, so as to be able to encompass the 'other' as potentially compatible at least to the extent of being a legitimate dialogical partner, involves the deep task of grappling with religious pluralism and the encounter of ideological and theological dialogue. That, as I indicated above, is the next substantive dialogical challenge.

I often find, in my research and thinking, that where I arrive at is where I should really begin. Or, having attained a goal, I find it is not the ending I might have expected, but really only a new beginning. The end of one journey brings me but to the start of another. So it is with this book: there is no resting on a laurel of satisfaction, but a further challenge of engagement and thinking inviting response; more work of research and writing that beckons.

---

[6] Ibid., 54.

[7] For example, see my 'Pluralism and Interreligious Engagement: The Contexts of Dialogue', in David Thomas with Clare Amos, eds, *A Faithful Presence, essays for Kenneth Cragg* (London: Melisende Press, 2003), 402–18.

Appendix

Introducing Islamic Scripture
Selected Passages from the Qur'an

The following selections have been chosen and grouped to facilitate a first study of the scripture of Islam, the Holy Qur'an. In the longer suras (chapters) there is much more to the content than the title of the passage would indicate, so titles should not be taken to denote subject matter. Indeed, individual suras may touch on many different topics, and topics will reappear in different suras. Many Muslims, including non-Arabic speakers, aspire to memorise the Qur'an in the original Arabic. Titles act as aids to the memory and help to retain the order of the suras.

This introductory guide includes a total of 30 suras representing about one-third of the contents of the Qur'an. It is widely recognised that of the 114 suras comprising the Qur'an, about 90 were delivered at Mecca and the balance either at Medina, or otherwise of unknown placing. In the Arabic Qur'an, suras are arranged in order of length from longest to shortest. English editions sometimes present the suras in a chronological framework, beginning with those that are believed to be the earliest.

I have grouped this representative selection of suras into six categories and given an indication as to the nature of the content of each. The Arabic title, in italics, is preceded by the number denoting the order of placement of the sura within the Qur'an. I have given this title first, followed by its English translation in parenthesis. This referencing should help you to locate the suras in whichever English-language edition you are using. The notations concerning content indicate an opening, or closing, or perhaps predominant theme of the sura.

By working your way through these passages in a good English edition of the Qur'an the first-time student of Islam should get some feel both for the Qur'an as a sacred text and for the substance of Quranic revelation, and so a sense of Muslim belief and religious values.

1. References to previous Scriptures and Legends

10. *Yusuf* [Joseph]; the story of Joseph is appealed to as a proof of the truth of the revelation.
18. *Al-Kahf* [The Cave]; a warning to those (Christians) who claim God has begotten a Son—the prophet is only a mortal.

7. *Al-A'raf* [The Heights]; echoes legends of the Torah.

2. References to the Calling of Muhammad

96. *Al-'Alaq* [The Blood Clots]; Muhammad's first call to 'read' (*recite*) the Qur'an.

97. *Qadr* [Qadr]; the Qur'an revealed on the 'night of power'.

74. *Al-Mudqathir* [The Cloaked One]; an admonition to those demanding material scriptures as a proof of Muhammad's mission.

70. *Al-Ma'arij* [The Ladders]; Judgement Day and its terrors.

73. *Al-Muzammil* [The Mantled One]; encouragement to Muhammad; early prescriptions for devotional practices.

69. *Al-Haqqa* [The Inevitable]; the Last Judgement is inevitable.

68. *Al-Qalam* [The Pen]; Muhammad is neither mad nor an impostor. Unbelievers warned.

3. The Mission of Muhammad

62. *Al-Jumm'a* [Friday or The Day of The Congregation]; Muhammad sent by God; Jews rebuked for not believing; exhortation to the Friday congregation.

61. *Al-Saff* [Battle Array]; believers must keep their word and fight for the faith; Jews and Christians rebuked.

57. *Al-Hadid* [Iron]; sovereignty of God; exhortation to embrace Islam.

56. *Al-Waqi'a* [That Which Is Coming]; description of the inevitable Day of Judgement.

54. *Al-Qamar* [The Moon]; warnings of impending judgement.

53. *Al-Najm* [The Star]; description of Muhammad's vision of his ascent into heaven; exalting the attributes of God.

52. *Al-Tur* [The Mountain]; punishments and rewards: the consequences of judgment.

51. *Al-Dhariyat* [The Winds]; the Day of Judgement is coming; vindication of Muhammad.

50. *Qaf* [Qaf]; proofs of future life; the Last Judgement and exhortation to believe.

47. *Muhammad* [Muhammad]; promises and exhortations.

4. The Authority of the Apostle

29. *Al-'Ankabut* [The Spider]; believers must be proved; exhortation to strive for the faith.

8. *Al-Anfal* [The Spoils]; who are the true believers?—exhortation to believe and to avoid treachery; plots and intrigues.

9. *Al-Tawba* [Repentance]; conditional immunity for idolaters; exhortation to fight rigorously against the infidels (pagan opponents of Islam).

5. The Messiah, the Son of Mary

19. *Maryam* [Mary]; the story of Mary, mother of Jesus, re-cast and set in an Islamic context.

3. *Al-Imran* [The Imrams]; unity of God; the Qur'an confirms and supersedes previous scriptures (Torah and Gospels); injunctions and exhortations to the faithful.

6. The Laws of God

17. *Al-Isra'* [The Night Journey]; allusion to the 'night journey' from the Sacred Mosque (at Mecca) to the Remote Mosque (at Jerusalem); the Qur'an as guide and glad tidings; revealed as occasion required; those who believe the Scriptures recognise it.

4. *Al-Nisa'* [Women]; Allah creates and watches over humankind. duties, roles, rights and relationships set out and defined; men are superior to women; Jews charged with perverting scripture; Christian doctrine of the Trinity denounced.

65. *Al-Talaq* [Divorce]; the laws of divorce; Arabs admonished to believe in Allah.

5. *Al-Ma'ida* [The Table]; prescriptions for rituals; variety of moral injunctions and religious exhortations.

66. *Al-Tahrim* [Prohibition]; instructions and exhortations to the Prophet; jealousies in his harem occasioned by his intrigue with the Coptic slave-girl Mary.

Glossary

This glossary is by no means an exhaustive list. The terms selected are predominantly, but not entirely, Arabic words that are of significance to understanding Islam and/or the related issues of interfaith dialogue. They appear also in the Index. Words that are in bold type in the text below indicate they are themselves glossary items.

Abbasid Name of the second great dynasty of Islam that was based in Baghdad and lasted from 750–1258CE.

Abu Bakr One of the first converts to Islam who became a close companion of Muhammad and was elected the first leader, or **Caliph**, of the Muslim community upon the death of Muhammad in 632CE. Abu Bakr died in 634CE.

Adab This is often translated as 'culture'. However, the word has a wide range of meaning around the notion of 'good manners', 'refined living' 'a cultured life' and so on. 'The basic Arabic root indicates the possession of refinement or good habits bequeathed down the ages'.[1]

Adhzan Sometimes spelt 'Adhan', this names the call to prayer traditionally proclaimed by the **Muezzin** from the **Minaret** of a mosque.

Allah The Muslim name for God, which comes from the Arabic *al-Ilah* meaning 'The God' or 'The Deity'. See also **Tawhid**.

Antisemitism This term, often written 'anti-semitism', means not 'opposition to Semites' as the term might at first glance suggest (and which technically would include all who identify with the Semitic language group of Aramaic, Arabic and Hebrew), but specifically a pathological antipathy to, even hatred of, Jews and things Jewish.

Arkan A word meaning 'supports' or 'basic elements', this term names the five 'pillars' of Islamic faith, namely the **Shahada**, the Creed, or profession of faith; **Salat**, the ritual act of prayer undertaken on a daily basis; **Sawm**, the act of fasting during the month of Ramadan; **Zakat**, the requirement to give alms on an annual basis at least; and **Hajj**, the great pilgrimage.

---

[1] Ian Richard Netton, *A Popular Dictionary of Islam* (London: Curzon Press, 1992), 19.

al-'Asr The afternoon prayer.

Aya This is the word for 'verse', specifically a verse within a chapter (**sura**) of the **Qur'an**.

Ayatollah In both Arabic and Persian this word means 'The Sign of God' and has come to be used as a title of esteem and rank bestowed on scholars, within the Iranian **Shi'a** world, who have achieved a high level of eminence in Islamic jurisprudence and/or theology.

al-Azhar Meaning the 'brilliant' or 'radiant', this term names the famous University and Mosque in Cairo that was founded in 969CE.

al-Bukhari The name of a most famous compiler of **Hadith** whose collection, referred to by his name, is often ranked by Muslims as a text whose importance and authority is second only to the **Qur'an**.

Caliph Also written as 'Khalifa'—which transliterates the Arabic—this is the name given to the Head of the Islamic community, initially the 'deputy' or 'successor' to Muhammad. Although embracing both a spiritual and political function in its initial application, the term took on a more political application.

Companions In Arabic *Sahaba*, this refers primarily to those who were the close friends and associates of the Prophet Muhammad, and more generally to the generation that saw him when he was alive.

Dar-al-Islam Meaning literally 'The Abode (or House) of Islam', this term technically denotes those countries or regions that are subject to Islamic law. More loosely, perhaps, it applies to those countries that may be said to be culturally, religiously and politically part of the Islamic world. The term contrasts with 'Dar-al-Harb', which translates as 'The Abode of War' and has been traditionally used to denote non-Islamic countries or regions.

Da'wah Meaning 'call' or 'invitation', this term denotes the missionary or propagandist motive and movement of Islam.

Dhimmi This Arabic term apples to those non-Muslims who lived in Muslim-ruled countries, but who were granted the status of 'an agreement of protection' (*dhimma*) which granted freedom of worship, the right of non-harassment and security from the state, provided certain taxes were paid and protocols observed.

Din (*or* Deen) The fundamental idea of 'faith' or 'religion' as such; that which concerns the spiritual life of humankind.

Eid (*or* **Id**) Feast, festival, holiday, of which there are two major ones in Islam, namely:

    Eid-ul-Adha The Feast of Sacrifice, occurring on the tenth day of the month of the **Hajj**;

    Eid-ul-Fitr The festival of the Breaking of the Fast (**Sawm**), which occurs at the conclusion of the month of **Ramadan**.

Eschatology From the Greek *eschaton* (last things), this term applies to religious notions of the 'end of time' or the 'Last Days' and allied ideas of ultimate human destiny.

Exclusivism A paradigm of interreligious relations, which holds that 'my religion' is the only true or right one thus excluding alternate possibilities to truth or to authentic religious identity.

al-Fajr The dawn or morning prayer of **Salat**, this term is also the name of the eighty-ninth chapter of the **Qur'an**.

al-Fatiha Meaning 'The Opening', this is the title of the first chapter of the **Qur'an**. It is a short hymn of praise and supplication which is used in Muslim daily prayers (**Salat**).

Fatima The daughter of the Prophet Muhammad and his wife Khadija, who married Muhammad's cousin **Ali** with whom she had two sons, **Hasan** and **Husayn**.

Fatwa This is the technical term for a formal legal judgement or opinion as issued by an Islamic law scholar.

Fiqh Originally a word meaning 'understanding' or 'knowledge', this term names Islamic jurisprudence which, in Sunni Islam, issues in four Schools of law (Hanafi, Hanbali, Maliki and Shafi'i) and in separate systems for the Shi'a world.

Gnosticism A form of religion or spirituality that places emphasis on secret knowledge (Greek: *gnosis*) to effect salvation in a context of a hard dualism that pits the world of light, spirit, truth and good, over against the world of darkness, materiality, falsehood and evil. Human beings are understood to be trapped within the later and so require a salvific figure or action to get them to the former.

Hadd Meaning literally 'boundary', 'edge' or 'limit', in the context of Islamic law it refers to divinely sanctioned punishment that may be meted out in regard to certain criminal acts that are deemed to transgress the limits of human behaviour as set by God.

Hadith This term denotes the record of the traditions (**Sunnah**) of doings and sayings of the Prophet Muhammad, and also the first Companions, which provides authoritative texts on matters of law, ritual, interpretation and application of Islamic values and ideas that are deemed second only in status to the Qur'an.

Hajj The great pilgrimage which takes place in the last month (Dhu 'l-Hijja) of the lunar calendar of Islam. It is generally reckoned as the fifth pillar (**Arkan**) of Islam.

Halal Means that which is permitted or lawful.

Hamas The radical Islamist group associated with the Palestine Liberation Organisation which utilises acts of violence and terror to advance its cause.

Hanif Someone who is a monotheist, in the Qur'an this term refers in particular to someone who, prior to Muhammad and not a Christian or Jew, nonetheless believes there is but one God. Muhammad is believed to have himself been a Hanif even before he commenced his Prophetic life.

Haram Means that which is prohibited as unlawful and/or sinful; that which is set apart as in a sanctuary or particularly sacred or religiously significant area to be treated with utmost respect and reverence.

Hasan ibn Ali Hasan was one of the sons of **Ali**, and so a grandson of the Prophet Muhammad. He became the second Shi'ite **Imam**, but abdicated his role as **Caliph** of the **Ummah**, so opening the door to the advent of the **Umayyad** dynasty.

Hijab This term names the veil or headscarf worn by Muslim women as both a customary practice and as a mark of identity and pride in being Muslim. Modest dress is a Quranic virtue, but the nature of that dress, especially as it applies to women, varies greatly in both place and time throughout the Muslim world.

Hizbollah This term means 'The Party of God', and it names a major Shi'ite Islamist movement.

Holocaust From a biblical term referring to a 'burnt offering' to God, this word names the event wherein twentieth century European **antisemitism** issued in the Nazi ideology that promoted the extermination of the Jews, among other so-called undesirables such as gypsies, homosexuals, and the mentally retarded. Approximately six million Jews perished in this European Holocaust.

Husayn ibn Ali The brother of **Hasan**, upon whose abdication Husayn became the third **Shi'a Imam**. Husayn fought the nascent **Umayyad** dynasty but was killed at the battle of **Karbala**, so dying a martyr for the Shi'a cause and setting the scene for the Shi'a passion narrative which annually commemorates the unjust death of Husayn, and the ongoing struggle (**Jihad**) between good and evil, right and wrong, true belief and falsehood.

Ijtihad Derived from the same Arabic root as **Jihad**, this term refers to the intellectual struggle in the task of preserving and thinking through the integrity of faith; it has more specifically the technical jurisprudential meaning of exercising independent judgement, unconstrained by case law or precedent already set.

Imam Meaning primarily 'prayer leader', this term of respect can be a title indicative of a loosely institutional role (as in a full-time Imam of a mosque) that, in function, may be akin to that of a Rabbi or Priest. However in Islamic understanding and practice there is no equivalence with the sanctioned religious specialists and leadership of religions such as Christianity, for there is no ordained status or priestly hierarchy in Islam. The term also applies in the **Shi'a** world to the line of leaders descendent from the Prophet Muhammad ending when the last was taken into **occultation**.

Iman The Arabic word that means 'faith' or 'belief', particularly the idea of 'right belief' by virtue of being Muslim.

Inclusivism The paradigm of understanding that holds that religious diversity, if not also the diversity of religions, is in some sense contained or included within one universalising perspective, namely, the perspective of whoever it is that holds the Inclusive paradigm.

al-'Isha The night prayer of **Salat**.

Isma'ili The name of the branch of Shi'a Islam which believes it was the seventh of the line of Imams who was occluded; hence this branch is also known as 'The Seveners'. A sub-branch of the Isma'ilis, the Nizaris, produced the paradigm and method of political assassination, as well as the term 'assassin', and also the title 'Agha Khan' which in modern times designates the leader of the group that has descended from the original.

Ithna 'Ashari The name of the majority branch of Shi'a Islam which believes it was the twelfth of the line of Imams who was occluded; hence this branch is also known as 'The Twelvers'.

Jahiliyya A state or period of 'ignorance', applied classically to the pre-Islamic period that pertained to Arabia, but ideologically extended by many to designate the state of the world or human existence that lies beyond true or pure Islam.

Jama'at-i Islami This term names a twentieth-century revivalist movement founded in India but which greatly impacted upon the formation and early development of Pakistan.

Jihad The root meaning is 'struggle' or 'striving' and the primary application is to the life of faith, maintaining and advancing one's standing as a good Muslim living according to the dictates of Allah; more widely interpreted as 'Holy War' it indicates that sometimes the struggle to uphold, advance, and apply one's faith, and protect the community of faith, requires an armed struggle.

Ka'ba This names the cubic stone building that stands within the Great Mosque of Mecca, which is regarded as the symbolic geographic heart of Islam by virtue of being itself an ancient shrine whose purpose originally, and restored through the actions of Muhammad, is to commemorate and honour the One and Only God.

Kafir This term designates someone who is an unbeliever or atheist.

Madrasa School or college, a place of Islamic education most usually linked to a mosque.

al-Maghrib The evening prayer of **Salat**, held at sunset, and also the name of North West Africa broadly speaking, Morocco more particularly—the place of sunset relative to Arabia.

Mahdi This term means, literally, 'The One who is Rightly Guided' and is applied within both Sunni and Shi'a Islam (though differently) to 'a figure of profound eschatological significance ... (whose) just rule will herald the approach of the end of time'[2]

Mecca This is the name of the holiest city in Islam (in Arabic, *Makkah*) on account of its association with the Prophet Muhammad, the beginnings of the Islamic religion, and being the location of the Ka'ba.

Medina The name of the second holiest city of Islam, from the Arabic *al-Madina*, this town is the birthplace of the Islamic community, the **Ummah**, prior to which it was called Yathrib.

Mihrab The indented niche in the mosque wall nearest to or facing Mecca, indicating the direction (**Qibla**) of prayer.

---

[2] Ibid., 156.

Minaret The tower on or next to a mosque and from which the call to prayer is issued by the **Muezzin** or broadcast by public address system.

Minbar The word for 'pulpit', this (usually) prominent feature in a mosque is where the **Imam** delivers the Friday sermon (*Khutba*).

Muezzin This is the name of the person—or rather the role undertaken—who issues the call (**adhzan**) to prayer from the **minaret** of a mosque.

Mufti Someone qualified in terms of both law and theology, to issue a **fatwa**.

Mullah A title of respect given to someone who has qualified, through years of study, as a 'master' in terms of religious and/or legal ability and acumen.

Muslim Brotherhood A twentieth-century Egyptian-based revivalist organisation that opposes westernisation and advocates the establishment of an Islamic State.

Occultation The Arabic term for this is *Ghayba* and it refers to the idea of something or someone being concealed or made to be hidden or absent. It is applied specifically to the **Shi'a** idea that **Allah** took the last **Imam** into hiding— so he has not died, but will one day return as the **Mahdi**.

Orthodox Church This names the branch of Christianity that emerged in the East in distinction to the branch that emerged in the West, the 'Catholic' Church. Both claim to express normative Christian belief (orthodoxy) and both claim universal applicability (catholicity). The Orthodox Church is, however, a family of Christian communities most usually each with strong national or ethnic identities, for example, Russian Orthodox, Serbian Orthodox, Greek Orthodox and so on.

Paradise In Arabic, *al-Janna* (the Garden), this is the idea of a heavenly afterlife where the privations and struggles of this life, for those who have lived in the way of God, will be more than compensated by a place of ease and delight. Whether the images that feed the imagination about the paradisical state are to be read literally, allegorically, metaphorically or symbolically, is a matter of debate.

Pluralism The paradigm of viewing the diversity of religions, and the variety of religious perspective, as varyingly complementary parts that together make up the whole of religious reality or truth, equally valid alternatives that achieve much the same end, or equally valid paths derived from the same essential divine source.

Qibla This names the direction of prayer towards the **Ka'ba** in Mecca.

al Quds Arabic for 'The Holy', this is the Islamic name for the city of Jerusalem. It is the third holiest city in Islamic thought, following Mecca and Medina.

Qur'an The holy scripture of Islam, given as a series of recitations voiced by the Prophet Muhammad during his lifetime, thence remembered and recorded for posterity.

Ramadan This is the ninth month of the Muslim lunar calendar, during which the annual dawn-to-dusk fast (**Sawm**) takes place.

Rushidun This term denotes the first four **Caliphs** (Abu Bakr, Umar, Uthman, and **Ali**) elected by the nascent Islamic community after the death of Muhammad.

Salat The ritual prayer that in the Sunni world occurs five times per day, in accordance with the tradition (**Sunnah**) as recorded in **Hadith**. The five prayer times are Morning (**al-Fajr**); Midday (**al-Zuhr**); Afternoon (**al-'Asr**); Evening or Sunset (**al-Maghrib**); and Night (**al-'Isha**).

Sawm The act of fasting which occurs during the month of **Ramadan**.

Shahada The profession of faith, or Creed, which is incorporated into **Salat** and which states: 'There is no god but God, and Muhammad is the Messenger of God'.

Shari'a This term refers to the Divinely given Law which guides and animates the Islamic life.

Shaykh (or Sheik) This is a title of respect and seniority given to a Muslim religious leader, tribal chief, or **Sufi** master.

Shi'a This is the Arabic term for 'party' and it refers to those who follow and accept the lineage and ideals of **Ali**, the fourth Caliph of the Ummah and the first **Imam** of the Shi'ism.

Sufism Islamic mysticism; the pietism that focuses upon the experiential dimension of Islam as a faith tradition.

Sunnah A word meaning 'trodden path', this term names the corpus of customary practices, or traditions, that derive from the Prophet Muhammad, and also from his Companions, and which is found in collections of **Hadith**.

Sunni The term naming the majority of Muslims, in distinction from the Shi'a, and means, in effect, one who follows the traditions (**Sunnah**) of the Prophet.

Sura A chapter of the **Qur'an**, each sura is comprised of verses (**aya**).

Tafsir This names the intellectual activity of exegesis, interpretation and commentary in respect of the **Qur'an**, and which classically has addressed matters such as 'grammar, identification or provision of proper names, textual ambiguities … lexicography, philology etc., all with the intention of clarifying the Qur'anic words themselves'.[3]

Tahrif The notion of alteration, distortion or corruption that has occurred to other scriptural texts that pre-date the **Qur'an**. This concept is frequently invoked 'to account, for example, for the disparity between the data about Jesus in the New Testament and that in the Qur'an'.[4]

Taliban A term that means 'student', this names the resurgent Islamist movement that emerged in Afghanistan late in the twentieth-century.

Tawhid The concept of 'unicity' or oneness that is the defining motif of deity and which informs much Islamic ideological thinking as it is applied to the community of believers in the One God.

Ulema Muslim religious and legal scholars who, in some contexts, comprise the grouping of Islamic intellectuals and academics regarded as those who are the custodians of the faith.

Umayyad The name of the first major dynasty (661–750CE) that followed the period of the four Caliphs (**Rushidun**) who had succeeded Muhammad, and which was based in Damascus.

Ummah This names the idea of a single community of Muslims although is more loosely applied simply to the social reality of a community, people, or nation that identifies as Islamic.

Umra This names a personal pilgrimage to Mecca undertaken at any time except during the **Hajj**, which therefore does not count in terms of the religious obligation associated with the Hajj proper,

Wahhabism A strict and rather puritanical form of Sunni revivalism that is prominent in Saudi Arabia and has significantly influenced the wider Islamic world in recent time.

---

[3] Ibid., 240.
[4] Ibid., 241.

Zakat This names the requirement of giving alms. It is one of the pillars (**arkan**) of Islam.

Zaydis The third major branch of **Shi'a** Islam after the **Ithna 'Asharis** and the **Isma'ilis**, it is prominent in the Yemen.

Zionism This names the Jewish movement, which emerged out of the context of European **antisemitism**, that sought the security of Jews and their political independence through re-settling, then reclaiming, the ancient homeland of Israel.

al-Zuhr The midday prayer of **Salat**.

Bibliography

Adas, Michael (ed.), *Islamic and European Expansion: The Forging of a Global Order.*
   Philadelphia: Temple University Press, 1993.
Ahmed, Akbar S., *Living Islam.* London: BBC Books, 1993.
———, *Islam Under Siege.* Cambridge: Polity Press, 2003.
Ali, Abdullah Yusuf, *The Meaning of the Holy Qur'an,* New edition with revised translation
   and commentary. Beltsville, MD: Amana Publications, 1989.
Ali, Maulana Muhammad, *A Manual of Hadith.* London: Curzon Press, 1988.
Ali, Tariq, *The Clash of Fundamentalisms: Crusades, Jihads and Modernity.* New York:
   Verso, 2002.
Arberry, A. J. *Sufism: An Account of the Mystics of Islam.* London: Unwin Hyman, 1979.
Ariarajah, S. Wesley, *Hindus and Christians: A Century of Protestant Ecumenical Thought.*
   Amsterdam: Editions Rodopi; and Grand Rapids, Michigan: Wm B. Eerdmans, 1991.
Armour, Rollin, Sr., *Islam, Christianity, and the West: A Troubled History.* Maryknoll, New
   York: Orbis Books, 2002.
Armstrong, Karen, *Islam: A Short History.* London: Phoenix Press, 2001.
Asad, Talal, *Formations of the Secular: Christianity, Islam, and Modernity.* California:
   Stanford University Press, 2003.
Azzam, Abd al-Rahman, *The Eternal Message of Muhammad.* Leicester: The Islamic Texts
   Society, 1993.
Barnes, Michael, SJ, *Religions in Conversation: Christian Identity and Religious Pluralism.*
   London: SPCK, 1989.
———, *Theology and the Dialogue of Religions.* Cambridge: Cambridge University Press,
   2002.
Bayfield, Tony, and Marcus Braybrooke (eds), *Dialogue with a Difference.* London: SCM
   Press, 1992.
Borrmans, Maurice, *Guidelines for Dialogue between Christians and Muslims.* Rome: PCID
   and New York: Paulist Press, 1990.
Bowker, John, *Voices of Islam.* Oxford: Oneworld Publications, 1995.
Brockopp, Jonathan E., *Islamic Ethics of Life: Abortion, War, and Euthanasia.* Columbia,
   South Carolina: University of South Carolina, 2003.
Brown, D. A., *A Guide to Religions.* London: SPCK, 1975.
Brown, Stuart E. (ed.), *Meeting in Faith: Twenty Years of Christian–Muslim Conversations
   Sponsored by the World Council of Churches.* Geneva: WCC Publications, 1989.
———, *The Nearest in Affection: Towards a Christian Understanding of Islam.* Geneva:
   WCC Publications, 1994.
Choudhury, Golam W., *The Prophet Muhammad: His Life and Eternal Message.* 2nd edn,
   Kuala Lumpur: WHS Publications, 1993.

——, *Islam and the Modern Muslim World.* 2nd edn, Kuala Lumpur: WHS Publications, 1994.

Clarke, Peter (ed.), *The World's Religions: Islam.* London: Routledge, 1990.

Cook, Michael, *Commanding Right and Forbidding Wrong in Islamic Thought.* Cambridge: Cambridge University Press, 2000.

Coulson, N. J., *A History of Islamic Law.* Edinburgh: Edinburgh University Press, 1990.

Cragg, Kenneth, *The Wisdom of the Sufis.* London: Sheldon Press, 1976.

——, *The Call of the Minaret.* London: Collins, 1986.

——, *Readings in the Qur'an.* London: Collins Liturgical Publications, 1988.

——, *Muhammad and the Christian: A Question of Response.* Oxford: Oneworld Publications, 1999.

Cragg, Kenneth and R. Marston Speight, *The House of Islam.* 3rd edn, California: Wadsworth, 1988.

D'Ambra, Sebastiano, *Life in Dialogue.* Zamboanga City, Philippines: Silsilah Publications, 1991.

Dawood, N. J., *The Koran,* London: Everyman Classic Edition, 1987.

Doi, 'Abdur Rahman I., *Shari'ah: The Islamic Law.* Kuala Lumpur and London: A. S. Noordeen, 1989.

——, *Women in Shari'ah.* Kuala Lumpur: A. S. Noordeen, 1990.

Eck, Diana L., *Encountering God. A Spiritual Journey from Bozeman to Banares.* Boston: Beacon Press, 1993.

Encounter in the Spirit: Muslim–Christian Dialogue in Practice. Geneva: WCC Publications, 1991.

Esack, Farid, *On Being a Muslim.* Oxford: Oneworld Publications, 1999.

Esposito, John L., *Islam: The Straight Path.* Expanded edition. Oxford: Oxford University Press, 1994.

——, *The Islamic Threat: Myth or Reality?* 2nd edn, New York: Oxford University Press, 1995

——, *What Everyone Needs To Know About Islam.* New York: Oxford University Press, 2002.

——, *Unholy War: Terror in the Name of Islam.* New York: Oxford University Press, 2002.

——, 'The Threat of Islam: Myth or Reality?' *Concilium,* Vol. 3, 1994, 39–47.

—— (ed.), *The Oxford Encyclopedia of the Modern Islamic World.* Oxford: Oxford University Press, 1995.

—— (ed.), *The Oxford History of Islam.* Oxford: Oxford University Press, 1999.

Faksh, Mahmud A., *The Future of Islam in the Middle East: Fundamentalism in Egypt, Algeria, and Saudi Arabia.* Westport, Connecticut: Praeger, 1997.

Farah, Caesar E., *Islam: Beliefs and Observances,* 7th edn, New York: Barrons Educational, 2003.

Feiler, Bruce, *Abraham: A Journey to the Heart of Three Faiths.* New York: William Morrow, 2002.

Firestone, Reuven, *Jihad: The Origin of Holy War in Islam.* New York: Oxford University Press, 1999.

Fitzgerald, Michael L. and Robert Caspar, *Signs of Dialogue: Christian Encounter with Muslims*. Zamboanga City, Philippines: Silsilah Publications, 1992.

Fortman, E. J., *The Triune God*. London: Hutchinson, 1972.

Forward, Martin, *Inter-religious Dialogue: A Short Introduction*. Oxford: Oneworld Publications, 2001.

Friedmann, Yohanan, *Tolerance and Coercion in Islam: Interfaith Relations in the Muslim Tradition*. Cambridge: Cambridge University Press, 2003.

Fuller, Graham E., *The Future of Political Islam*. New York: Palgrave Macmillan, 2003.

Gaudeul, Jean-Marie, *Encounters and Clashes: Islam and Christianity in History*. Rome: Pontifico Instituto di Studi Arabi e Islamici, 1990.

Gioia, Francesco (ed.), *Interreligious Dialogue: The Official Teaching of the Catholic Church (1963–1995)*. Boston: Pauline Books and Media/Pontifical Council for Interreligious Dialogue, 1997.

Goddard, Hugh, *Muslim Perceptions of Christianity*. London: Grey Seal, 1996.

——, *Christians and Muslims: From Double Standards to Mutual Understanding*. Richmond, Surrey: Curzon Press, 1995.

Haykal, Husein, *The Life of Muhammad*. Trans. Ismail Raji al-Faruqi. Kuala Lumpur: Islamic Book Trust, 1993.

Hick, John, and Brian Hebblethwaite (eds.), *Christianty and other Religions*. London: Collins Fount, 1980.

Hourani, Albert, *Arabic Thought in the Liberal Age*. Oxford: Oxford University Press, 1970.

Inamdar, Subhash C., *Muhammad and the Rise of Islam: The Creation of Group Identity*. Madison, Connecticut: Psychosocial Press, 2001.

Inter-religious Dialogue: A Paradox? Zamboanga City, Philippines: Silsilah Publications, 1991.

Ipgrave, Michael (ed.), *The Road Ahead: A Christian–Muslim Dialogue*. London: Church House Publishing, 2002.

Ismail, Salwa, *Rethinking Islamist Politics: Culture, the State and Islamism*. London and New York: I. B. Tauris, 2003.

Kamali, Mohammad Hashim, *Principles of Islamic Jurisprudence*. Revised edn, Cambridge: Islamic Texts Society, 1991.

Karawan, Ibrahim A., *The Islamist Impasse*. International Institute for Strategic Studies. Adelphi Paper 314. London: Oxford University Press, 1997.

Kepel, Gilles, *The Revenge of God: The Resurgence of Islam, Christianity and Judaism in the Modern World*. Cambridge: Polity Press, 1994.

Kimball, Charles, *Striving Together: A Way Forward in Christian–Muslim Relations*. Maryknoll, New York: Orbis Books, 1991.

Leaman, Oliver, *A Brief Introduction to Islamic Philosophy*. Cambridge: Polity Press, 1999.

Lecker, Michael, *Muslims, Jews and Pagans: Studies in Early Islamic Medina*. Leiden: E. J. Brill, 1995.

Lewis, Bernard, *The Jews of Islam*. London: Routledge Kegan Paul, 1984.

——, *The Crisis of Islam: Holy War and Unholy Terror*. New York: Modern Library, 2003.

Lewis, Bernard (ed. and trans.), *Islam: From the Prophet Muhammad to the Capture of Constantinople, I: Politics and War.* New York: Oxford University Press, 1987.

Lings, Martin, *What is Sufism?* Cambridge: The Islamic Texts Society, 1993.

Lochhead, David, *The Dialogical Imperative: A Christian Reflection on Interfaith Encounter.* London: SCM Press, 1988.

Ludwig, Theodore, *The Sacred Paths.* New York: Macmillan, 1989.

McAmis, Robert Day. *Malay Muslims: The History and Challenge of Resurgent Islam in Southeast Asia.* Grand Rapids, Michigan: William B. Eerdmans, 2002.

Macquarrie, John, *The Mediators.* London: SCM Press, 1995.

Martin, Richard C., *Islam: a cultural perspective.* New Jersey: Prentice Hall, 1982.

Mawdudi, Abdul, *Toward Understanding Islam.* London: The Islamic Foundation, 1989.

Mitri, Tarek (ed.), *Religion, Law and Society: A Christian–Muslim Discussion.* Geneva: WCC Publications, 1995.

Mohamad, Mahathir, *Terrorism and the Real Issues.* Hashim Makaruddin (ed.), Malaysia: Pelanduk Publications, 2003.

Momen, Moojan, *An Introduction to Shi'i Islam.* New Haven and London: Yale University Press, 1985.

Naipaul, V. S., *Among the Believers: An Islamic Journey.* London: Picador, 2003.

Nasr, Seyyed Hossein, *Islam: Religion, History, and Civilization.* New York: HarperSanFrancisco, 2003.

Nazir-Ali, Michael, *Frontiers in Muslim–Christian Encounter.* Oxford: Regnum Books, 1991.

Nettler, Ronald L., and Suha Taji-Farouki (eds.), *Muslim–Jewish Encounters: Intellectual Traditions and Modern Politics.* Amsterdam: Harwood Academic Publishers, 1998.

Netton, Ian Richard, *A Popular Dictionary of Islam.* London: Curzon Press, 1992.

Neusner, Jacob, and Tamara Sonn, *Comparing Religions Through Law: Judaism and Islam.* London: Routledge, 1999.

Neusner, Jacob, Tamara Sonn and Jonathan E. Brockopp, *Judaism and Islam in Practice: A Sourcebook.* London: Routledge, 2000.

Nielsen, Jørgen S., *Muslims in Western Europe.* Edinburgh: Edinburgh University Press, 1992.

Nielsen, Jørgen S. (ed.), *Religion and Citizenship in Europe and the Arab World.* London: Grey Seal Books, 1992.

Parrinder, Geoffrey, *Jesus in the Qur'an.* Oxford: Oneworld Publications, 1995.

Phipps, William E., *Muhammad and Jesus: A Comparison of the Prophets and Their Teachings.* London: SCM Press, 1996.

Peters, F. E., *A Reader on Classical Islam.* Princeton, New Jersey: Princeton University Press, 1994.

Piscatori, James P., *Islam in a World of Nation-States.* Cambridge: Cambridge University Press, 1994.

Pranger, Jan Hendrik, *Dialogue In Discussion: The World Council of Churches and the Challenge of Religious Plurality between 1967 and 1979.* IIMO Research Publication 38, Utrecht-Leiden, 1994.

Pratt, Douglas, *Religion: A First Encounter.* Auckland: Longman Paul, 1993.

——, *Identity and Interaction: Islam and the Challenge of Interreligious Dialogue*
Adelaide: The Charles Strong Memorial Trust, 2000.

——, *Rethinking Religion: Exploratory Investigations.* Adelaide: ATF Press, 2003.

——, 'Christian–Muslim Relations: Perceptions of Encounter and Perspectives on
Dialogue'. Number 4 in the series *CSIC Occasional Papers: Christian–Muslim
Reflections*, Centre for the Study of Islam and Christian–Muslim Relations, Birmingham
UK (Dec. 1995).

——, 'Christian-Muslim Encounter: A New Zealand Perspective'. *Encounter: Documents
for Muslim–Christian Understanding*, Pontificio Istituto di Studi Arabi e d'Islamistica,
Rome (No. 263, April 2000).

——, 'Pluralism and Interreligious Engagement: The Contexts of Dialogue', in David
Thomas with Clare Amos (eds.), *A Faithful Presence, essays for Kenneth Cragg*,
London: Melisende Press, 2003.

Race, Alan, *Interfaith Encounter: The Twin Tracks of Theology and Dialogue*. London:
SCM Press, 2001.

Rahman, Fazlur, *Islam*. 2nd edn, Chicago: University of Chicago Press, 1979.

Reeber, Michel, *Islam, Islamism and Secularity*. Centre for the Study of Islam and
Christian–Muslim Relations, Birmingham, UK, (Paper No. 2, November 1990).

Richardson, C. C., *The Doctrine of the Trinity*. Nashville: Abingdon, 1958.

Rippin, Andrew, *Muslims. Their Religious Beliefs and Practices*. Volume 1. London:
Routledge, 1991.

——, *Muslims. Their Religious Beliefs and Practices*. Volume 2. London: Routledge,
1993.

Robinson, Neal, *Discovering the Qur'an: a contemporary approach to a veiled text*.
London: SCM Press, 1996.

——, *Islam: A Concise Introduction*. Richmond, Surrey: Curzon Press, 1999.

Samartha, Stanley J. (ed.), *Dialogue Between Men of Living Faiths*. Geneva: WCC, 1971.

Shepard, William, 'Islam and Ideology: Towards a Typology', *International Journal of
Middle East Studies*, 19 (1987): 307–36.

——, 'Sayyid Qutb's Doctrine of *Jahiliyya*', *International Journal of Middle East Studies*,
35 (2003), 521–45.

Siddiqui, Ataullah, *Christian–Muslim Dialogue in the Twentieth Century.* London:
Macmillan and New York: St Martin's Press, 1997.

Siddiqi, Muhammad Zubayr, *Hadith Literature*. Cambridge: Islamic Texts Society, 1993.

Smart, Ninian, *The Religious Experience of Mankind*. London: Fontana, 1969.

Stillman, Norman A. , *The Jews of Arab Lands: A History and Source Book*. Philadelphia:
The Jewish Publication Society of America, 1979.

Swidler, Leonard, John B. Cobb Jr., Paul F. Knitter and Monika Hellwig, *Death or
Dialogue? From the Age of Monologue to the Age of Dialogue*. London: SCM Press
and Philadelphia: Trinity Press International, 1990.

The Challenge of Dialogue – Papers from the Meeting of the Dialogue Working Group.
Geneva: WCC Publications, 1989.

Thomas, David with Clare Amos (eds.), *A Faithful Presence: Essays for Kenneth Cragg*. London: Melisende Press, 2003.

Van Gorder, A. Christian, *No God But God: A Path to Muslim–Christian Dialogue on God's Nature*. Maryknoll, New York: Orbis Books, 2003.

Waines, David, *An Introduction to Islam*. Cambridge: Cambridge University Press, 1995.

Ward, Keith, *The Concept of God*. Oxford: Basil Blackwell, 1974.

Watt, W. Montgomery, *Islamic Philosophy and Theology*. Edinburgh: Edinburgh University Press, 1987.

——, *Muslim–Christian Encounters: Perceptions and Misperceptions*. London: Routledge, 1991

——, *The Formative Period of Islamic Thought*. Oxford: Oneworld Publications, 2002.

Watt, W. M. and R. Bell, *Introduction to the Qur'an*. Edinburgh: Edinburgh University Press, 1990.

Wingate, Andrew, *Encounter in the Spirit: Muslim–Christian Dialogue in Practice*. Geneva: WCC Publications, 1991.

Wistrich, Robert S., *Anti-Semitism: The Longest Hatred*. London: Mandarin, 1992.

Ye'or, Bat, *The Dhimmi: Jews and Christians under Islam*. Cranbury, New Jersey: Associated University Presses, 1985.

Zakaria, Rafiq, *The Struggle Within Islam: The Conflict Between Religion and Politics*. London: Penguin, 1989.

Zebiri, Kate, *Muslims and Christians: Face to Face*. Oxford: Oneworld Publications, 1997.

Zubaida, Sami, *Islam: The People and the State. Political Ideas and Movements in the Middle East*. London: I. B. Tauris, 1993.

Index